BRAND AID

brand aid

a quick reference guide to solving your branding problems and strengthening your market position

BRAD VANAUKEN

AMACOM AMERICAN MANAGEMENT ASSOCIATION

New York • Atlanta • Brussels • Buenos Aires • Chicago • London
Mexico City • San Francisco • Shanghai • Tokyo • Toronto • Washington, D.C.

This publication is designed to provide accurate and authoritative information in regard to the subject matter covered. It is sold with the understanding that the publisher is not engaged in rendering legal, accounting, or other professional service. If legal advice or other expert assistance is required, the services of a competent professional person should be sought.

Library of Congress Cataloging-in-Publication Data

VanAuken, Brad.
Brand aid : a quick reference guide to solving your branding problems and strengthening your market position / Brad VanAuken. — [Second edition].
    pages cm
Includes bibliographical references and index.
ISBN 978-0-8144-3473-4 (hardcover) — ISBN 0-8144-3473-8 (hardcover) — ISBN 978-0-8144-3474-1 (ebook) 1. Brand name products—Management. 2. Branding (Marketing) 3. Trademarks—Design. I. Title.
HD69.B7V36 2015
658.8'27—dc23
                                                                    2014033826

About AMA
American Management Association (www.amanet.org) is a world leader in talent development, advancing the skills of individuals to drive business success. Our mission is to support the goals of individuals and organizations through a complete range of products and services, including classroom and virtual seminars, webcasts, webinars, podcasts, conferences, corporate and government solutions, business books, and research. AMA's approach to improving performance combines experiential learning—learning through doing—with opportunities for ongoing professional growth at every step of one's career journey.

Printing number
10 9 8 7 6 5 4 3 2 1

CONTENTS

FOREWORD

What is a brand, really? In my thirty-plus years working in this industry, I've observed the following: Every brand is a promise, and everything is a brand—from products and services to institutions and communities.

Building, maintaining, and growing a brand was once all about trust. And trust is something that is earned over time and performance. So the challenge used to be simpler: Demonstrate what your brand believes in, then prove it over time through actions across all touchpoints.

Today, the challenges of building a brand are more complex. We're now short-term thinkers, in chase of the next shiny object. Our time is limited. Our attention spans are even shorter. Additionally, the ecosystem in which brands live has evolved. It's a barter system. To get what we need from the consumer, we have to give them something, too. We have to give them a meaningful experience. To that end, we barter with entertainment, utility, and shared values. The entertainment and utility bring them into the brand, and the shared values make them stay.

So the key to engaging and inspiring consumers today is to make a brand stand for something bigger than its products, to make it share a cultural relativity that connects on a deeper level.

As chief executive of Partners + Napier, an ad agency with offices in New York City, San Francisco, and Rochester, New York, I've had the privilege to work with many great brands through a lot of different stages. As a consequence, I've read countless books on the subject of launching, growing, and building brands.

This new edition contains all the bits of wisdom and insight Brad has garnered as a veteran of branding, as well as new insights and in-depth information on all the new influences that have exploded in the evolving brand landscape in recent years—from the analytic, such as the importance of big data and social media, to the more fundamental humanistic elements, such as storytelling, social responsibility, and meeting basic human needs.

You'll find detailed and extensive coverage of critical aspects that most branding books tend to overlook: from creating consumer brand insistence to nontraditional brand marketing techniques that work, and what it takes to develop a fully functional, empowered, well-running building organization, to the thirty-five most common brand problems and twenty-one keys to success.

I met Brad for the first time when he was the brand manager of an e-learning brand that we were pitching. Through the course of the pitch process, I sensed that he would be a great client. I also sensed that there was much that I could learn from him. I was impressed not only with the extensive knowledge he had of his brand, but also with the insights he brought to every working session, and his ability to understand the big-picture landscape of branding as well as the subtle nuances that are so critical. And indeed, he proved to be a great client—working with us as a true collaborator, letting us become an extension of his team.

As our relationship evolved over the years, he remains a steadfast friend, adviser, and industry colleague whom I truly respect. I've never had a meeting with Brad, even an impromptu one at Starbucks, where I did not glean at least one nugget of invaluable advice.

My father used to say, "Be prepared; be overly prepared." Because in life a lot of people are going to be smarter than you, but not a lot of people are going to be really prepared. Now I say that to my kids all the time—"You're smart, but did you prepare for it?"

With this new edition of *Brand Aid*, Brad VanAuken gives us a comprehensive and insightful look at what it really takes to build, nurture, and grow a brand today—as well as what it takes to build and cultivate a brand-driven organization.

So who should read this book? Everyone involved in any facet of the branding process—whether you're just launching your career or, like me, you have thirty-plus years in the field.

More than a manual of dos and don'ts, it's a catalyst, a map for optimal brand health, and a truly insightful and substantive book on the changing brand landscape. Brad has written it in a way that breaks down the issues and simplifies them, while uncovering new and big insights, providing the preparation needed for any reality today or eventuality that may come your way tomorrow.

Everyone who knows me knows that much of what I've learned about leadership, I learned playing basketball—whether it was as a player or from my coaches. For me, within my ad agency, the key is building bench strength. I want everyone on my team, regardless of his or her role, to be prepared. To that end, you can be sure that all the employees at Partners + Napier will have a copy of this invaluable reference tool on their desks. As well, I've made a tradition of giving a book a year to clients and colleagues, and this will be my book for 2014.

Sharon Napier, CEO
Partners + Napier
A Project: WorldWide Agency

PREFACE

Today, brands are ubiquitous. In the past decade and a half, I have helped to brand not only companies and their products and services, but also colleges and universities, high schools, municipalities, professional and trade associations, restaurants, sports teams, museums, orchestras, libraries, magazines, health systems, continuing care retirement communities, and a wide variety of other entities. For better or for worse, almost everything in the world is now branded.

Why has this marketing discipline become so popular? In an age of increasing product commoditization and choice, the brand is an easy way for people to break through the clutter. It helps them simplify certain choices in their lives. And brands are increasingly fulfilling peoples' needs for affiliation and identification—needs that traditional institutions are struggling to meet as well as they used to.

Senior management interest in brands has soared for a variety of reasons:

- Studies have shown that more and more categories are moving toward commoditization as companies a) use increasingly sophisticated customer research to understand and address customer needs, and b) are able quickly to determine and emulate the best practices of their competitors. A strong brand can help combat category commoditization and the resulting downward pressures on price.

- Manufacturers want to obtain increased leverage vis-à-vis retailers (this is a relationship the manufacturer can own with the consumer).

- Brands provide a flexible platform for growth (beyond current categories).

- Deregulation in several industries (notably, the utilities) has resulted in a need for differentiation.

- There is increased competition for consumer dollars.

• The emergence of the Internet has changed commerce.

Branding also becomes a critical issue for businesses that are spun off from the parent company (such as AT&T's Bell Labs, now Alcatel-Lucent) and as more and more companies merge or acquire one another. The brand identity of the new combined enterprise becomes critical.

Organizations have discovered that brands are perhaps their most important assets (along with their people) for a number of reasons. There is increasing evidence and consensus that strong brands deliver the following benefits to organizations:

• Increased revenues and market share

• Decreased price sensitivity

• Increased customer loyalty

• Additional negotiating leverage with business partners

• Increased profitability

• Increased stock price and shareholder value

• Increased clarity of vision

• Increased ability to mobilize an organization's people and focus its activities

• Increased ability to expand into new product and service categories

• Increased ability to attract and retain high-quality employees

If brand management is new to you or your organization, you most likely need a quick but comprehensive overview of the key elements necessary for successful brand building. (I certainly would have found this information very helpful when I assumed the role of director of brand management and marketing for Hallmark Cards.) So, with this in mind, I have written this book using what I've learned from a wide variety of sources—books, seminars, consultants, industry benchmarking studies, my own consulting on this subject, and, most important, hands-on experience establishing brand management functions and brand building cultures at Hallmark Cards and at Element K (now Skillsoft), a leading online learning company.

I wrote this book to be a thorough but pithy quick reference guide to all of the most important aspects of brand management and marketing. I have included every concept, template, formula, worksheet, research finding, "rule of thumb," checklist, and assessment tool that I have found to be useful in building strong brands throughout my thirty-plus years as a marketing practitioner and brand strategy consultant. Feel free to read the book a chapter at a time or to zero in on the topics that are of greatest interest to you.

Most chapters end with a brand management checklist. Use this checklist to identify the areas where your brand practices are strong and where they may be weak. Also use it to identify brand management activities and approaches that are new to you. The checklist takes the form of questions. The more questions to which you can answer "yes," the better you are doing. After answering all the questions, it should be obvious which areas of brand practice require your attention. If you have answered no to a question, it should be clear what the associated action step should be. If it is not clear, you should at least be able to identify the general area in which you need help and the type of resources that may be of help to you.

Appendix B contains information about online resources to help you further explore topics in much greater detail than can be covered in this book. Also, the boxed "Did You Know?" items scattered throughout the book feature interesting facts, rules of thumb, and other handy information you may find useful as you manage your brand. Finally, I have included brand examples and case studies from a variety of industries and product/service categories throughout the book to illustrate key points.

New in This Revised Edition

While the first edition of the book included a chapter on brand building on the Internet, it did not include reference to blogs or social media, as those came into popular use between 2001 and 2010. (I wrote the original book between 1999 and 2001. It was published in 2003.) So, as you might imagine, I have completely rewritten this chapter, which is now titled "Online Brand Building."

Since I wrote the first edition of the book, shared values, social responsibility, sustainability, brand storytelling, neuromarketing, and big data have surged in popularity with marketers. I have added something about each of these developments in this edition. I added information on private label brands and on upscale consumers and their desires. I also included more in-depth information on basic human needs, fears, and other behavioral motivators.

Based on a burgeoning demand for brand architecture strategy by clients that have grown through mergers and acquisitions, I have expanded my coverage of that topic. I have added information on how to differentiate commodities and how to create "category of one" brands, a particularly powerful but seldom-used branding concept.

I now include brand archetypes and a couple of other new elements in brand positioning statements, which are reflected in the new edition of the book. I have also added a section summarizing the six most powerful sources of brand differentiation. And, finally, I have added many new brand examples featuring more contemporary brands.

I have extensively revised the book, but the importance of branding has not changed, nor have its core tenets, so you will find some older material and examples from the first edition of the book. I have not eliminated "evergreen" material that continues to be relevant today.

DID YOU KNOW?

- *In December 1993, Charles Cobb purchased the Pan Am trademark for $1.32 billion.*

- *Disney paid more than five times book value for Capital Cities/ABC.*
  (Source: Don E. Schultz and Anders Gronstedt, "Making Marcom an Investment: Market-Driven Accounting System Splits Spending into Business-Building and Brand-Building Activities," Marketing Management, Fall 1997, p. 45.)

- *In 1988, Philip Morris Co. acquired Kraft Foods for $12.9 billion— $11.6 billion over book value.*

Book Overview

Part 1 is an introduction to brand management, and it assumes no prior knowledge of brand management. Chapter 1 begins with a story that communicates the importance of brand management in a simple but compelling way, and that reinforces *the brand's essential role* in creating emotional connections and building relationships.

The next chapter, in order to establish a common working vocabulary (something brand managers must do within their organizations), defines a number of *brand-related terms* as a quick reference.

Part 1 ends with Chapter 3 and an overview of the *brand management process*, which serves to put the rest of the book in perspective. Marketing practitioners who have unsuccessfully searched for such an overview will find this visual and verbal presentation, and the context it provides, to be very helpful. The remainder of the book roughly follows this brand management process.

Part 2 covers brand design. Brand management must start here—with a thorough understanding of the *target consumer*, as covered in Chapter 4. Do brand marketers understand the consumer's benefit structure (including functional, emotional, experiential, self-expressive, cost-of-entry, and differentiating benefits) and how it varies by consumer segment? Do they know how to acquire and analyze this information? I include summaries of basic human needs and fears in this chapter.

Before marketers can design and position the brand, they must also have a thorough *understanding of the competitive set*. As Chapter 5 describes, the best benefit for a brand to deliver is one that is very important to the consumer, one for which your organization has unique capabilities, and one that competitors are not adequately addressing.

Chapter 6 covers the "meat" of *brand design*—defining the brand essence, promise, archetype, personality, and positioning. Seven components of brand design are discussed: target consumer, frame of reference, brand essence, brand promise, brand archetype, brand personality, and brand positioning. The chapter includes templates and exercises to develop each of these brand design components and also features three brand positioning case studies.

Chapter 7, which covers the codification of the brand design, addresses the key practical considerations when designing or revamping the *brand identity system and standards*. It also covers brand naming and the importance of color selection in brand identity development, and highlights tools that can aid in creating brand identity consistency throughout the enterprise.

Part 3 focuses on building the brand, and it begins by showing the reader how to create brand insistence. Chapter 8 gets to the heart of brand building. It presents a model that my company, BrandForward, has adopted for *creating consumer brand insistence* in detail. This model is based on extensive research across multiple product and service categories, and it demonstrates that five common elements drive consumers to insist upon a particular brand: awareness, accessibility, value, relevant differentiation, and emotional connection. This chapter focuses on different brands to emphasize the importance of each driver (for instance, Coca-Cola: the power of accessibility; McDonald's: the importance of consistent icon repetition; Harley-Davidson: the power of emotional connection building). The chapter concludes with a case study on managing brand equity.

Chapter 9 covers the basics of translating a chosen brand strategy and position into effective *advertising*. This chapter discusses choosing an advertising agency and development of the agency brief, advertising effectiveness evaluations (for print, radio, television, outdoor, and overall), and advertising "rules of thumb." It also includes an overview of advertising research and a quick advertising assessment tool.

Chapter 10 provides brief examples of more than sixty different types of *nontraditional brand marketing techniques that work*, including those applicable to small businesses and business-to-business organizations. The categories include membership organizations, larger-than-life brand owners, ingredient branding, museum and factory tours, and flagship stores. This chapter also features a list of considerations in getting the news media to cover your story, and it briefly touches upon customer relationship management (CRM) and creative problem solving and ideation techniques.

Chapter 11 covers eleven important areas of *online brand building*: the brand website, the importance of content, the power of blogs, search engine optimization, online advertising, using social media, web analytics, e-mail marketing, online public relations, mobile apps, and QR codes.

Chapter 12 then focuses on what may be the most important and difficult component of brand management within a large enterprise—the nonmarketing aspects of brand building: *developing the brand building organization*. This is a topic most academicians, consultants, and other nonpractitioners nearly always overlook. The chapter answers the all-important questions: How can we make the brand promise real? How can we get our organization to deliver against the promise? How can we align all that we do with the brand's positioning?

Chapter 13, on *integrated brand marketing*, outlines all the components that must be integrated to consistently deliver against the brand promise. It covers traditional marketing elements, such as product, packaging, pricing, distribution, advertising, promotion, and publicity. It also covers human resource and organization design components that must be aligned in support of the brand's promise, and presents an overview of the most important integrative mechanisms.

Brands are more than names and logos that are applied to products and services. They are the source of integrated consumer experiences. Chapter 14 addresses how to create those experiences and gives several examples of situations in which the *total brand experience* has been created. A simple list of questions is provided to help you optimize your total brand experience. Finally, the chapter presents an overview of effective crisis management, or what to do when the brand experience goes awry.

Part 4 covers the "R" in brand ROI—leveraging the brand for increased revenues and profits. I focus on two ways of generating a return: through *brand extension* and *by leveraging the brand globally*. Chapter 15 discusses ways to leverage a brand's equity and prolong its life by extending the brand into new product and service categories, and touches upon the most likely brand extension pitfalls and how to avoid them. Chapter 16 begins by highlighting the advantages of global branding, and then discusses the most important considerations in building global brands.

Part 5 addresses *brand metrics*. Most organizations conduct ongoing market (consumer and competitor) research to help them position and reposition their brands. Others monitor and measure their brands' equities. Some organizations also measure the effectiveness of specific marketing programs. Chapter 17 covers the spectrum of *brand research* (from logo recognition and recall to brand extension), emphasizing in-depth qualitative techniques that lead to a better understanding of consumer needs.

How can you manage what you haven't measured? Chapter 18 provides a detailed look at *brand equity measurement*. It is based on BrandForward's brand insistence model, which incorporates the latest thinking on brand equity measurement. The model includes the five brand equity drivers covered in Chapter 8 as well as measures of usage, preference, consideration set ranking, loyalty, and vitality.

Part 6 covers two miscellaneous brand management topics: the relationship of brand management issues to *organization age and size*, and *legal issues* in brand management. Chapter 19 looks at how older, larger companies differ from younger, smaller companies on a number of dimensions and how those differences affect the brand management issues they are likely to encounter. These key dimensions include leadership, size, business scope, brand structure, organization infrastructure, corporate culture, marketplace, decision making, financial resources, primary marketing method, brand identity, brand awareness and esteem, and brand differentiation.

Chapter 20 focuses on the most important concepts marketing managers should understand about trademark law and protection. It also covers trade dress, trade secrets, false or deceptive advertising, and intellectual property issues on the Internet.

Finally, Part 7 serves as a *brand management summary*. Chapter 21 outlines thirty-five of the most *common brand problems* that organizations encounter in managing, building, and leveraging their brands. It briefly analyzes each problem and offers practical suggestions on how to address the problem. These real-life problems are based on the experience of marketing practitioners in a variety of organizations.

The book's final chapter features twenty-one *keys to success* in brand building. The chapter includes a quick brand health assessment and my prognostications about the future of branding.

The first of the book's three appendixes explains the value of a brand *audit*. Through a brand audit, an organization can assess the strengths, weaknesses, opportunities, and threats of its brand and it brand management practices. Appendix A outlines the components of a brand audit, offers suggestions on what to look for when selecting an outside brand auditor, and features a quick (six question) brand health assessment.

Appendix B contains a list of online brand management and advertising resources, including URLs for a wide variety of articles and publications on brand management and advertising.

Finally, Appendix C is a list of references and further readings, citing more than 160 books, papers, and articles that I referenced to write this book, which represent some of the best-written documents available on various aspects of brand management and marketing.

ACKNOWLEDGMENTS

As I have discovered, although writing a book is a somewhat daunting task, it is not an entirely solitary task. Lance D'Amico, Julianne Hanes, and Jeff Kuzmich provided valuable input and feedback related to their areas of expertise. Lance Teitsworth squeezed time out of his busy schedule to help me with an illustration. I am indebted to my business partner, Dan Vandenberg, for his contributions to the chapters on "Brand Research" and "Brand Equity Measurement." I am particularly grateful to Amy Kelm for writing the foreword to the first edition of the book and to Sharon Napier for writing the foreword to this edition. Niels Buessem and Susan Stim provided invaluable help in editing the first edition of the book. And I would like to thank James Bessent, Karen Brogno, Cindy Durand, and Randi Minetor for their help in editing the second edition of the book. Finally, I am grateful for Ellen Kadin's support from the very beginning of the *Brand Aid* project.

"Developing a Brand Building Organization" was published previously as an article of the same title in the *Journal of Brand Management* 7, no. 4 (March 2001), pp. 281–290. I am grateful to Henry Stewart Publications for permitting me to reprint it here.

This book is the composite of years of experience coupled with extensive research. I am grateful to all of those individuals and organizations whose expertise and research findings have made this a more useful book. I have attempted to cite every source as precisely as possible. If I have made an oversight, please let me know and I will rectify the situation in the next edition.

Brad VanAuken

PART 1
Introduction to Brand Management

1

a brand is a friend

BUSINESS LEADERS talk about the importance of maintaining strong brand equity, but is there consensus on what brand equity is? Some people say it's everything associated with the brand that adds to or subtracts from the value it provides to a product or service. Others emphasize the financial value of the brand asset. Still others stress the consumer loyalty or price premium generated by brand equity. Some even talk about the permission and flexibility a brand gives an organization to extend into new product and service categories. While all of these opinions are very important parts of brand equity, I think the following story best illustrates what brand equity is.

Imagine you are having lunch with a longtime and very good friend. Several times throughout the lunch, she makes disparaging and sarcastic remarks that make you feel bad. You think to yourself, "This just isn't like her. She must be having a bad day." You meet with her again a week or two later, and again she acts ornery and negative. You think to yourself, "Something must be going on in her life that she's really struggling with. Maybe she is having difficulties with her job or her health or her marriage or her children." You may even ask her if everything is all right. She snaps back, "Of course it is."

Your interaction with her continues in this vein over the next couple of months. You continue to try to be supportive, but she's definitely getting on your nerves. After many meetings and much interaction, you finally decide that she's a changed person and someone with whom you prefer to spend less and less time. You may get to this point after a few months, or perhaps even after a year or more. She doesn't change, and eventually the relationship peters out.

Now consider for a moment that the person you first had lunch with is the same person as before, with one exception: She is a total stranger to you. You haven't met her previously and she is not your dear friend. I would guess that after enduring many caustic comments and being insulted a few times at that lunch, your first impression wouldn't be very positive. In fact, you'd probably be inclined not to get together with that person again. You'd probably walk away from that lunch thinking, "What a miserable person. I hope I don't run into her again."

In both of these scenarios it is the same person behaving the same way in the same situation. Yet in the first scenario, you are very quick to forgive the behavior. In fact, you feel a lot of concern toward her. In the second scenario, you can't wait for the lunch to be over and you hope never to see the person again.

In the first scenario, the person was a longtime good friend. She had a lot of equity with you. In the second scenario, she had no equity at all. You see, if people or brands have a lot of equity—that is, if you know, like, and trust them—you will "cut them a lot of slack" even if they repeatedly fail to meet your expectations. If a person, product, service, or organization has no equity with you, no emotional connection, and no trust, then you are much less inclined to forgive unmet expectations.

DID YOU KNOW?

"Familiarity . . . more often breeds liking."

(Source: Raj Raghunathan, Ph.D., Sapient Nature, January 17, 2012.)

Declining brands tend to lose buyers while the brands' loyalty and purchase rates stay stable among remaining buyers.

(Source: Andrew Ehrenberg, "Description and Prescription," Journal of Advertising Research, November/December 1997, p. 19.)

In most product categories, price is the primary purchase incentive for no more than 15 percent to 35 percent of all customers.

(Source: Kevin J. Clancy, "At What Profit Price?" Brandweek 38, no. 25, June 23, 1997, pp. 24–28.)

Brand equity creates a relationship and a strong bond that grows over time. It is often so strong that it compensates for performance flaws, whether an out-of-stock situation, poor customer service, a product that falls apart, inconvenient store hours, or a higher-than-average-price. In the end, you want to deliver good quality and good value, innovation, relevant differentiation, convenience, and accessibility with your brand. However, we must never forget that building brand equity is like building a close friendship. It requires a consistent relationship over time, trust, and an emotional connection.

TEN SIGNS THAT PEOPLE DO NOT UNDERSTAND MARKETING

1. *They never think about the customer and that individual's motivations and needs.*
2. *They define marketing as sales support.*
3. *They use the terms* sales *and* marketing *interchangeably.*
4. *They use the terms* marketing *and* advertising *interchangeably.*
5. *They think about marketing as a cost center or overhead rather than as an investment.*
6. *They only think of marketing as its tools and tactics, not as an integrated process that delivers on a strategy.*
7. *There is no well-thought-out media plan.*
8. *They believe marketing should copy whatever the competitors are doing.*
9. *They think anyone can do marketing, ignoring that it is a discipline based on training and experience.*
10. *They can't see the link between marketing strategy and business strategy.*

2

....

understanding the language of branding

IT IS IMPORTANT to establish a common brand management vocabulary in your organization. Establishing this common vocabulary will ensure that people can communicate with fewer misunderstandings. More important, it will help communicate and reinforce key brand management principles.

I worked with organizations in which different managers used different terms to describe positioning the brand. Terms ranged from "essence" and "promise" to "position" and "unique value proposition." This caused great confusion. I worked with other organizations that struggled with the differences among master brand, family brand, parent brand, umbrella brand, corporate brand, brand, subbrand, endorsed brand, product brand, etc. The aim is to agree on one set of terms and to simplify the brand architecture.

Brand

The American Marketing Association describes a brand as a "name, term, sign, symbol, or design, or a combination of them, intended to identify the goods and services of one seller or group of sellers and to differentiate them from those of competition."[1]

More important, *a brand is the source of a promise to the consumer.* It promises relevant differentiated benefits. Everything an organization does should be focused on enhancing delivery against its brand's promise.

Combining a few different definitions, a brand is the name and symbols that identify:

- The source of a relationship with the consumer

- The source of a promise to the consumer

- The unique source of products and services

- The single concept that you own inside the mind of the prospect (according to brand management experts Al Ries and Laura Ries, in their book *The 22 Immutable Laws of Branding*)

- The sum total of each customer's experience with your organization

Finally, another way to think about brands is that they are personifications of organizations and their products and services. In this way, brands can hold certain values, have specific personalities, possess admirable qualities, stand for something, make promises, and create emotional connections with people.

THE ORIGIN OF BRANDS

Brands date back to earliest recorded history when they were used to indicate the origin of a product and information about its quality. As far back as 2250 BCE, researchers have found evidence of brands being used by craftspeople and merchants in trade. They often took the form of seals featuring pictoral symbols and text. Brands (stamping with embers or hot irons) were also used to identify harlots or wrongdoers and to identify lifestock ownership.

(Source: Karl Moore and Susan Reid, "The Birth of Brand: 4000 Years of Branding," Business History 50, no. 4, July 2008, pp. 419–432.)

Brand Equity

Brand equity is the commercial value of all associations and expectations (positive and negative) that people have of an organization and its products and services due to all experiences of, communications with, and perceptions of the brand over time. This value can be measured in several ways: as the economic value of the brand asset itself, as the price premium (to the end consumer or the trade) that the brand commands, as the long-term consumer loyalty the brand evokes, or as the market share gains it results in, among many others. From an economist's perspective, brand equity is the power of the brand to shift the consumer demand curve of a product or service (to achieve a price premium or a market share gain).

To use a metaphor, brand equity is like a pond. People may not know how long the pond has been around or when it first filled with water, but they know that it supports life, from ducks to deer. It also may provide recreation, irrigation, even human drinking water. Clearly it is a valuable resource. But many people take the pond for granted. It seems as if nothing can diminish its supply of water, yet we sometimes notice that it rises with the spring rains or lowers after a long drought or overuse for irrigation.

Similarly, brand equity is a reservoir of goodwill. Brand building activities consistently pursued over time will ensure that the reservoir remains full. Neglecting those activities or taking actions that might deplete those reserves will reduce the reservoir, imperceptibly at first, but soon all too noticeably until it is too late and all that is left is mud.

This illustrates a chronic difficulty in brand management. Brand equity is critically important to a company's success, yet because of its reservoir-like nature, it is often taken for granted, overly drawn upon, and not adequately replenished, especially in times of crisis or to meet short-term needs.

BRAND IMAGE

Brand image is the totality of perceptions resulting from all experience with and knowledge of the brand. It is how consumers perceive the brand.

BRAND ASSOCIATIONS

Brand associations are anything consumers associate with the brand in their minds. As David Aaker, "guru" of brand management, points out, these associations could be organizational, product related, symbolic, or personified. If there is a strong brand connection with a specific retail outlet, the associations could also be based on the retail experience.

Other brand equity components not listed here but covered in detail in Chapters 8 and 18 include awareness, accessibility, value, relevant differentiation, emotional connection, preference, usage, loyalty, and vitality.

Brand Positioning

Brand positioning is the way the brand is perceived within a given competitive set in the consumer's mind. Ideally, it is a function of the brand's promise and how the brand compares with other choices with regard to quality, with innovation, perceived leadership, value, prestige, trust, safety, reliability, performance, convenience, concern for customers, social responsibility, and technological superiority. Relevant differentiation is the most important aspect of brand positioning.

One could argue that brand essence, promise, archetype, and personality are all a part of the brand positioning. Given that, brand positioning is very similar to what I refer to as *brand design* in Chapter 3.

Brand positioning elements can be intentional and crafted by the marketer—for instance, as written in the brand positioning statement. The brand essence, promise, archetype, and personality can also exist "in the mind of the consumer." Ideally, what is in consumer's minds is congruent with the intended brand positioning. If not, hopefully the brand management team is actively managing the brand so that congruence will occur.

BRAND ESSENCE

This is the *heart and soul of a brand*—a brand's fundamental nature or quality. Usually stated in two to three words, a brand's essence is the one constant across product categories and throughout the world. Some examples are:

Nike: Authentic Athletic Performance

Hallmark: Caring Shared

Disney: Fun Family Entertainment

Disney World: Magical Fun

Starbucks: Rewarding Everyday Moments

The Nature Conservancy: Saving Great Places

Typically, it is rare for an organization's brand essence and slogan to be the same. For instance, Nike's essence—Authentic Athletic Performance—was translated to the following two slogans: "Just do it!" and "I can." The Nature Conservancy's brand essence, however, also served as its previous slogans: "Saving the Last Great Places" and "Saving the Last Great Places on Earth." Its current slogan is "Protecting nature. Preserving life."

Kevin Keller, brand expert and author of the popular book *Strategic Brand Management*, has coined the term "brand mantra," which is very closely related to brand essence. The "mantra" concept reinforces the role of brand essence in internal communication. According to Keller:

> [Brand mantra should] define the category of business for the brand and set brand boundaries. It should also clarify what is unique about the brand. It should be memorable. As a result it should be short, crisp, and vivid in meaning. Ideally, the brand mantra would also stake out ground that is personally meaningful and relevant to as many employees as possible.[2]

BRAND DNA

This term has been used in a variety of ways; however, it is similar to the brand's essence. It is the core stuff of which the brand is made, including its core values, competencies, and passions.

BRAND PROMISE

To be successfully positioned in the marketplace, a brand must promise differentiated benefits that are relevant and compelling to the consumer. The benefits can be functional, experiential, emotional, or self-expressive. A brand promise is often stated as:

Only [brand name] delivers [benefit] in [product or service category].

Sometimes, with corporate brands, it is stated as:

[Brand name] is the (trusted/quality/innovative) leader in [benefit] in the [product or service category].

To be believable, brand promises require compelling proof points (and what advertising professionals call "reasons to believe") in support of the brand's promise. A brand promise must:

- Address important consumer needs
- Leverage your organization's strengths
- Give you a competitive advantage through differentiation
- Inspire, energize, and mobilize your people
- Drive every organizational decision, system, action, and process
- Manifest itself in your organization's products and services

As respected marketing consultant Kristin Zhivago once said:[3]

The simple truth about branding—a brand is not an icon, a slogan, or a mission statement. It is a promise—a promise your company can keep. First you find out, using research, what promises your customers want companies like yours to make and keep, using the products, processes, and people in your company. Then you look at your competition and decide which promise would give you the best competitive advantage. This is the promise you make and keep in every marketing activity, every action, every corporate decision, every customer interaction. You promote it internally and externally. The promise drives budgets and stops arguments. If everyone in the company knows what the promise is, and knows that they will be rewarded or punished depending on the personal commitment to the promise, politics and personal turf issues start to disappear.

The brand promise should drive organizationally, mission, and strategy; communication; operations, systems, and logistics; products and services; and values and behaviors.

UNIQUE VALUE PROPOSITION

A brand's unique value proposition is what makes it unique and compelling to its target customers. In this way, a brand's unique value proposition is similar to its promise. One could say that unique value propositions are very important to brands and that brands should promise and deliver on those unique value propositions.

BRAND PERSONALITY

Brand personality refers to adjectives that describe the brand (such as fun, kind, sexy, safe, sincere, sophisticated, cheerful, old-fashioned, reliable, progressive, etc.). How consumers perceive a brand's personality is often discovered through qualitative research by asking people to describe the brand as if it were a person or an animal.

BRAND ARCHETYPE

If the brand personality is composed of a set of adjectives that describe the brand as if it were a person, the brand archetype goes a level deeper to identify the primary quality or motivation that underlies the brand's view of the world and its behavior. In *The Hero and the Outlaw: Building Extraordinary Brands Through the Power of Archetypes*, Margaret Mark and Carol S. Peterson focus on twelve archetypes that drive the brand. In his book *Winning the Story Wars*, Jonah Sachs provides examples of seven archetypes—the pioneer, the rebel, the magician, the jester, the captain, the defender, and the muse. We use twenty-seven different archetypes when we work with clients. Example archetypes include achiever, advocate, explorer, guide, healer, poet, sage, trickster, and wizard, among others.

> *TIP*
> *For nonprofit organizations loath to use the word "brand" (because of its corporate or business overtone/connotation) but who still want to actively manage their brands internally and externally, consider using "promise" instead. For instance, talk about "managing our promise" or "delivering our promise," or state that "[name's] promise is. . ."*

Brand Identity

Brand identity is a combination of visual, auditory, and other sensory components that create recognition, represent the brand promise, provide differentiation, create communications synergy, and are proprietary.[4] Some people define brand identity more broadly to include almost everything in a brand's design, including essence, promise, personality, and positioning. The more specific definition used in this book reflects the most common usage of the term, especially as used by firms focused on the creation of brand identity systems and standards.

Names and nomenclature, logotypes, symbols and other graphic devices, distinctive shapes and colors, brand voice and visual style, sounds, jingles and other mnemonic devices, typography, theme lines or slogans, and characters that are uniquely associated with a brand are all components of a brand's identity.[5] Textures, scents, flavors, and other sensory elements also can be components of a brand's identity.

BRAND PORTFOLIO

Brand portfolio is the mix of brands and subbrands owned by an organization. This portfolio should be actively managed to ensure effective, efficient brand management. For example, P&G, Unilever, and Kraft Foods Group all have a very large portfolios of brands; General Motors manages Buick, Cadillac, and other brands; Hallmark manages the Hallmark, Shoebox, and Crayola brands, among others; Darden restaurant group manages the Red Lobster, Olive Garden, LongHorn Steakhouse, Bahama Breeze, Seasons 52, The Capital Grille, Eddie V's, and Yard House brands. Marriott brands include Marriott Hotels & Resorts, Courtyard, Fairfield Inn & Suites, Residence Inn, JW Marriott, the Ritz-Carlton, and others.

BRAND ARCHITECTURE (OR BRAND STRUCTURE)

Think of brand architecture as a brand's family tree or its hierarchy. It is how an organization organizes the various named entities within its portfolio and how they relate to each other. Ideally, the brand architecture is simple, with no more than two levels: brand and subbrands. In fact, brand/subbrand is the type of architecture most often used. It takes many forms, mostly based upon the type of name used for the subbrands. Some organizations add a third level: named products. But any more than two levels can be confusing.

The four general types of architecture are:

1. Master brand

2. Brand/subbrand

3. Endorsed brand

4. Separate (stand-alone or independent) brands

Brand architecture addresses the following:

- Number of separately named entities
- Criteria for becoming a separately named entity
- Levels of relationships between separately named entities
- Naming and other brand identity conventions for each level

Corporate Brand. Corporate brand is the brand bearing the company name. It is always the highest in a brand hierarchy. Examples are Ford, Hewlett-Packard, IBM, General Motors, 3M, and Kodak.

Master Brand. Master brand is the dominant, highest-level brand in a brand hierarchy. Corporate brands are typically master brands (unless they are largely invisible by design, such as P&G or Unilever). As the Ford example points out, the same brand can be a corporate, master, and parent brand.

Parent Brand. Parent brand is a brand that is extended into more than one product category. It may or may not be the same as the corporate brand. Examples are Ford and Honda.

Parent brands offer the following advantages:

- Less expensive new product launches
- Trust/assurance
- Marketing economies of scale

Subbrand. A subbrand is a new brand that is combined with a parent or corporate brand in the brand identity system. The subbrand can make the parent brand more vital and relevant to a new consumer segment or within a new product category. Examples are Ford Taurus and Honda Accord.

Endorsed Brand. Endorsed brand is the primary name the consumer uses to refer to a product. It is a brand that is endorsed by the parent or corporate brand in the brand identity system. The parent brand is also identified with the product; however, the endorsed brand is given much greater visual weight than the parent brand. In this situation, the corporate or parent brand lends credibility or assurance to the endorsed brand without overpowering it with its own associations. An example is Shoebox, a tiny division of Hallmark.

Private Label

Private label describes products or services that are manufactured or otherwise sourced by one company to be sold under another company's brand name. Private label manufacturers can be large national brand manufacturers that use their excess manufacturing capacity to supply store brands, or smaller manufacturers that focus on creating store brands for others, or major retailers or wholesalers who manufacture their own store brands, or regional manufacturers that concentrate on providing private label brands for specific markets. Many retailers across a variety of categories have created their own store brands. According to the Food Marketing Institute, nearly all grocers offer their own store brands. And store gross margins are significantly higher (35 percent) for store brands than for nationally advertised brands (25.9 percent).[6]

Often, retailers use private label brands to offer lower-priced alternatives to nationally advertised brands; however, retailers are increasingly creating their own premium store brands. Offering store brands decreases the leverage that nationally advertised brands have vis-à-vis retailers, which makes it even more important for national advertisers to strengthen the equity of their brands to maintain leverage in the marketplace. Historically, people perceived private label brands to be "knock-offs" of nationally advertised brands, but increasingly, people perceive them to be acceptable alternatives to nationally advertised brands. And loyalty to a store brand translates to loyalty to a store.

Trade Dress

Trade dress refers to aesthetic elements that provide legal protection for a brand's identity. For example, Coca-Cola's bottle shape is a part of its trade dress, as are Absolut Vodka's bottle shape and Harley-Davidson's engine sound.

Brand Extension

Brand extension means applying the existing brand to new products, services, or consumer segments. If done by combining an existing one with a new brand, the new is called a subbrand. Executed properly, brand extensions can broaden and clarify the meaning of the brand. Improperly done, they can dilute or confuse the brand's meaning. Examples are Crayola (from crayons to markers and pens) and Jell-O (from gelatin to pudding).

Marketing Plan

A marketing plan is a request for funds in return for a promised level of incremental revenues, unit sales, market share, or profits.[7] One can develop marketing plans for products, services, market segments, or brands. The critical components of a marketing plan include the following:

- *Summary.*

- *Objectives* (e.g., attract new consumers, create new uses, increase share of requirements, incent trial, encourage repeat purchase, encourage add-on purchase, increase awareness, increase loyalty, change value perception, increase emotional bond, or extend into new product and service categories).

- *Situation Analysis:*
  - Market analysis
  - Competitive context
  - Customer profile (e.g., segments, needs, attitudes, behaviors, insights)

- *Strategies and Tactics* (touching upon all key marketing components that will be used: product, packaging, pricing, distribution, advertising, publicity, sales promotion, and selling). Be specific.

- *Operations Considerations* (e.g., impact on plant capacity, or need for new assets).

- *Financial Projections:*
  - Pro forma profit-and-loss statements, balance sheets, cash flows, etc.
  - Funds required to execute plan

- *Supporting Customer Research* (including qualitative research, concept testing, volumetric modeling, and market test results).

- *Risks and Contingency Plans.*

BRAND PLAN

A brand plan is similar to a marketing plan. Its objectives focus primarily on changing or improving brand equity components. Increased market share is a frequently specified brand objective. Others include:

- Brand awareness
- Brand accessibility
- Brand value
- Brand relevant differentiation
- Brand emotional connection

- Brand vitality
- Brand loyalty
- Brand personality
- Other brand associations

3

brand management process: an overview

THE BRAND management process starts with a deep understanding of consumers and competitors. You need to fully understand the consumer benefit structure by segment, including which benefits are cost of entry and which are differentiating. In-depth qualitative consumer research will help uncover this information. You will also need to know which benefits each of your competitors delivers in consumers' minds. Ultimately, you will need to know which benefits are important, personally relevant, unique and differentiating, purchase motivating, and appropriate for your brand. You also need to know that consumer benefits can be functional, emotional, experiential, or self-expressive. Once you acquire all this knowledge, you can begin to design your brand.

Designing Your Brand

In brand positioning or design, there are five components to be addressed:

1. *Target Audience.* Define the target customer.

2. *Brand Essence.* Articulate the "heart and soul" of the brand.

3. *Brand Promise.* Develop the relevant, differentiating benefits the brand promises to deliver to its target audience.

4. *Brand Archetype.* Identify the driving motivation behind the brand.

5. *Brand Personality.* Describe the brand as if it were a person.

As you address these five components (especially brand promise) you need to define your brand's competitive frame of reference and map out how it is positioned against competitors. (Figure 3–1 is a brand positioning statement.)

Figure 3–1. Brand positioning statement of The Nature Conservancy.

The Nature Conservancy

Target Audience:

1. Affluent people who are concerned about environmental conservation

2. Opinion leaders

Brand Essence:

Saving Great Places

Brand Promise:

Only The Nature Conservancy works in creative partnership with local communities in the U.S. and abroad to conserve the most important natural places for the benefit of future generations.

Brand Archetypes:

Scientist, advocate, and achiever

Brand Personality:

- Results-oriented, action-oriented
- Effective
- Entrepreneurial
- Focused
- A good ally, a reliable partner
- Possessing integrity
- Businesslike, professional
- Hardworking, persistent, tireless, dedicated
- Positive, constructive, nonconfrontational
- Science-driven

Although this may sound like a linear process, it is actually iterative and even organic. In the end, though, you will have determined each of the elements of your brand's design.

Figure 3–2 provides an overview of the brand management process.

Once the brand is designed, this design must drive all your consumer communication, all your other marketing elements, and your organization's design, particularly the company culture. It must also drive what Michael Porter, Harvard Business School professor and thought leader, calls the "customer value chain." (According to the "value chain" concept, each activity an

Figure 3–2. Brand management process.

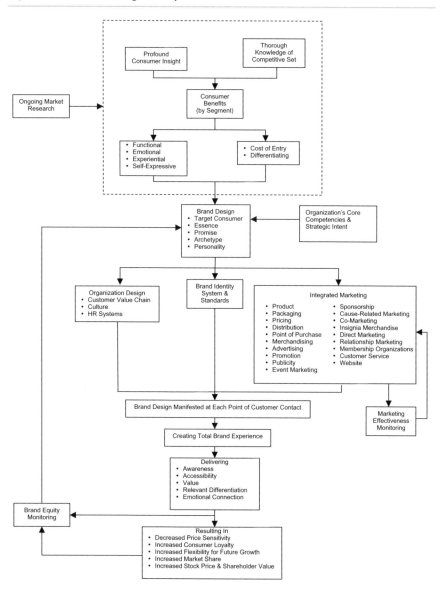

organization undertakes should lead to added value to its target consumers. If it doesn't, it should be reevaluated and possibly eliminated.[1])

The brand design should be directly translated into and supported by the brand identity standards and systems. This process ensures that the brand design is realized at each point of contact with the consumer, resulting in a total brand experience. If done right, a brand and the experience it delivers transcend the brand's products and services. In essence, you are selling the brand experience more than anything else.

All of this should deliver awareness, relevant differentiation, value, accessibility, and emotional connection—the key components in creating brand insistence.

Ultimately, strong brand equity should result in price premiums, decreased price sensitivity, increased consumer loyalty, increased flexibility for future growth, increased market share, and increased shareholder value.

THE MOST IMPORTANT TASKS OF A BRAND MANAGEMENT FUNCTION

- *Develop and execute brand plans, including brand marketing plans.*
- *Build brand awareness.*
- *Position the brand for sustainable competitive advantage.*
- *Transform the organization's leadership team into brand champions.*
- *Transform all employees into brand champions.*
- *Measure and actively manage your brand's equity.*
- *Actively manage the brand's identity, including enforcement of its guidelines and standards.*
- *Legally protect the brand.*
- *Always keep the brand customer-focused.*
- *Design and implement plans to create emotional connection between your brand and its customers.*
- *Develop and execute brand loyalty programs.*

Research That Supports the Brand Management Process

There are many types of research that aid in the brand management process. Some are ongoing, while others are only conducted periodically or as needed. Ongoing research includes brand equity, marketing effectiveness, and competitive monitoring, among other categories of research.

MONITORING BRAND EQUITY

Brand equity monitoring should highlight changes in consumers' attitudes, preferences, and behavior regarding your brand. It should also play a diagnostic role, giving insight into the whys those changes occur. While some brands, such as Coca-Cola, monitor brand equity on an ongoing basis, many brands conduct a more comprehensive brand equity "snapshot" every year or two.

MONITORING MARKETING EFFECTIVENESS

Marketing effectiveness monitoring takes many forms—from simple testing of advertising copy to using an ongoing system to identify the relative effectiveness of each element in your marketing mix, including estimates of return on marketing investment. It can be even more detailed, including analysis of effectiveness against different marketing objectives, such as customer retention, share of requirements, category buying rate, in-store capture, and conversion rates.

COMPETITIVE MONITORING

Competitive monitoring can take many forms, from dialy panel studies and market tours to product preference testing and POS (point of sale) data analysis—chain-specific data or from ACNielsen (Scan Track) or IRI (DataServer, FasTrac, and InfoScan).

Onetime or periodic research includes attitude and usage studies, in-depth qualitative consumer research, focus groups, conjoint analysis, Perception Analyzer testing, recognition and recall tests, concept testing, benefit testing, and test markets.

BRAND EXTENSION RESEARCH

A brand is an asset, and to provide strong shareholder value, assets must be leveraged. Brand extension is the primary way of doing that. Brand extension can be a powerful way to optimize the performance of your brand, but it also can be a complicated endeavor. Brand extension and brand extension research are discussed in detail in Chapters 15 and 17.

BRAND MANAGER COMPETENCIES AND RESPONSIBILITIES

Brand Manager Competencies

- *Strong ability to influence behaviors and perceptions without formal authority*
- *Respected throughout the organization*
- *Strong written and verbal persuasion skills*
- *Adequate analytical skills*
- *Customer research experience*
- *Strong intuition about human behavior and motivation*

- *Good project management skills*

Brand Manager Responsibilities
- *Identify, refine the brand's "unique value proposition."*
- *Monitor, measure, and manage brand equity/strength.*
- *Increase brand awareness, relevant differentiation, value, accessibility, and emotional connection.*
- *Develop brand plan.*
- *Monitor progress against brand plan.*
- *Be responsible for results against brand plan.*
- *Drive brand understanding and support organization-wide.*
- *Champion/drive initiatives that support delivery of the brand promise.*
- *Develop brand messaging—elevator speech, tagline, campaign themes, proof points, etc.*

Brand Identity Manager Competencies
- *Strong ability to influence behaviors and perceptions without formal authority.*
- *Respected throughout the organization.*
- *Likable.*
- *Assertive.*
- *Ability to say "no" in a nice way.*
- *Some understanding of brand identity standards and systems.*

Brand Identity Manager Responsibilities
- *Manage the brand architecture.*
- *Establish brand architecture and naming decision rules.*
- *Establish brand identity standards including cobranding standards.*
- *Maintain brand identity consistency.*
- *Chair the brand identity council/team/board.*
- *Help manage brand identity transitions resulting from mergers and acquisitions.*
- *Help determine identities for new brands/subbrands.*
- *Anticipate and accommodate new brand identity needs.*

PART 2
Designing the Brand

4

understanding
the consumer

ORGANIZATIONS EXIST for one purpose—to meet human needs. Thriving organizations do that exceedingly well. Venerated organizations have managed to meet evolving human needs over a long period of time. All of an organization's revenues and profits result from one thing—customers who are willing to pay money for products and services that meet their needs. Therefore, any brand management initiative, any marketing initiative, and indeed any business or organizational initiative must start with a solid understanding of the customer.

Defining the Target Customer
Focus is an important part of a brand's success. Brands focus on a target customer and often narrow their focus to a particular customer need segment. As mentioned in Chapter 3, customer targeting is the first step in brand design. Everything else emanates from that. So let us start with how to identify your brand's target customers.

Look for customers who meet the following criteria:

- They have an important need, and your brand meets that need.
- Your brand has the potential to be preferred by them.
- There is something about your brand that they admire.
- They have the potential to provide your organization with ample revenues and profits over the long run.

• Your organization can grow by building a long-term relationship with and increasingly fulfilling the evolving needs of these customers.

At a minimum, you should identify and understand the following target customer attributes:

- Demographics
- Lifestyle
- Needs/desires
- Hopes/aspirations
- Fears/concerns
- Product purchase behavior
- Product usage behavior

BASIC HUMAN NEEDS

As branders, it is useful to understand the basic needs that drive human emotions and behaviors. Abraham Maslow's hierarchy of needs addresses this requirement, as does Artur Manfred Max Neef's classification of fundamental human needs. Albert T. Poffenberger, Ph.D., devotes an entire chapter to "An Inventory of Human Desires" in his book *Psychology in Advertising*, published in 1925.

I have been a student of basic human needs for the better part of thirty years.

Here is my list of basic human needs, going from survival needs to such higher-order needs as self-actualization and enlightenment (compiled and revised over time from numerous sources):

1. Appetite/hunger
2. Safety/security
3. Physical comfort
4. Health/well-being
5. Sexual gratification
6. Competence/mastery
7. The desire to matter
8. Ability to contribute/make a difference
9. The desire to be heard/understood
10. Respect
11. Recognition
12. Self-esteem/sense of self-worth
13. Affection
14. Friendship
15. Sense of belonging
16. Control
17. Autonomy
18. Freedom

19. Creative expression/
   playfulness

20. Growth

21. Meaning

22. Beauty

23. Wholeness/oneness

As marketers and crafters of brand strategy and messaging, we should be cognizant of the underlying needs that drive human behaviors, including brand purchase and usage behaviors. The next time you craft strategy for your brand, think about which of these fundamental human needs your brand fulfills and then make sure you are reinforcing that need fulfillment with the brand and its messaging.

FEAR MOTIVATES

Unfortunately, fear is still the primary motivator among humans. I say unfortunately because I would hope that one day we would transcend our fears and be motivated primarily by our highest dreams and visions. It would lead to a much more utopian world.

Nevertheless, here is a partial list of some of our most common fears (in no particular order):

- Flying
- Heights
- Intimacy
- Crowds
- Rejection
- Change
- Damnation
- Clowns
- Spiders
- Drowning
- Being discovered as an imposter
- Dying
- Dark
- Commitment
- Making a mistake
- Abandonment
- The unknown
- Public speaking
- Germs
- Snakes
- Wild animals

And marketing messages certainly play off fear. Consider the opposite of each of these marketing claims. With our brand, you will feel:

- Safer
- As though you have more social status
- More beautiful or handsome

- More attractive to others
- Sexier
- More virile
- Smarter
- More likable
- As though you are a better mother or father
- As though you are a better husband or wife
- As though you are a better breadwinner/provider for your family
- More competent in your work
- More unique
- More lovable
- More loving
- More compassionate
- As though your life has more meaning
- Like you are making a difference in the world

So what underlies this ability to appeal to people through their fears and insecurities at a deep emotional level? People do not feel completely at ease in their own skins or in this world of ours. They feel insignificant, inferior, unlovable, inconsequential. It all relates to their self-esteem and their belief in the benevolence or cruelty or indifference of the universe. Does my life have any meaning at all? Do I matter? Does anyone really care about me? It also relates to the notion of judgment. Will I be judged to be worthy or not? Am I a good person or a bad person? Do I deserve to be loved? Do I deserve anything good in my life?

I could get metaphysical at this point and say that the solution is nonjudgment and nonattachment and transcending the sense of self and feeling connected to everyone and everything and being loving in all that you do. I guess I did just say that. However, my point is, until people wake up to a new way of seeing the world, fear is the primary motivator on which many a successful marketing campaign has been built. Just observe successful salespeople, ministers, politicians, lobbyists, or advertising campaigns. The importance of fear as a motivator will become crystal clear.

AUTOMOBILE PURCHASES AND SELF-IMAGE REINFORCEMENT

Research has shown that at least some people choose specific automobile brands to reinforce their self-image, project a certain social status, and enhance their self-esteem. They also choose them to "fit in" with their chosen social group. Other factors contribute to choice, including constraints such as income and capacity to acquire.

Think about this. What might each of these brands say about the purchaser's self-image and intended social group/status:

Audi	BMW	Chevy
HUMMER	Jeep	Mercedes-Benz
MINI Cooper	Subaru	Tesla
Toyota	Volvo	

Source: Liza-Jane Sowden and Martin Grimmer, "Symbolic Consumption and Consumer Identity: An Application of Social Identity Theory to Car Purchase Behavior" (Australian and New Zealand Marketing Academy Conference 2009), http://www.duplication.net.au/ANZMAC09/papers/ANZMAC2009-206.pdf.

BEHAVIORAL ECONOMICS

Behavioral economics is a relatviely new branch of economics. It explores how and why people behave in seemingly irrational ways. The discipline is at the intersection of psychology and economics. Several very interesting books have been written on this subject in the past few years. One of the findings is that people are often motivated more by what is "right" than by what is in their own self-interest. That is, morals and values often override self-interest. This is why Liberal Democrats and Conservative Republicans sometimes support policies that do not seem to be in their own self-interests. This is an important insight for marketers that are trying to create compelling brands and persuasive messages.

PEER PRESSURE

In 1951, psychologist Solomon Asch conducted conformity experiments at Swarthmore College. He found that within peer groups, there is great pressure to conform to group norms and follow others in the group. This is especially true among younger people and people who have lower self-esteem.[1] If marketers can establish brand usage as a group norm, it can create increased brand usage and loyalty within that group. In the late 1990s, Hallmark ran an advertising campaign that encouraged people to turn over greeting cards to make sure the Hallmark name was on the back. Not all people cared if the card was Hallmark branded, but they worried that the recipient might.

THE DOVE CAMPAIGN FOR REAL BEAUTY

"The Dove brand is rooted in listening to women. Based on the findings of a major global study, The Real Truth About Beauty: A Global Report, Dove launched the Campaign for Real Beauty in 2004. The campaign started a global conversation about the need for a wider definition of beauty after the study proved the hypothesis that the definition of beauty had become limiting and unattainable. Among the study's findings was the statistic that only 2 percent of women around the world would describe themselves as beautiful. Since 2004, Dove has employed various communications vehicles to challenge beauty stereotypes and invite women to join a discussion about beauty. In 2010, Dove evolved the campaign and launched an unprecedented effort to make beauty a source of confidence, not anxiety, with the Dove Movement for Self-Esteem."

Dove's Campaign for Real Beauty website

To Dove's credit, this campaign does not play off of a woman's fear that she is not beautiful, but rather celebrates the truth that everyone radiates beauty in her own way. This ad campaign is based on a more enlightened view of the world.

THE POWER OF FOCUS

The power of brands lies in focus. Very few, if any, brands can be all things to all people within a product or service category. That is why segmentation is important. Ideally, a brand or subbrand focuses only on the customer segment that it can best serve. It becomes an expert provider of products and services to that segment. I am a firm believer that in today's business environment, the most robust brands will be those that:

- Focus on one customer group.
- Become intimate with that group.
- Strive to meet more and more needs of that group.
- Cocreate products and services with the group.
- Epitomize what that group stands for.

Although we most often think of brands as targeting specific customer groups, different brands can also target different needs for the same people. For instance, different needs are driving your purchase decision at different times, and you are very likely to consider a different set of restaurants (or brand) for each of the following situations:

- Catching a quick bite to eat on your way to work in the morning

- Taking your children out to eat

- Celebrating a special occasion with a loved one

- Staying on your diet and losing weight

Techniques to Better Understand the Customer

Understanding your customer is a never-ending process. Here are some simple ways to do so:

- Conduct ongoing customer research, from focus groups and depth interviews to anthropological and quantitative research techniques (see Chapter 17 on brand research).

- Conduct customer satisfaction surveys.

- Maintain and monitor customer service/support mechanisms (e.g., help lines, e-mail support).

- Establish and monitor social media devoted to different customer groups/segments.

- Establish and consult with customer advisory boards.

- Establish customer membership organizations. Participate in and monitor their events. Harley-Davidson executives are masters at this technique. They attend—and ride in—HOG (Harley Owners Group) rallies, talk with their customers at those rallies, observe new product accessories, and after every HOG rally, debrief back at the office for new product ideas and other action items.

- Have key executives/managers participate in sales calls.

- Have key executives/managers occasionally rotate through frontline customer service positions.

- Hire employees who are also passionate customers. (There is one danger with this approach. Even if you are a passionate brand customer, don't assume that all other customers are just like you.)

Because of their extensive market research, people who develop new products (marketers and marketing researchers) often understand the market (including deep customer insights) better than anyone else in the organization. Seek them out to gain a better understanding of your brand's customers and their needs.

ENVIRONMENTAL SCANNING

For most businesses, environmental scanning can also be very helpful in staying abreast of the latest customer, industry, and societal trends. "Environmental scanning" is a fancy term for the following process:

- Reading a broad cross section of books and publications of relevance to your business

- Monitoring any other relevant media

- Keeping very close track of the emerging trends by counting the number of times certain ideas, needs, or concepts are referenced

- Seeking to better understand emerging ideas, needs, or concepts— those that are steadily increasing in frequency and intensity

---

DID YOU KNOW?

Through carefully researched consumer insight, John Deere was able to significantly increase sales of its lawn tractors. Most men really admired the brand but believed that it was "too much for them." They could never justify buying a John Deere for themselves. Here's the insight. When their wives were made aware that eight out of ten men would prefer a John Deere lawn tractor if given the option, sales significantly increased. The way in was through the gift giver.

(Source: Barry Krause, "Advertising Agency's View on Corporate Branding," presented at the American Management Association's Corporate Branding conference, San Francisco, February 24, 1999).

Market Segmentation

Market segmentation is often necessary to effectively meet the needs of different customer groups. Different segments will value different aspects of your products, services, and brands differently. You should have a good understanding of the following dimensions of each market segment:

- Its overall size and its growth rate

- Its price sensitivity

- The benefits that are most and least important to it

- How well it is served by existing products and brands

- How brand-loyal it is

- How it selects and purchases the product
- How accessible it is
- The distribution methods it prefers
- How it uses the product
- Its product usage/replacement rate
- Its longevity and projected evolution over time

Markets can be segmented in the following ways:

- *Product Usage Segmentation.* For instance, some people use baking soda to deodorize their refrigerators, while others use it as a surface soft scrub, to treat insect bites or itchy skin, or as a toothpaste.

- *Purchase Behavior Segmentation.* In many industries, four groups that often emerge to one degree or another are:
  1. Brand-loyal consumers
  2. Convenience-driven consumers
  3. Price-driven consumers
  4. Consumers that enjoy seeking out new brands and products within the category

- *Benefit Segmentation.* People might buy a sailboat to race, for a day sail, to cruise on a vacation, to live aboard, to entertain friends, or as a second home.

- *Price Segmentation.* Price segmentation will yield higher overall revenues and profits if designed properly. Airlines have made a science out of price segmentation. First-class travelers pay more. Business travelers with tight schedules will be less price sensitive. Tourists with fixed budgets, flexible schedules, and a long planning horizon will look for lower fares. Some people will only travel taking advantage of last-minute seat-filling bargain prices. Other last-minute travelers have no choice and behaviorally (but probably not attitudinally) are virtually price insensitive. Seats are less expensive on slower days (Saturdays, December 25, etc.).

- *Lifestage Segmentation.* There is a system of segmenting adults into eight distinct mindsets using a specific set of psychological traits and demographics that are proven to drive consumer behavior. Consult: Strategic Business Insights VALS (values and lifestyles) at www.strategicbusinessinsights.com/vals/ustypes.shtml, and Yankelovich MONITOR at thefuturescompany.com/what-we-do/us-yankelovich-monitor.

• *Cohort Group Segmentation.* Refers to people who were born at approximately the same time and who have experienced the same events at the same lifestages.

• *Psychographic Segmentation.* Refers to segmenting people based on their values, attitudes, and lifestyles.

• *Geographic Segmentation.* Segmenting people according to their geographic location can help target people in the same socioeconomic bracket who may share interests or concerns.

• *Geodemographic Segmentation.* Refers to segmenting people based on their location—typically zip or postal code—and demographics, such as age and income. Consult: Nielsen PRIZM and Nielsen's other segmentation tools (www.claritas.com/MyBestSegments/Default.jsp) and CACI's ACORN (acorn.caci.co.uk).

As the previous list illustrates, consumers can be segmented on many dimensions. The trick is to arrive at a segmentation scheme that relates to differences in purchase motivations and behaviors. Different brands are designed to appeal to different needs with unique points of difference. It is important to understand the consumers for whom your brand will mean the most and who will have the highest likelihood of responding to your brand messages.

WHAT DO UPSCALE CUSTOMERS WANT?

- *High quality, including choice materials, fine craftsmanship, and superior aesthetics*
- *Outstanding customer service, including attentiveness, respect, courtesy, and civility*
- *Exclusivity, rarity, and unique privilege of ownership*
- *Brands that confer status*
- *History, pedigree, and a well-told brand story*
- *Minimized risk*

Business-to-Business Customers

For B2B (business-to-business) organizations, understanding the purchase decision-making process is usually more complicated. Decisions are often made by teams or committees comprising people from different functions. Some people initiate the purchase order or request for proposal (RFP).

Others are gatekeepers, influencers, decision makers, purchasers, and users. Each has a different role in the process at a different point in the process. They often focus on different product, service, and brand attributes, and they respond to different types of appeals. Also, they usually rely on different sources for their information. An astute B2B marketer should understand how best to get to each of these individuals, what angle to emphasize in the communication, and in what verbal style to communicate (see Figure 4–1).

Figure 4–1. B2B purchaser motivations.

These purchaser motivations are usually present in B2B buying situations:

- Price
- Perceived quality
- Technical specifications
- Warranties
- Other service or postsale support
- Financial stability of the seller
- Buyer's past experience
- Organizational policies
- Fear of making a mistake
- Friendship
- Seller's interest in buyer's business
- Persuasiveness of seller

Source: Gabriel M. Gelb, Gelb Consulting Group, Inc. (now Endeavor Management Company — http://endeavormgmt.com/gelb-consulting), "The Nuts and Bolts of Business-to-Business Marketing Research."

For instance, in a corporation considering e-learning (online learning) solutions, the chief learning officer (CLO) may be the primary decision maker for enterprisewide solutions; however, many others are typically a part of the process, too:

- The chief financial officer (CFO) may have suggested that e-learning be investigated as a cost-saving measure and may have final approval of the purchase.

- General managers whose employees will be beneficiaries of the training will have their own point of view.

- The chief information officer (CIO) may have an opinion regarding the technology training components of the solution.

- The HR vice president may want to know how e-learning fits into the organization's overall approach to human capital management.

- There may even be a group of end users set up to evaluate each of the alternatives considered.

- Lawyers may provide their opinions on aspects of the proposal.

- And, depending on the organization, the list of stakeholders in the decision-making process may be extensive.

A marketer will have to decide which audiences are the most important, how many different types of communications are necessary, and how much the brand needs to be built with each stakeholder. As resources are always finite, decisions on reach vs. frequency for each audience will be necessary.

In B2B situations, once one decision maker has been identified through research, it is very useful to ask that person, "Who else in your organization is involved in the decision-making process?"

Business markets can often be segmented by Standard Industrial Classification (SIC) code. Various publications and other sources provide information by SIC code, including U.S. Industrial Outlook, the U.S. Census of Manufacturers, the D&B Business Information Report, and mailhouses.

In organizations with a wide variety of products and services serving multiple markets, business units are often formed around different customer groups. Another approach to serving different markets is to create the role of segment marketing manager. Segment marketing managers become experts in their assigned markets through primary and secondary research and develop (and execute) integrated marketing plans (including product requirements) for their assigned markets. These people often interact in a matrix fashion with the product managers.

WARMTH AND COMPETENCE

Customer loyalty expert Chris Malone and social psychologist Susan Fiske evaluated forty-five companies over ten separate studies, including Amazon, Chobani, Dominos, Hershey's, Johnson & Johnson, Lululemon, Sprint, and Zappos. They discovered that people make quick judgments about two things: 1) What are their intentions toward me? 2) How capable are they in carrying out those intentions? These concerns are summarized as warmth and competence. They apply to people's judgments of other people, but also their assessments of businesses, products, and brands. What is the takeaway for brands? They need to be both warm and competent to succeed, the most important of which is warmth. Put another way, worthy intentions drive loyalty.

(Source: Chris Malone and Susan Fiske, The Human Brand: How We Relate to People, Products, and Companies, San Francisco: Jossey-Bass, 2013).

Techniques to Retain Customers

The "lifetime value of the consumer" concept is based on the fact that it is much more cost-effective to keep a good consumer than to attract a new one. For large-ticket items (e.g., automobiles) or items that require frequent purchase over time (e.g., breakfast cereals), the lifetime value of a consumer can be very high. So, encouraging young customers to buy your products and services will help your business to remain healthy over time and to create a longer lifetime value of the customer.

DID YOU KNOW?
Customers share bad brand experiences with approximately twice as many people as they do good brand experiences.

Among the techniques for keeping good consumers are:

- Database marketing
- Special services
- Product customization
- Personal touches
- Legendary service
- Communication that reinforces previously made purchases (especially to overcome post-purchase anxiety or doubts over large-ticket items)
- Programs that reward loyalty and heavy brand consumption
- Avoiding programs that encourage brand switching

Use the checklist in Figure 4–2 to assess the efficacy of your brand management practices in the area covered by this chapter. The more questions to which you can answer "yes," the better you are doing. The checklist also serves as a brief summary of the material covered in the chapter.

Figure 4–2. Checklist: Understanding the consumer.

	YES / NO
Do you conduct customer research frequently?	___ ___
Do you use in-depth, qualitative consumer research techniques (such as laddering, hidden-issue questioning, and symbolic analysis) to better understand your consumer's needs and motivations as they relate to your brand?	___ ___
Do you know who your customers most frequently rely on to gather information about your products and services? Do you know which of these sources "carry the most weight" with them?	___ ___
Do you know the process customers use to select and purchase products and services in the product/service categories your brand serves?	___ ___
Do you know how people are using your products and services?	___ ___
Do you fully understand how consumers experience your product or service when using it? Do you know what emotions it evokes? Do you know how it makes them feel? Are you aware of all the sensory components of its use? Does it stimulate their thinking? Do you know what comes to their minds when using it?	___ ___
Do you know what problems people encounter when they use your products and services?	___ ___
Have you experienced your brand side by side with your consumers?	___ ___
Do you keep track of household participation, units per household, and average price (as components of category dollar sale growth)?	___ ___
Do you know what drives brand preference and insistence within your categories?	___ ___
Do you know what other brands your customers considered before they bought your brand? Do you know what it was about your brand that caused them to choose it?	___ ___
Do you know all the reasons why customers switch from your brand to other brands?	___ ___
When your product or service is not available in a certain store (out of stock or not carried), do you know what portion of your brand's consumers switch brands, switch stores, or postpone their purchases?	___ ___

Do you know how involved consumers are with your brand? Do consumers have an opinion about your brand?   ___ ___

Do you have a thorough understanding of how the market for your brand's product and services is segmented? Do you know which segments your brand best serves? Do you know which segments are likely to provide the most long-term business potential for your brand?   ___ ___

Do you know which customers are the most valuable to your organization?   ___ ___

For business-to-business organizations: Do you understand the customer organization's decision-making process? Do you know how to reach the decision makers?   ___ ___

Have you calculated the "lifetime value" of your customers? Have you done the same by consumer segment?   ___ ___

Have you identified a specific set of simple questions that separates your customers into different customer need segments?   ___ ___

Is your brand attractive to younger consumers? Does the average age of your brand's consumer remain constant instead of creeping up over time?   ___ ___

Do you frequently monitor what people are saying about your brand in social media and other online forums?   ___ ___

Do you know how people talk about your products and services when they recommend them to others?   ___ ___

Do you invite customers and potential customers to provide input to new product development?   ___ ___

Do your organization's systems and databases have a unified view of who your customers are?   ___ ___

Does your organization have a CRM (customer relationship management) system? Is everything driven off of one relational database?   ___ ___

Does your organization capture, learn from, and evolve based on consumer complaints? Are there mechanisms in place to ensure that happens?   ___ ___

Do you share customer information broadly throughout the organization? Do you post customer research and insights on an intranet or extranet site for employees?   ___ ___

5

understanding
the competition

WHEN A COMPANY positions its brand in a customer's mind, it is positioning that brand against other brands. It is critical to understand the strengths, weaknesses, opportunities, and threats of each of those competitors along with the industry structure itself. (In fact, wise organizations dedicate a person to understanding the competition.)

This knowledge about your competition is necessary because you want to *uniquely* "own" an important benefit in your customer's mind. Ideally, this benefit is one that your competitors have not addressed and cannot easily address in the future. Better yet, the benefit you own should be one that takes advantage of your competitors' Achilles' heels.

At a minimum, you should collect the following data on each key competitor:

- Key business objectives, goals, and strategies

- Sales, sales growth, profitability, market share, and other key financial measures

- Brand equity including brand awareness, usage, preference, relevant differentiation, quality, value, accessibility, vitality, personality, key associations, emotional connection, and loyalty

- Product and service offerings

- Pricing and distribution

- Major customers

- Corporate culture
- Organization charts
- Sales organization and compensation
- Share of voice/marketing, budget/advertising spend

Sources of Competitive Information

Important sources of competitive information include:

- Competitor websites.
- Press releases. There are free online services that can send you daily e-mail messages with press releases on topics of interest to you.
- Industry analyst reports.
- Financial analyst reports. (If you have a Charles Schwab or Fidelity account, you can use their research functions to view company research reports from a wide variety of financial analysts.)
- News clipping services.
- ORC International (www.orcinternational.com) and Avention (www.avention.com) consulting and research services.
- Harte Hanks (www.hartehanks.com), Hoovers (www.hoovers.com), and other company databases.
- Online database searching services, such as FirstSearch, ProQuest, and Lexis-Nexis Academic Universe.
- Services that track advertising spending.
- Search engines and intelligent agents.
- Online chat rooms, bulletin boards, and discussion groups.
- Product/brand review websites, e.g., epinions.com (Chapter 11 has more).
- Trade magazines.
- Trade shows.
- Competitor direct mail campaigns. Add a friend or relative to their lists.
- Your field sales force. Responding to the information they send from the field will encourage them to send more.
- Ex-employees from competitors' firms. They may be under your employ now, or they can be identified from job search databases.

- Current customers. Many of them will pass on competitive communications they receive.

- Primary and secondary research (qualitative and quantitative, including brand equity studies). Make sure to investigate syndicated studies. Syndicated studies are typically published by large research firms such as ACNielsen, Harris Interactive, and Forrester Research. An example is IntelliQuest's Computer Industry Media Study.

- Purchase and use a competitors' products (i.e., become a customer). Your entire management team should do this; it is an excellent way to understand competitors' customer experiences.

- Market tours. If you work in retail, visit stores that carry your competitors' products and talk with the sales associates about their products and services and what the companies are like to work with.

- Competitive intelligence firms.

This chapter has focused on how to better understand your brand's competition. Use Figure 5–1 to assess the efficacy of your brand management practices in regard to competition. The more yes answers you have, the better you are doing.

Figure 5–1. Checklist: Understanding the competition.

	YES / NO
Have you identified your brand's primary competitors for each market segment in which your brand operates?	___ ___
Have you carefully analyzed of your competitors' strengths, weaknesses, opportunities, threats?	___ ___
Do you fully understand the brand equities of your competitors?	___ ___
Do you know how loyal your competitors' customers are, which of their customers are less loyal than others, and why?	___ ___
Is there someone responsible for competitive intelligence in your organization?	___ ___
Does your management team buy and use competitive products?	___ ___
Does someone in your organization track competitor news and announcements on a daily basis?	___ ___
Do you share competitive data throughout the organization?	___ ___

6

....

brand design

IF A BRAND is the personification of an organization or that organization's products and services, it must have a personality and an identity. There are four major components of brand design on which you must focus once you have identified the target customer: 1) brand essence, 2) brand promise, 3) brand archetype, and 4) brand personality. Let's begin with brand essence.

Brand Essence

Brand essence is the timeless quality that the brand possesses. It is a brand's "heart and soul." The essence is usually articulated in the following three-word format: *adjective, adjective, noun.* For instance Nike's essence is "authentic athletic performance," Post-it's essence is "fast, friendly communication," and Disney's is "fun family entertainment."

BRAND ESSENCE EXERCISE

When I conduct workshops on brand positioning for organizations, I always warm up the participants with an exercise that demonstrates what brand essence is. I divide the group into teams of three to four people. Each team is given five minutes to define the essence of a well-known personality. (Some people I frequently use are Madonna, Arnold Schwarzenegger, Bill Clinton, George W. Bush, John Ashcroft, Marilyn Manson, Abraham Lincoln, Albert Einstein, Adolf Hitler, Mother Teresa, Wolfgang Amadeus Mozart, and Nelson Mandela.) While there is much discussion and debate, most groups are able to agree on an essence within five minutes. The essences are always distinct for each personality assigned. (Well, almost always. In one workshop, a group defined Madonna's essence as "audacious sexual chameleon." Another group assigned to Bill Clinton indicated they had arrived at the same essence for him. Perhaps they were copying the adjacent group's notes!)

Most of the essences that teams craft "ring true" with the larger group of participants in a given workshop and are fairly consistent across workshops in different organizations. The exercise reinforces the power of having a strong and well-known essence and personality.

Occasionally, brand essences take a slightly different form. Hallmark's essence is "caring shared," The Nature Conservancy's is "saving great places," and Ritz-Carlton's is "ladies and gentlemen serving ladies and gentlemen."

Figure 6–1 defines what a brand essence is and what it is not.

Figure 6–1. *Brand essence.*

A Brand Essence Is . . .	A Brand Essence Is Not . . .
The "heart and soul" of the brand.	A name.
Elegant in its economy of words. Take one word away and it loses its meaning.	An advertising theme line or slogan (The Nature Conservancy's essence being a notable exception).
A constant, timeless and enduring. It will not change over time, across geographies, or in different situations.	A brand promise.
Aspirational yet concrete enough to be meaningful and useful. For instance, Hallmark's essence is "caring shared," not "greeting cards" (a product category description that lacks the aspirational quality) or "enriching people's lives" (aspirational but not concrete enough to be useful).	
Extendable.	A product or service (category) description.

When Xerox neared the brink of failure in the mid-2000s, its brand essence was "The Document Company,"[1] which may have been one source of the company's problems. It was a very limiting product/business description (especially in the digital age), not an extendable timeless quality.

Method's "Our Story" section of its website says that "Eric (Ryan) knew people wanted cleaning products they didn't have to hide under their sinks. And Adam (Lowry) knew how to make them without any dirty ingredients. Their powers combined, they set out to save the world and create an entire line of home care products that were more powerful than a bottle of sodium hypochlorite. Gentler than a thousand puppy licks. Able to detox tall homes in a single afternoon." So, what is the brand's essence? I think it is pretty clearly "powerful, nontoxic cleaning."

Brand Promise

The brand promise is the most important part of a brand's design. A brand must promise a relevant, compelling, and differentiated benefit to the target customer. (People often confuse benefits with attributes and features. The brand must promise a benefit, not an attribute or feature.) The benefit may be functional, emotional, experiential, or self-expressive. (Who am I? What do I value? What are my convictions? With whom do I associate? To what do I aspire?) Nonfunctional benefits are the most desirable, however, as they appeal to people on a visceral level and are the least vulnerable to competitive copying. The benefit must focus on points of difference, not points of parity.

The ideal benefit has the following three qualities (see Figure 6–2):

1. It is extremely important to the target consumer.

2. Your organization is uniquely suited to deliver it.

3. Competitors are not currently addressing it (nor is it easy for them to address it in the future).

In their book *Creating Brand Loyalty: The Management of Power Positioning and Really Great Advertising*, Richard Czerniawski and Michael Maloney indicate that the most powerful benefits tap into people's deeply held beliefs, exploit your competitors' vulnerabilities, or overcome previous concerns people had about your brand, its product/service category, or its usage.[2] From my experience, the most powerful benefits give people hope that they can overcome or transcend their anxieties, fears, problems, or concerns.

COMPETITIVE COPYING

The easiest thing for a competitor to copy is a price reduction or discount. Almost as easy to copy are advertised (or otherwise communicated) product and service features. The things least easy to copy are consumer benefits that are based on proprietary consumer research or behind-the-scene systems, logistics, or customer service training. For instance, if frontline service employees are trained to internalize the brand promise and are empowered to deliver it in whatever way makes sense given the situation, that is much less easy for a competitor to observe and copy. The way a company interacts with different consumers differently through database marketing is also less visible (and often highly effective).

Figure 6–2. *Crafting the most powerful brand benefit.*

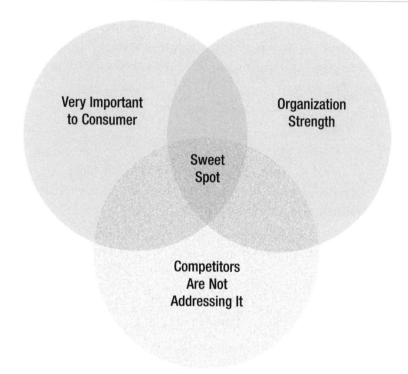

The following steps should enable you to identify the optimal brand benefit:

● Review previous product and brand research.

● Conduct qualitative research (e.g., focus groups, one-on-one interviews) to better understand the target customer's attitudes, values, needs, desires, fears, and concerns, especially as they relate to your brand's product/service category. In this step, you can develop short benefit statements and run them by the target customer iteratively to get a feel for which are most compelling.

● Compile a list of twenty to forty possible benefits.

● Do research that quantifies the importance of each of the possible benefits to your target customer, together with that customer's perceptions of how your brand and each of its competitors deliver against those benefits (to identify the most important benefits that your brand could "own").

COMPETITIVE FRAME OF REFERENCE

Often, exploring different competitive frames of reference will help you choose the most powerful brand benefit. Here are some questions to help you determine your brand's optimal frame of reference:

- Within what product/service category does our brand operate?
- Within which product and service categories do our customers give us "permission" to operate today? Do they give us more permission than we give ourselves?
- Does our brand stand for something broader than its products and services? Does that give our brand permission to enter new product and service categories?
- What compromises do we make with our customers that we take for granted but that might cause our customers to pursue alternative solutions to meet their needs?
- What could another company give our customers that would cause them to become disloyal to our brand?
- Could another brand within our category credibly insert its name into our brand's promise/positioning statement?
- What are the most likely substitute products for our product?
- What could neutralize our point of difference?
- What could make our point of difference obsolete?
- What could "kill" our category?

Consider, for example, the various frames of reference from which Coca-Cola could choose, from most narrow to most broad (see Figure 6–3).

Figure 6–3. *Frames of reference for Coca-Cola.*

Frame of Reference	Potential Competitors	Potential Point of Difference
Cola	Pepsi, RC Cola	?
Carbonated beverage (soda pop)	7 Up, Dr. Pepper	?
Soft drink	Crystal Light, Gatorade	?

Nonalcoholic beverage	Chocolate milk, root beer float	?
Beverage	Wine, beer	?
Liquid refreshment	Water, bottled water	?
Psychological refreshment	A walk in the woods, yoga, a swim	?

Now consider how Hallmark Cards' "differentiating benefits" might vary for each of the frames of reference listed in Figure 6–4.

Figure 6–4. *Frames of reference for Hallmark Cards.*

Frame of Reference	Potential Product Categories
Greeting cards	Greeting cards
Social expression products	Note cards, invitations, electronic greetings, enhanced e-mail
Caring and sharing	Flowers, candy, gift baskets, romantic cruises, family portraits, family scrapbooks, children's books, children's educational activities, family games, massage oil
Community building	Interpersonal relationship workshops, marriage enrichment courses, planned communities

And, interestingly, Cirque du Soleil did not define its competition as "other circuses," but rather as "every other show in town."[3]

Find out how choosing alternative frames of reference will alter competitive sets, products and services, and points of difference. Broadening your brand's frame of reference can help you:

1. Identify a strong point of difference within your current narrower frame of reference. (For instance, Pepsi chose to "own" psychological refreshment as a point of difference over Coca-Cola.)

2. Identify logical avenues for brand growth.

3. Identify potential substitute products and other competitive threats.

To create a "category of one" brand, one must choose a preemptive frame of reference so that the brand is the only one in its consideration set. Rather than differentiating the brand by choosing a differentiating benefit within a current product/service category or frame of reference, one differentiates the brand by identifying or creating an entirely new product/service category or frame of reference that is highly compelling. The new category is set up so that the brand in question is the only one within that category (Figure 6–5).

Figure 6–5. *Creating "category of one" brands.*

Brand Category	Broadest Category	Narrower	Category-of-One	Category-of-One Tagline or Key Message
Rensselaer Polytechnic Institute	University	Technological University	University that changes the world through technological creativity	Why not change the world?
American University	University		University whose students and professors are federal government insiders	Our WONK status sets us apart
Paul Smith's College	College		College for people who love to live and play in the Adirondack wilderness	THE COLLEGE OF THE ADIRONDACKS
Naropa University	University	Religious-affiliated university	University that focuses on personal transformation	Transform Yourself, Transform the World
The Strong	Children's museum	Top-tier (no. 3) children's museum in the world	The first museum in the world dedicated to the study and exploration of play	The National Museum of Play

For the sake of simplicity and focus, I state a brand's promise as follows:

Only [brand] delivers [relevant differentiated benefit] to [target customer].

Use of the word *only* is very important. It forces you to choose a benefit that only your brand can deliver.

Occasionally, clients will ask why they can't craft the brand promise as, "[Brand] is the best at delivering [relevant differentiated benefit] to [target customer]." The problem with this approach is that being the best may not change a customer's purchase behavior if other brands deliver against the chosen benefit to a sufficient degree.

Others may use a form that incorporates the frame of reference, such as "Only [brand] delivers [relevant differentiating benefit] to [target customer] within the [product/service category]." Although the frame of reference exercise can help to identify potentially powerful differentiating benefits, incorporating it into the brand promise itself is not helpful. Here are some brand promises of well-known brands (see also Figure 6–5):

- Only Volvo delivers assurance of the safest ride to parents who are concerned about their children's well-being.

- Only Harley-Davidson delivers the fantasy of complete freedom on the road and the comradeship of kindred spirits to avid cyclists.

- Only The Nature Conservancy has the expertise and resources to work in creative partnership with local communities in the United States and internationally with exceptional range and agility to conserve the most important places for future generations.

- Only the Boy Scouts of America instills values in boys, resulting in a more successful adulthood on a massive nationwide scale through a proven fun program.

A brand promise must be (and should be tested to be):

- Understandable

- Believable

- Unique/Differentiating

- Compelling

- Admirable or Endearing

Once crafted and agreed to, the brand promise should be delivered at each point of contact with the consumer. So everyone in your organization should know your brand's promise.

VOLVO BRAND STRATEGY

In the late 1990s to mid-2000s, Volvo Car executives believed the brand position of the "ultimate safe car" for families was too limiting and began to extend the brand into the performance car segment targeted at men. Results were disappointing. When Ford bought Volvo in 1999, it pushed the brand into the crowded luxury brand market. Ten years later, sales were down 20 percent from where they were when Ford first purchased the brand.

Volvo Car Corporation was then acquired by China's Zhejiang Geely Holding Group Co. Under this new ownership, in August 2011, Volvo Car announced a new global brand strategy—"Designed

Around You," focusing on a position of human-centric luxury cars that are safe and dependable.

In November 2013, Volvo Car Corporation announced a new brand strategy designed to revive the brand in the United States after a decade of declining demand. According to Automotive News, "The new focus is on 'Scandinavian' design, safety, environmental leadership, and 'clever functionality' reflected in state of the art—yet simple—infotainment systems."

Volvo's primary brand association is still "safety." And safety is still most valued by parents with children living at home. And Volvo is still one of the most trusted automobile brands. Any repositioning must be congruent with and build on its reputation as the "ultimate safe car."

Sources:
David Kiley, "Volvo Goes Beyond Safety" Bloomberg Businesssweek, March 22, 2007, www.business-week.com/stories/2007-03-22/volvo-goes-beyond-safetybusinessweek-business-news-stock-market-and-financial-advice.

Patrick Lefler, "Is Volvo's New Brand Strategy Going to Stress Luxury or Safety?" Customer Think (blog), August 19, 2010, customerthink.com/is_volvo_s_new_brand_strategy_going_to_stress_luxury_or_safety/.

"Volvo Car Corporation Announces a New Brand Strategy—'Designed Around You,'" company news release, August 23, 2011, www.volvocars.com/intl/top/corporate/news/pages/default.aspx?itemid=307.

Richard Truett, "Volvo Outlines Strategy for U.S. Revival," Automotive News, November 7, 2013. www.autoweek.com/article/20131107/CARNEWS/131109872.

Brand Archetype

Whereas the brand personality uses adjectives to describe the brand as if it were a person, the brand archetype, based on Jungian archetypes, indicates the brand's driving force or motivation. Margaret Mark and Carol Pearson, in their book *The Hero and the Outlaw: Building Extraordinary Brands Through the Power of Archetypes*, describe twelve archetypes in great detail—the innocent, the explorer, the sage, the hero, the outlaw, the magician, the regular guy/gal, the lover, the jester, the caregiver, the creator, and the ruler. We use twenty-seven different archetypes when we work with clients.

As an example, in *Winning the Story Wars*, Jonah Sachs describes the defender archetype as "defending that which is sacred but may be lost." The archetype's qualities are "strong, sensitive, selfless, and resolute" and its values are "justice, perfection, and wholeness." Famous defenders include "John Muir, Jane Goodall, Ronald Reagan, the Tea Party, Greenpeace, and the Boy Scouts." He says that "while defenders are indispensible in any society, they are often the last to accept needed change."[4]

Brand Personality

Each brand should choose an intended personality based on the brand's aspirations and its customers' current perceptions of the brand. The personality is usually communicated in seven to nine adjectives describing the brand as if it were a person.

A brand's personality and values are often a function of the following:[5]

- The personality and values of the organization's founder (assuming the person had a strong personality and values)

- The personality and values of the organization's current leader (again, assuming this individual has a strong personality and values)

- The personalities and values of the organization's most zealous customers/members/clients

- The brand's carefully crafted design/positioning

- Some combination of the above

Although personality attributes vary considerably by product category and brand, strong brands tend to possess particular personality attributes. In general order of importance, strong brands are:

- Trustworthy

- Authentic

- Reliable ("I can always count on [brand name]!")

- Admirable

- Appealing

- Honest

- Representative of something (specifically, something important to the customer)

- Likable

- Popular

- Unique

- Believable

- Relevant

- Known for delivering high-quality, well-performing products and services

- Service-oriented

- Innovative

Employees are also an important factor in communicating the brand's personality in organizations in which the organizational brand is used. This is why companies are increasingly recruiting, training, and managing their employees to manifest their brands' promises.

Repositioning a Brand

Brand repositioning is necessary if one or more of these conditions exist:

• Your brand has a bad, confusing, or nonexistent image.

• The primary benefit your brand "owns" has evolved from a differentiating benefit to a cost-of-entry benefit. (For example, for airlines cost-of-entry benefits would be safe flights, needed routes, and required times.)

• Your organization is significantly altering its strategic direction.

• Your organization is entering new businesses and the current positioning is no longer appropriate.

• A new competitor with a superior value proposition is entering your industry.

• Competition has usurped your brand's position or made it ineffectual.

• Your organization has acquired a very powerful proprietary advantage that must be worked into the brand positioning.

• Corporate culture renewal dictates at least a revision of the brand personality.

• You are broadening your brand to appeal to additional consumers or consumer need segments for whom the current brand positioning won't work. (This should be a "red flag" since it could dilute the brand's meaning or make it less appealing to current customers or even alienate them.)

You follow the same steps and address the same brand design components when repositioning a brand as you do when first designing the brand. But brand repositioning is more difficult than initially positioning a brand because you must first help the customer "unlearn" the current brand positioning (easier said than done). Three actions can aid in this process:

1. Carefully crafted communication

2. New products and packaging that emphasize the new positioning

3. Associations with other brands (e.g., cobranding, comarketing, ingredient branding, strategic alliances) that reinforce the new brand positioning

You should not rely on an advertising agency, a brand consulting company, or your marketing department to craft your corporate or organizational brand's design. This is so critical to your organization's success that its leadership team and marketing/brand management leaders should develop it themselves, preferably with the help of a brand positioning expert.

> ### *REBRANDING FOOTJOY*
>
> *FootJoy is a well-known golf brand (67 percent of golfers use it) recognized for having comfortable, exceptionally high-quality products that stay dry in wet conditions. FootJoy sells shoes, gloves, outerwear, socks, and accessories.*
>
> *Traditionally, FootJoy focused is messages on its superior product features and functionality; however, it knew it needed to create a more emotional connection with its customers. FootJoy retained us to help create this emotional connection. Through qualitative research, we learned that FootJoy was perceived to be a golf-centric brand that is for people who are serious about golf. We discovered that it had the potential to be a strong aspirational brand as it possessed all the qualities to which serious golfers aspire. The result was a new tagline (The Mark of a Player) that underpinned a new advertising campaign, making FootJoy a badge that says, "I am a serious golfer."*

Conducting a Brand Positioning Workshop

Frequently, a brand design is not embraced by the organization because the leadership team was not actively involved in the process at every step along the way. Often, outside experts will design a brand based on separate interviews with key stakeholders. This input does not allow for disagreement, debate, discussion, or consensus building among the stakeholders. Brand positioning involves highly facilitated, well-prepared sessions in which all the key stakeholders (typically organization leaders and marketing executives) are "locked in a room" until they reach a consensus on all the key elements of brand design: the target customer and the brand essence, promise, archetype, and personality. Figure 6–6 is the brand positioning statement template that we use in our brand positioning workshops.

Figure 6–6. Brand positioning statement template.

Brand Essence
[Adjective] [adjective] [noun] (the "heart and soul" of the brand, its timeless quality, its DNA)

Brand Promise
Only [brand]

Delivers [unique and compelling benefit or shared value]

To [target customer description]

In the [product or service category] (establishing the competitive "frame of reference")

In the context of [market condition or trend that makes the benefit or value even more compelling]

Because [proof points or "reasons to believe"]

Brand Archetype

Choose one or two archetypes (what drives or motivates the brand, as related to Jungian archetypes).

Brand Personality

Choose six to ten adjectives that describe the brand as if it were a person.

If the brand is an organizational brand, we also specify the brand's (organization's) mission, vision, and values.

Taken together, these elements of the brand positioning statement should inform all brand decisions and its communication strategy and become important components of creative briefs.

BRAND POSITIONING CASE STUDY:
Element K

I became the vice president of marketing at Element K, a leading e-learning company, in September 2000. Earlier that year, U.S. Equity Partners acquired ZD Education from Ziff Davis and renamed it Element K. Element K has four business units: Element K Online (e-learning), Element K Courseware (computer training courseware publishing), Element K Journals (journal publishing), and Element K Learning Center (Rochester, NY–based computer training center).

When I joined Element K, there was virtually no awareness of the brand by our target customers: corporate chief learning officers. And we intended to take the company public after the turbulent market of late 2000 stabilized. My objective was simple: to quickly and aggressively build brand awareness and differentiation to make Element K the number one preferred e-learning brand.

When I was at Element K, the e-learning market was an increasingly crowded space with hundreds of relatively new companies vying for a greater share of the market and industry leadership. Since then, the market has grown rapidly and consolidated considerably. In 2013, the e-learning market is worth $23.8 billion in the U.S. alone, while the learning management system (LMS) space is about $2.55 billion, of which Skillsoft has a $414 million share. Worldwide, the e-learning market is projected to grow to $51.5 billion by 2015.

This growth is fueled by the many advantages that e-learning offers vis-à-vis traditional classroom training:

- There is great flexibility in where and when to train.

- People can learn at their own pace.

- E-learning is especially effective for decentralized organizations with geographically dispersed workforces.

- You can train an unlimited number of employees.

- Training is "on demand," decreasing cycle time significantly.

- E-learning is a fraction of the cost of classroom training.

Element K's e-learning solution is fully hosted on the Internet. We had large up-front fixed costs associated with developing our instructional design methodology, 800+ online courses, and a robust learning management system. But variable costs were low: Providing access to our e-learning solution was as simple as giving someone an ID for access to the site. The cost of adding servers was almost the only variable cost (cost that increases with increased usage/volume). For this reason, we increasingly focused on delivering enterprisewide solutions to Fortune 1000 companies and similarly large organizations in which the number of users was substantial with each sales agreement. Simply put—our business model favored large numbers of students.

Most of the companies vying for business in this segment of the e-learning space, if they even had any semblance of consistent messaging, directed one of the following messages at corporate officers:

- We offer a complete, integrated solution.

- Our e-learning can improve your organization's performance. It produces good business results.

- High-profile clients are very pleased with our solution.

Every company seemed to be saying the same things, and there was way too much clutter to break through. We therefore embarked on qualitative and quantitative research to identify the key decision makers and the most powerful differentiating benefit for Element K to own. In our qualitative research (one-on-one interviews and mini-groups) we found that the primary decision maker is the senior-most executive with enterprisewide training responsibility, often bearing the title of CLO (chief learning officer). In this research, we also explored people's needs, desires, fears, concerns, and other perceptions regarding training in general and e-learning in particular. From that, we developed thirty-three different brand benefit statements, which we reviewed with people toward the end of each session. We added, eliminated, and revised statements after each round of feedback. In the process, we gained a major insight, which led to Element K's brand positioning: *People have an underlying concern that, despite all of its potential advantages, e-learning lacks the human touch.* In particular they were concerned that, with e-learning:

- You lose the personal attention only an instructor can offer.
- It is harder to ask questions.
- Feedback is not possible.
- Students may feel isolated.
- You lose peer-to-peer learning.
- There is no peer pressure to attend or complete the course.
- There is not enough personal attention available.

Based on insights from the qualitative research, we developed quantitative research to measure the importance of the wide variety of brand benefits to the target customer. This research also quantified each brand's perceived delivery against each benefit. In this way, we were able to identify the most important benefits and the benefits for which Element K had the biggest relative (and absolute) advantage.

While several benefits were higher in importance, all of them were benefits that would quickly become "cost of entry" benefits (such as affordable price, quality content, and ease of use). E-learning with the human touch was validated to be important. More important, it provided Element K with the biggest advantage. While two-thirds of the respondents believed that Element K integrates the human element into e-learning, only one-third and one-quarter, respectively, believed Element K's two primary competitors did the same (see Figure 6–7).

This benefit was particularly powerful for Element K to "own" for the following reasons:

- It addresses one of the major fears about e-learning. (Fear is a particularly powerful motivator.)

Figure 6–7. *Identifying the key benefit.*

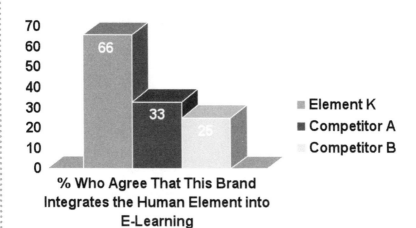

% Who Agree That This Brand
Integrates the Human Element into
E-Learning

- Element K had a substantial advantage in this area, according to the research.
  - Element K delivered on this promise at multiple levels, including:
    - The way the student experience was designed.
    - The way the training administrator experience was designed.
    - Its comprehensive support services.
    - Its participation management services.
    - The way the salespeople interact with customers (friendly, low pressure, consultative selling).
    - Within the corporate culture itself. (Element K is naturally service-oriented, which is sustainable because it is built into the corporate DNA.)
- Element K's most formidable competitor was generally known to be pushy and arrogant and only interested in "making the sale." (This was a part of the firm's corporate culture.) This positioning would indirectly and subtly bring this weakness to mind.
- Element K's customers found the company to be very easy to work with. (There was extensive anecdotal evidence that Element K had won many contracts based on this fact alone.)
  - It felt "right" and was quickly embraced by every employee.

Here is what we now say about Element K:

Element K brings a unique understanding of how people learn to the business of training. Our understanding comes from a twenty-year heritage of innovation in adult career learning for leading corporations. Today, you'll find it in our best-in-class e-learning solution—over 800 courses integrated with a state-of-the-art learning management system, all delivered with a human touch.

This statement is believable because of Element K's rich heritage as a company of training professionals, founded by two university professors who wanted to make adult training more interesting and interactive. As training professionals committed to multiple training modalities (including classroom instruction), Element K would want to share and address these concerns. The company is now committed to building "the human touch" into everything it does, from the way the sales force interacts with potential customers and the services offered to current customers, to the enhancements made to our learning management system and the personality characteristics looked for when hiring new employees.

SELF-IMAGE AND BRANDING

Most people view themselves in the context of a wide variety of identity elements:

- *Race/ethnicity*
- *Gender*
- *Sexual orientation*
- *Age*
- *Intelligence*
- *Physical characteristics*
- *Health*
- *Fitness*
- *Attractiveness*
- *Personal values*
- *Personality attributes*
- *Competencies/talents*

- *Vocation*
- *Avocations/hobbies*
- *Religious beliefs*
- *Nationality*
- *Place of residence*
- *School affiliations*
- *Political party affiliation*
- *Other organizational affiliations*
- *Income level*
- *Wealth level*
- *Social class*
- *Peer or social group affiliation*

Many of the identity elements interact with and reinforce (or conflict with) one another. People often emphasize the elements that are the most advantageous in a given context. Each of these identity elements contributes to a sense of self, and each could be an entry point for brand alignment and self-image reinforcement.

BRAND POSITIONING CASE STUDY:
Rensselaer Polytechnic Institute

Rensselaer Polytechnic Institute, founded in 1824, was the first degree-granting technological university in the English-speaking world. Rensselaer was established "for the purpose of instructing persons, who may choose to apply themselves, in the application of science to the common purposes of life." Since Rensselaer's founding, its alumni have impacted the world in many significant ways, including:

- Inventing television
- Creating the microprocessor
- Managing the Apollo project that put the first man on the moon
- Founding Texas Instruments/creating the first pocket calculator
- Creating e-mail (including using the @ symbol)
- Inventing baking powder
- Inventing the Reach toothbrush
- Building the Brooklyn Bridge
- Building the Panama Canal
- Inventing the Ferris wheel

Yet, for all of its accomplishments, in the late 1980s and early 1990s, Rensselaer was not well positioned (to prospective students) compared with its world-renowned rival, MIT, or even schools such as Caltech, UC Berkeley, and Carnegie Mellon. Many state universities (e.g., Purdue, University of Illinois at Urbana, etc.) offered exceptionally strong technical programs at significantly lower costs than private universities. Ivy League schools and other first-tier liberal arts universities were building their math, science, and engineering programs. And most states had public universities that provided respectable engineering programs. This increasingly competitive landscape left Rensselaer in a positioning "no-man's-land." I was on Rensselaer's alumni board of directors and national admissions committee at the time. We worked with the school to conduct research to better understand the college selection process. We interviewed students (and their parents), some of whom chose to attend Rensselaer and some of whom didn't. We explored what factors were most important in their decision-making process as well as their perceptions of Rensselaer as compared with other schools. And we conducted focus groups with alumni and businesspeople to better understand their impressions of Rensselaer.

Almost everyone who knew of Rensselaer perceived it to be a first-rate technical school. Many put it in the same class as MIT. People "in the know" were genuinely impressed with the school and the caliber of its students, its academics, and its research. But there were drawbacks:

- Rensselaer is in Troy, New York (which lacks the appeal of, say, Boston or California).

- Rensselaer is not as well known or prestigious as MIT. It does not have the same name cache.

- Rensselaer costs more than state engineering schools (though after factoring in financial aid, costs can be comparable).

- Rensselaer was known to be a "boot camp." It's been said that "you don't go there to have fun."

- The curriculum was perceived to be too narrow compared with liberal arts schools.

- The school had a lopsided male to female ratio (13:1 when I attended in the mid-to-late 1970s, and a 3:1 ratio today).

- A significant portion of Rensselaer's students (mostly those who had used Rensselaer as a backup school to MIT and others) felt inferior to students at their first-choice schools.

Furthermore, those with no connection to the school had no impression of the school. Awareness was also nil among the general U.S. population.

These were significant hurdles. And yet, looking at the school itself, there were also a number of very strong advantages, which include:

- A rich history by alumni of major contributions to society

- A vital, engaged campus community

- A strong student leadership development program

- Innovations in entrepreneurship, with one of the first and perhaps best known business incubators and a strong student entrepreneurship program

- Award-winning innovations in educational techniques

- Thriving interdisciplinary research centers

- Programs that ranked among the best available in the world
- An increasingly strong reputation throughout the world

(Interestingly, the university's reputation was stronger in many other countries than it was in the U.S. Midwest!)

Also, the university had embarked on a significant long-term commitment to enhance the student experience, addressing everything from administrative procedures, counseling, and breadth of course offerings to quality of instruction, the male-to-female ratio, and campus aesthetics. And, gauging from student surveys over time, the efforts were producing significant results.

Here are the key insights that led to Rensselaer's very powerful current positioning:

- Rensselaer's students have always been serious about their chosen fields of endeavor and their studies.

- Rensselaer's faculty, students, and alumni want to make a difference in the world.

- Rensselaer is and has been a leader in technological innovation.

- Rensselaer's alumni, throughout the school's history, have made major, lasting contributions to society.

- Rensselaer was emerging as a leader in entrepreneurship, especially technological entrepreneurship.

- "Technological creativity" seemed to capture the essence of the school and the spirit of those associated with the school throughout its now 190-year history.

- Rensselaer wanted its new positioning not only to capture the school's unique competitive advantages, but also to inspire its students and give them confidence. (In the mid-to-late 1970s, under George Low's leadership, the school informally adopted the slogan, "Rensselaer: Where imagination can achieve the impossible." For a short time after that, the school used the slogan, "Rensselaer: For minds ahead of their time.")

So, Rensselaer's tagline—"Why not change the world?"—was born.

Confident? Yes.

Aspirational? Yes.

Inspirational? Yes.

Accurately reflecting the school's strengths and those of its alumni? Yes.

An invitation to like-minded individuals and organizations to "come join Rensselaer in its quest"? Yes

Effective in recruiting an increasing number of highly qualified students? Yes.

Rensselaer's entering freshman classes are the most qualified and talented in the last few decades. Each class seems more qualified than the one before. As one measure, the class of 2005 arrived on campus with an average SAT score of 1307, 25 points over that of the previous class. And in the three years between 2005 and 2008, applications went from 5,500 to 11,000. In 2013, more than 16,100 high school students applied for admission to Rensselaer and the average SAT critical reading and math score for the admitted group averaged 1408.

And the most important question: Are students satisfied with Rensselaer and its recently articulated positioning? Yes.

Today, Rensselaer is thriving. In early 2001, it received a gift of $360 million—the largest single gift (at that time) ever made to a university. In 2004 it built a $82 million Center for Biotechnology and Interdisciplinary Studies to expand its research portfolio; in 2008 it built a $200 million Experimental Media and Performing Arts Center to showcase its world-leading electronic arts program; in 2009 it built a $92 million East Campus Athletic Village; and in 2013 it established its $100 million Computational Center for Nanotechnology Innovations (CCNI), featuring the seventh most powerful supercomputer in the world.

CASE STUDY:
GEICO Direct Insurance

When BrandForward conducted its insurance industry brand equity study, it uncovered a few things about the insurance industry:

• The insurance industry is highly fragmented. While there are dozens of companies whose names consumers recognize, less than a handful receive significant unaided first mention.

• While there is high behavioral loyalty, there is low attitudinal loyalty.

• Consumers have a low emotional connection to insurance brands.

• Fewer than one in five people said that their insurance company "has never disappointed them." (One sign of emotional connection.)

• Although consumers perceive differences among insurance companies, they don't perceive those differences to be significant. Price and rates are among the most important points of difference between companies, suggesting the category is commodity-like for many consumers.

• The following are the most important consumer benefits in the insurance industry. Of these benefits, consumers perceive only two of them to be addressed to any large degree:
- Paying claims fairly and promptly
- Good rates/prices
- Honest, trustworthy representatives
- Accessible, available representatives
- Knowledgeable, competent representatives
- Easy-to-understand policies
- Financial stability of company

• The following benefits have the widest variation in delivery and therefore provide the greatest opportunities for differentiation:
- Representatives who provide unbiased recommendations (all insurance categories)
- Good rates/prices (all categories)
- Knowledgeable, competent reps (life insurance)
- Honest, trustworthy reps (life insurance)
- Ability to establish a personal relationship (home and auto insurance)
- Strong overall reputation (financial services)

• The sales representative's and claims adjuster's points of contact with consumers are critical to the success of insurance company brands.

• The most brand preference exists in the auto insurance category (roughly a third with "no preference"), and the least brand preference exists in the financial services category (two-thirds with "no preference").

• At the time, State Farm was the preferred brand by a wide margin (especially in home and auto insurance). It also has a wide lead in the emotional connection it has created with consumers.

• GEICO was an "up-and-coming" brand in auto insurance (see Figure 6–8).

• Prudential was the preferred life insurance brand.

Figure 6–8. GEICO, the up-and-coming brand that has arrived.

While State Farm seemed to be doing many things right, almost all the other insurance companies seemed to lack any significant brand equity. But this story is not about State Farm. It's about GEICO Direct, at the time a virtually unknown auto insurance brand. And this is a very simple, short story: GEICO began to advertise its brand at a level that was the talk of the industry. And its message was very simple: "You could save 15 percent or more on car insurance!" (See Figure 6–9.)

Figure 6–9. GEICO's original simple message.

In brand building, focus is everything, and GEICO focused on one product segment—auto insurance—and one benefit—low price. And it did so again and again and again with a disciplined consistency. And its brand equity and market share increased at rates unknown to other insurance brands. In an industry with little brand equity or differentiation, GEICO decided to build its brand by aggressively focusing on an important brand benefit: low price. Its success was that simple—and consistent enough so that its current campaign focuses on the fact that "everyone knows" that "15 minutes can save you 15 percent or more on car insurance." (In general, I would not recommend trying to own "low price" as a point of difference. Typically, it is not a sustainable point of difference.

Nor does it usually contribute to building brand equity. Given where the insurance industry was when GEICO launched its campaign, it was an effective entry point from which to eventually add other messages.

REPOSITIONING RCI

Part of Wyndham Worldwide, RCI is a global leader in vacation time-share exchange networks. Interval International is its primary competitor. While smaller than RCI, Interval International had successfully positioned itself as the "quality" vacation timeshare exchange network. RCI retained us to help reposition the RCI brand. After poring over the research, it became clear that the category's primary benefit is choice. People who invest in timeshare exchange networks do so to expand their choices. It also was clear that RCI offered significantly more choices in more places around the globe. Furthermore, RCI offered many more different types of properties not available through competitors. We helped the company see that "maximum choice" was the benefit to own in the industry and that it had unmatched proof points against this claim. We knew that "maximum choice" would trump "a smaller number of high-quality properties" for most people (and affiliated resorts) when selecting a vacation timeshare exchange network (partner). We also worked with RCI to identify ways to expand the company's choices and to rectify system and process barriers to offering greater choice.

Use the checklist in Figure 6–10 to assess the efficacy of your brand management practices in the area covered by this chapter. The more questions to which you can answer "yes," the better you are doing. The checklist also provides a brief summary of the material covered in the chapter.

Figure 6–10. Checklist: Brand design.

YES / NO

Have you carefully defined your target customer on the following dimensions: demographics, lifestyle, values, attitudes, product usage, and buying behavior? ___ ___

Are these customers a good target for your brand in terms of?

- Market size, profitability, and growth rate

- Importance of your brand's promise to them

- Their alignment with your brand's values (i.e., your brand stands for something that is important to them)

- The opportunity for add-on sales through brand extension
- Their potential loyalty to the brand   ___ ___

Do you have profound insight into your consumer's values and motivations?   ___ ___

Have you considered the intangible ways in which your brand adds value to the consumer?   ___ ___

Can you articulate your brand's competitive frame of reference? Can you describe the universe within which it operates?   ___ ___

Do you know what benefits your competitors' brands own in consumers' minds?   ___ ___

Have you mapped your brand's delivery of key category benefits against competitive brands' delivery of those same benefits? Did you overlay that with a consumer importance scale?   ___ ___

Do you have a clear understanding of the things competitive brands do that your brand should and would never do?   ___ ___

Do you fully understand the decision-making process (rational or not) that the consumer uses to purchase your brand?   ___ ___

Do you know how different consumer segments perceive your brand differently?   ___ ___

Have you defined the role, target consumer, essence, promise, archetype, and personality for your brand?   ___ ___

If your brand is not the leader in its category, can you identify a way to redefine, reframe, or narrow the category so that your brand can be the leader in the redefined category?   ___ ___

Do you know what the most important problem is that your brand solves for your customers?   ___ ___

Do you have a vision or dream for your brand? Do you know what you'd like it to become well into the future?   ___ ___

Do you know what story your brand tells? Can you articulate its myth?   ___ ___

Do you know what your brand's timeless qualities are?   ___ ___

Is your brand dynamic? Does it learn, grow, mature, adapt, and improve over time?   ___ ___

Is your brand's essence aspirational and inspirational, yet concrete enough to own a position in the consumer's mind?   ___ ___

Does your brand embody certain beliefs, values, attitudes, and behaviors that evoke widespread admiration and devotion? ___ ___

Do you have absolute clarity regarding what your brand stands for and how it is unique and compelling to consumers? ___ ___

Can you identify the one word your brand owns in consumers' minds? ___ ___

Do you know what consumers would miss most if your brand ceased to exist? ___ ___

Do you know what deeply felt human needs your brand addresses? ___ ___

Is your brand's promise believable? ___ ___

Can you readily verbalize the proof points to your brand's promise? ___ ___

Have you identified brand benefits that are invisible to your competitors (and therefore extremely difficult to imitate)? ___ ___

Is your brand defined broadly enough to outlive specific product categories and provide flexibility for ongoing extension? ___ ___

Has your brand struck the optimal balance between maintaining a strong heritage and reinventing itself for the future? ___ ___

Have you considered narrowing your brand's focus to clarify meaning and gain market share? ___ ___

Can you identify the opportunities you have sacrificed to maintain clarity regarding your brand's promise and positioning? ___ ___

Have you considered "pruning" businesses that are not congruent with your brand's essence and promise? ___ ___

Do you have brand strategies consistent with the brand's promise—product, pricing, distribution, communications, etc.? ___ ___

Do you find you are spending most of your time creating sustainable competitive advantages (vs. matching competitive moves) with your brands? ___ ___

Is your brand so well positioned that there are no acceptable substitutes for your products and services? ___ ___

Did you know that competitors can and often will reposition your brand when repositioning theirs? Do you know how they are trying to do this? Are you doing something about it? ___ ___

7

brand identity system and standards

WHEN MOST people think about a brand's identity, they usually think about the name, the logo, and maybe the tagline. But the identity consists of so much more than that: It includes typestyles, colors, symbols, attitude and personality, brand voice and visual style, sounds and other mnemonic devices, characters and other spokespeople, product design, package design, and the list could go on and on. The most powerful brands have a consistent brand voice and visual style from product design and packaging to retail environment and external communication.

Companies such as Procter & Gamble have always practiced the traditional model of brand management. These companies manage a large portfolio of stand-alone brands (e.g., Bold, Bounty, Ivory, NyQuil, Pepto-Bismol, Scope, Folgers, Pringles) and market them as separate entities. While brand management is highly effective for those companies, it requires substantial marketing resources. Today, more and more manufacturing companies are discovering the power of using their corporate brand names (e.g., General Electric, IBM, 3M, Ford) to market their products. These companies have discovered that it is highly efficient to leverage the corporate brand name. The name offers quality assurance and familiarity at a minimum, as well as a coherent umbrella promise (example: 3M—Innovative Solutions), if executed properly.

Brand Architecture

Brand architecture, or brand structure, was covered in more detail in Chapter 2. Although situations vary greatly and company brand structures are much more complicated than the ideal, in general an efficient and effective brand structure leverages the corporate brand as the parent brand (e.g., Honda Accord, Canon EOS Rebel, Apple iPhone) and includes subbrands targeted to different consumer need segments. This two-level structure, executed correctly, can maximize consumer communication and efficiency, and clarify the definition of the corporate brand, making it more vital to an increasingly wider group of consumer segments. That said, brand architecture is a highly complex issue, especially for organizations that span multiple product/service categories and are the result of mergers and acquisitions. Some important considerations in developing and revising brand architecture are:

• Make sure that the architecture is based on a careful analysis of key internal and external audiences and *not* on internal organization structures, egos, and people's need for control.

• Be very sure to outline the role of the various levels in the brand hierarchy from the outset.

• Think through the extent to which the various brands will link to the parent brand:
  1. By name only (endorsed, subbrand)
  2. Through common design elements
  3. By sharing the same essence
  4. By sharing the same positioning and differentiating benefits

I tend to believe that the various brands should almost always relate to the parent brand in the first three ways but not always in the fourth, especially if the brands span a wide variety of product categories or are targeted at completely different customer segments.

SAMPLING OF OUR CLIENTS' BRAND ARCHITECTURE ISSUES

• *Should we have one brand or two?*

• *How should our brand promise play out at each level of branding?*

• *How many levels of branding should there be, and how does each level manifest itself?*

• *How can we reduce our brand architecture down from five levels of branding to two levels of branding?*

• *What is the architecture that creates the most coherent portfolio?*

- *How is each subbrand positioned against every other subbrand?*
- *How do we transition a product out of the architecture?*
- *How should category descriptors and product descriptors be handled vis-à-vis the architecture?*
- *How do we create more consistency in brand endorsement?*
- *Should these two brands be combined?*
- *Which brand's identity system should be dominant?*
- *How will we determine the identities of new products, services, and programs?*
- *How do we create naming coherence across our brands?*
- *Should our organization build a dominant umbrella brand?*
- *If so, should there be other subbrands?*
- *If so, which ones?*
- *What should the dominant umbrella brand be?*
- *If there is a transition in the umbrella brand, how should this transition occur?*
- *Should we combine these subbrands into one brand?*
- *Should we change our subbrand structure to better match the way our consumer segments are evolving?*
- *How do we address naming of internal programs?*
- *What do we do with our newly acquired brands? How should they fit into our portfolio?*
- *How do donor-named entities (supported by large donations) fit into the brand architecture?*
- *How should we cobrand with strategic partners?*

Brand Naming

Brand naming is extremely important. Many of you are probably working with brands that already have been named, but in case you are not, here are a few pointers on naming brands:

- *People only refer to a person or product using one, or at the most, two names.* For instance, I am either Brad or Brad VanAuken. No one calls me Alan Bradley VanAuken (with the exception of my mother, who called me by this name when she was upset with me when I was a boy). It is just too hard to remember, too cumbersome to say, and just unnecessary. Likewise, a car is either a Taurus or a Ford Taurus. People say, "I drive a Honda" or "I drive a Honda Accord." Few say, "I drive a Honda Accord EX." People rarely remember more than three levels of names. Saturn was simple. Chrysler New Yorker Fifth Avenue and Oldsmobile Cutlass Ciera were less easy to remember (and can anyone remember what company made the Oldsmobile?). How is a Chrysler New Yorker Fifth Avenue different from a Chrysler New Yorker Salon? How was an Oldsmobile Cutlass Ciera different from an Oldsmobile Cutlass Supreme, or how were both of them different from an Oldsmobile Toronado or an Oldsmobile 88 Royale? It got very confusing very quickly.

• *Products run into trouble when they have multiple levels of names.* For instance, Hallmark coproduced social expression software with Microsoft. Greetings Workshop was produced by Microsoft and Hallmark Connections (in some cases, as a subset of another suite of products from Microsoft, with additional names). What did consumers remember? What did they ask for? Did each consumer use the same name? It might have been easier to call this venture "Hallmark Greetings Workshop (brought to you by Microsoft)" or "Microsoft Greetings Workshop (featuring Hallmark cards)."

• *Coined names are preferred if you have sufficient resources to build their meaning.* Coined names (such as Xerox, Kodak, etc.) are distinct and can be designed to be easy to read, write, and pronounce. It is unlikely that another brand would be confused with one with a coined name. Because coined names require significant communication over time to build their meaning, they are best reserved for parent brands or other brands that are extremely important to the organization and that will be around for a very long time.

• *Many organizations opt for associative descriptive names.* Associative descriptive names, which may be partly descriptive, usually allude to a key brand benefit. Examples include Amazon, Sir Speedy, Road Runner, Lean Cuisine, Sprint, BrandForward, DieHard, and Aris Vision Institute. These names work quite well and immediately allude to the brand's benefit. If you want to get into a product or business quickly with a name that helps reinforce the product's or business's primary benefit, while still maintaining some level of uniqueness, this is the preferred naming option.

• *Generic descriptive names are least desirable.* They are not distinctive in consumers' minds and they can't be protected legally. Interestingly, among the online companies with generic names, such as Auctions.com, Business.com, Buy.com, Computer.com, eToys.com, Food.com, Furniture.com, Garden.com,

Mall.com, Mortgage.com, Pets.com, or Stamps.com, many have gone out of business. (Others have subsequently purchased many of these URLs and are trying their luck at them. So much for all those once exorbitantly expensive URLs!)

Generic descriptors are frequently used for subbrands, when you want most of the credit to go to the parent brand. For instance, at Element K (now Skillsoft), branding structure featured generic descriptor subbrands because (a) Element K was a new brand that we needed to build quickly, (b) resources were too limited to build multiple brands, and, most important, (c) we were touting a blended solution across all of our products and businesses.

> **DID YOU KNOW?**
> *Suggestive brand names assist with recall of brand benefits that are suggested by the names, but inhibit recall of other subsequently advertised brand benefits.*
>
> (Source: Kevin Lane Keller, Susan E. Heckler, and Michael J. Houston, "The Effects of Brand Name Suggestiveness on Advertising Recall," Journal of Marketing 62, January 1998, pp. 48–57.)

In summary, *coined names* are used for products and services that are distinctive, that provide sustainable competitive advantages, and that will receive substantial marketing support over time. *Associative descriptive names* are used for important products or services, but primarily those that need to have their meaning built quickly or that will not receive the sustained level of marketing support required of coined names. *Generic or descriptive names* are reserved for subbrands that are not mission critical.

Strong names allude to the benefit, such as Amazon, Smart Car, Duracell, or Best Buy. Ideally, any name you choose should be short, easy to spell, and easy to pronounce. Say the name out loud and see how easily it rolls off the tongue and how pleasing it is to the ear. Pay attention to cadence, rhythm, and balance. Alliteration and repetition of sounds can add to the strength of the name. Consider Best Buy, Kodak, and Coca-Cola. I prefer a two-syllable word starting with a strong consonant and possessing rich vowel sounds.

Here are two points to consider when naming your brand:

- Names formed from acronyms or initials are up to 40 percent less memorable than any type of pronounceable word, real or coined.[1]

- Perhaps the worst names of all are those built from generic word parts such as "com" and "sys" and "compu" (WorldCom, UniSys). These names seem to be confused with every other brand name created from similar word parts and they are very difficult to recall.

Naming Decision Trees

Organizations with more than one brand should develop decision trees to aid people in naming new products and services. The decision tree (see Figure 7–1) should outline when an existing brand should be used and when a new brand is necessary. (One of the more exhaustive branding/naming decision trees that I have seen is in Nicholas Ind's book, *Living the Brand*.) It should also identify the type of brand to be created (e.g., subbrand, endorsed brand) and the naming convention for that brand (e.g., coined, associative/descriptive), which should be based on the following factors:

- Importance of the new product or service to the market and to the organization

- Projected life span of the new product or service

- Unique differentiating benefits delivered by the new product or service

- Intent and capacity to communicate the new brand in a significant way over time

In general, new brands should be created only when a new product or service delivers on a different brand promise from one of the organization's existing brands. To do otherwise is costly and confusing to consumers.

Brand Logos

It is at least as important for a logo to be recognizable as it is for it to be readable. Often, people are only able to get a quick glance at the logo, and then only at a distance. In those instances, recognition, not readability, is all that counts. That is why it is so important to integrate recognizable icons, shapes, type fonts, and colors into a logo's design.

Some logos were created during the era of big department stores and were designed as signatures to fit on the side of buildings. As a result, these logos tend to be more square in orientation than they are horizontal. Many of these logos now seem outdated (if they haven't been updated). Hallmark's logo belongs to this class (see Figure 7–2); however, Hallmark has since moved the crown closer to the Hallmark signature to increase the logo's horizontal orientation. Others were designed as corporate logos to reinforce leadership and stability (AT&T, IBM). Many of these logos now seem cold and sterile. Some logos are more fun, communicating more of a personality (Apple, MTV, eBay). Google breaks all of the rules by frequently changing its logo to commemorate a particular holiday or season.

Figure 7–1. Brand naming decision tree.

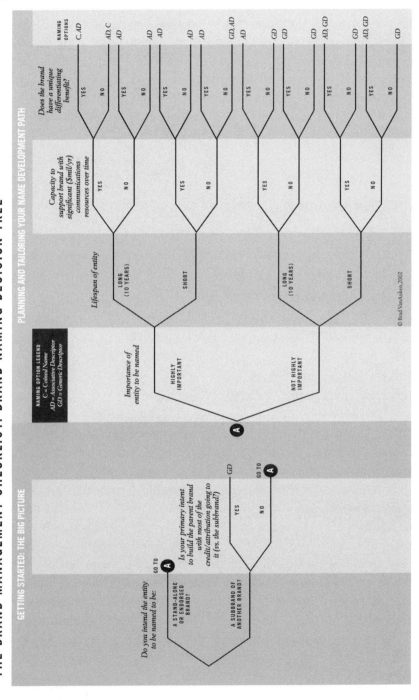

Today, logos must be designed assuming they will be used in multimedia environments (TV, Internet, etc.). That means colors, animation, and sound sequences should be considered. Examples include NBC, Intel, Yahoo (animation), Harley-Davidson (engine sound), and Maxwell House. Many social media brands (such as Facebook, Google +, LinkedIn, Pinterest, Tumblr, and Twitter) have square versions of their visual identity that are used as online buttons.

***Figure 7–2.** Hallmark logo.*

The Importance of Color

Color is an important consideration in your brand identity system. Colors have a significant impact on people's emotional state. They also have been shown to impact people's ability to concentrate and learn. They have a wide variety of specific mental associations. In fact, the effects are physiological, psychological, and sociological. For instance:[2]

- Nonprimary colors are more calming than primary colors.
- Blue is the most calming of the primary colors, followed closely by a lighter red.
- Test takers and weight lifters perform better in blue rooms.
- Blue text increases reading retention.
- Yellow evokes cheerfulness. Houses with yellow trim or flower gardens sell faster.
- Reds and oranges encourage diners to eat quickly and leave. Red also makes food more appealing and influences people to eat more. (It is no coincidence that fast-food restaurants often use these colors.)
- Pink enhances appetites and has been shown to calm prison inmates.
- Blue and black suppress appetites.

- Children prefer primary colors. (Notice that children's toys and books often use these colors.)

- Forest green and burgundy appeal to the wealthiest 3 percent of Americans, and often raise the perceived price of an item.

- Violet is often associated with spirituality, royalty, and quality.

- Orange is often used to make an expensive item seem less expensive.

- Red clothing can convey power.

- Red trim is used in bars and casinos because it can cause people to lose track of time.

- Most people (76 percent) associate "speed" with the color red.[3]

- White is typically associated with being cool, clean, and fresh.

- Red is often associated with Christmas, and orange with Halloween and Thanksgiving.

- Red and black are often associated with being sexy and seductive and are favored by porn sites. Red and black also have a high association with fear and terror.

- Black clothes make people look thinner (as most people know).

- Black is associated with elegance, sophistication, and mystery.

- Black is the favorite color of Goths.

- "Fun" is most associated with orange, yellow, purple, and red.

- "Trust" is most associated with blue and white.

- "High quality," "high technology," and "reliability/dependability" are most associated with black and blue.

FAVORITE COLORS OF AMERICAN CONSUMERS

1. *Blue*	5. *Pink*
2. *Red*	6. *Purple*
3. *Green*	7. *Orange*
4. *White*	8. *Yellow*

(Source: Carlton Wagner, Wagner Color Response Report, (Santa Barbara, CA: Wagner Institute, 1988).

- Men's favorite color is blue (57 percent), then green (14 percent); women's favorite colors are blue (35 percent) and purple (23 percent).[4]

Colors also have a functional impact on readability, eyestrain, the ability to attract attention, and the ability to be seen at night. These factors are important in choosing colors for signing, website pages, print ads, and other marketing media.

- The most visible color is yellow.

- The most legible of all color combinations are black on yellow and green on white, followed by red on white. (It is no surprise that most traffic signs use these color combinations.)

- Black on white is easiest to read, on paper and computer screens.

- "Hard" colors (red, orange, and yellow) are more visible and tend to make objects look larger and closer. They are easier to focus on. They create excitement and cause people to overestimate available time.

- "Soft" colors (violet, blue, and green) are less visible and tend to make objects look smaller and farther away. They aren't as easy to focus on. They have a calming effect, increase concentration, and cause people to underestimate remaining time.

Usually, it is advantageous for a brand to consistently "own" certain colors that provide an additional recognition cue. The George Eastman House International Museum of Photography and Film in Rochester, New York, has taken a different but equally effective approach. Eastman House wanted to communicate that it is a fun and vibrant organization that offers much more than artistic black-and-white photography. So, the "e" icon in its logo appears in a rainbow of colors. Each business card features the logo in a different color. The name itself only appears in black and white.

Obviously, colors are an important part of any brand identity system. Testing the effect of a new brand identity system's colors is well advised. It is important to consider that color associations will vary by individual and especially by cultural context and a person's previous experiences with the colors. All the impacts of colors are equally true of music, scents, and sounds. For instance, studies have identified that music affects supermarket sales, mental concentration, achievement on standardized tests, factory productivity, clerical performance, and staff turnover, among other things.

QUEVEDO ENDODONTICS

Dr. Quevedo needed a new brand identity for his endodontic practice after parting ways with his previous practice partner. Typically, dentists refer their patients to endodontists when they arrive with painful acute conditions that require immediate root canal procedures. We conducted research with dentists and endodontic patients to understand how decisions are made in the category. We discovered that Dr. Quevedo offered the following unique benefits that are very important to dentists and patients:

- *Dentists: Because Dr. Quevedo uniquely scheduled appointments for mornings but left afternoons open for emergency situations, dentists liked to refer patients to him because he could alleviate their patients' pain on the same day.*

- *Patients: Even though endodontic surgery is painless, patients associate root canals with pain. Dr. Quevedo has a very calming presence and a sedation certification unique in his market.*

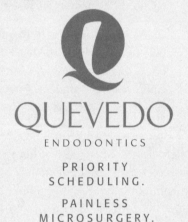

QUEVEDO
ENDODONTICS

PRIORITY
SCHEDULING.

PAINLESS
MICROSURGERY.

The primary place where the brand manifests is on the referral form that is given to patients by their dentist. For this reason, we decided to include a brand tagline for both the dentist and the patient on the referral form.

An amusing and challenging element of this project is that Dr. Quevedo wanted to include a space that looks like a perfect root canal within the Q, as an inside joke with dentists.

Tools to Maintain Brand Identity Consistency

To ensure that external audiences are hearing consistent messages about the brand, companies often "script" their sales and their service organizations. At Element K, to reinforce its brand positioning, the marketing department worked with company management and the ad agency that developed its "E-Learning with the Human Touch" campaign to craft a detailed script (with a PowerPoint slide presentation and other aids). There were then sales and service organizations required to memorize those scripts.

In addition to scripts, organizations use the following tools to ensure brand identity consistency across the enterprise (and by business partners):

• *Published Brand Identity System and Standards.* These standards used to be printed hard copy manuals and CDs, but more recently they're featured on intranet sites, which offer the advantage of instant, low-cost universal updates and digital access. They usually include brand architecture, brand style guides, naming conventions, and a naming decision tree.

• *Brand Photo Libraries.*

• *Brand Message Guidelines.* These procedures are often divided into dos and don'ts sections, such as: *Do say "Make a Xerox branded photocopy,"* but *don't say "Make a Xerox."*

• *Brand Management Intranets.* Internal sites usually include the following items:
- Brand essence, promise, and personality statements
- Brand pricing guidelines
- Brand distribution guidelines
- Brand research summaries
- Brand management contact information
- Examples of recent brand ads

Brand management intranet sites *sometimes* include the following items:

• Video clip of corporate officers talking about the importance of living the brand

• Video clip of customers talking about the brand

• Recognition of people and activities throughout the organization that have delivered the brand promise

• Brand history, myths, and legends

• Quizzes and other fun exercises designed to teach employees about the brand and its promise

• *Digital Brand Asset Management Systems.* More and more organizations are using digital asset management to maintain consistency and control throughout their enterprise. These systems are typically fully hosted on the Internet by third parties (cloud services model). They provide the ultimate control over decentralized sales and marketing organizations (or retail networks) that develop localized advertising, promotions, and other marketing programs. Two firms that specialize in digital brand asset management include Imation (www.imation.com) and Saepio (www.saepio.com).

● *Naming a Brand Identity Manager or Specialist.* This is also an extremely helpful management practice. This person reviews and approves all new executions of the brand and its subbrands and all new interpretations of its identity. This person should be well respected throughout the organization, possess strong interpersonal skills, and should be assertive and persuasive.

● *Creating a Cross-Divisional Brand Identity Council.* Such a council, composed of key design (and editorial) managers from departments and divisions throughout the organization, is also very helpful. The council raises awareness of brand identity issues, builds a consensus around their resolution, becomes a "brain trust" for the brand's identity, and provides peer pressure for interpreting the brand accurately and consistently.

Use the checklist in Figure 7–3 to assess the efficacy of your brand management practices in the area covered by this chapter. The more questions to which you can answer "yes," the better you are doing. The checklist also provides a brief summary of the material covered in the chapter.

Figure 7–4. Checklist: Brand identity system and standards.

	YES / NO
Is your brand's name proprietary? Does it differentiate the brand instead of just describing its products and services?	___ ___
Is your brand's name suggestive of a key differentiating benefit, but not too narrow so as to decrease the brand's ability to claim new benefits in the future?	___ ___
Do consumers like your brand's name? Is it memorable?	___ ___
Do you have comprehensive brand identity system and standards that address all uses of your brand's identity elements?	___ ___
Are the system and standards actively in use?	___ ___
Are they available in digital form?	___ ___
Are all business units and subbrands subject to those standards, with none outside the jurisdiction of the standards?	___ ___
At a minimum, does the system include standards for the visual identifier, color, typography, backgrounds, contrast, staging area, relative size, positioning, key applications, and unacceptable uses?	___ ___

Is your logotype horizontally shaped? That orientation delivers the greatest visual impact and is a functional necessity when the logotype is used in retail environments.   ___ ___

Will your system work globally? The meanings of specific words, colors, and symbols in different countries are especially important to understand.   ___ ___

Does your system include distinctive shapes, colors, typestyles, and voices?   ___ ___

Does your brand own a color that is different from that of your major competitor?   ___ ___

Does your system include a slogan or jingle?   ___ ___

Does it include sounds and other mnemonic devices?   ___ ___

Is your system effective in multimedia environments?   ___ ___

Does it address cobranding, comarketing, brand licensing, and strategic alliance and sponsorship situations?   ___ ___

Have you designed the brand portfolio, including a subbrand structure?   ___ ___

Is your brand hierarchy simple enough for consumers to easily understand (preferably no more than two levels)?   ___ ___

When your brand hierarchy has two or more levels, do you know which name (corporate, parent, endorsed, or subbrand?) the consumer uses to refer to each product or service offered by your organization?   ___ ___

Do you have criteria to help you decide when you can use an existing brand, when a completely new brand is needed, and when a subbrand is the right choice?   ___ ___

Do you find that all of your subbrands are distinctive? Are you certain that no two subbrands in your portfolio meet the same consumer needs and deliver the same benefits?   ___ ___

Are your subbrand names distinct from one another so that they are not confused for one another?   ___ ___

Do you use existing brands whenever possible to meet new consumer needs or to enter new product categories, offering instant assurance and maximizing communication efficiency (provided that doing so doesn't dilute the meaning of the original brand)?   ___ ___

Are you increasingly leveraging your corporate brand as a parent brand?   ___ ___

Are there simple and consistent ways in which subbrands relate to corporate or parent brands?   ___ ___

Are there simple rules for when a brand is endorsed by a corporate or parent brand and when it is not?   ___ ___

Does everyone agree on what names, symbols, colors, visual styles, voices, etc., are used across all applications, subbrands, and product lines on behalf of the parent brand and its identity? In each point of contact with the consumer (advertising, retail environment, product packaging, etc.), have you decided how much emphasis will be placed on the parent brand vs. the sub-brand? Have you decided which elements will be associated with the parent brand and which with the subbrand?   ___ ___

Is the system functional for all intended uses?   ___ ___

Does your system address internal applications (memos, employee newsletters and other internal publications, computer screensavers, etc.)?   ___ ___

Does the system reinforce intended brand associations?   ___ ___

Have you built at least nine random, nonfunctional design elements into your brand's trade dress to make it easier for you to legally protect your brand?   ___ ___

Do you confer with intellectual property lawyers when designing new products and brands to ensure that what you've created has maximum protection under the law?   ___ ___

Do you have an ongoing process set up to proactively protect your brand's identity against dilution or confusion, including regular reviews of possible competitive infringements?   ___ ___

Do you have a corporate brand identity council (or another process) to manage the brand identity on an ongoing basis?   ___ ___

Do you conduct periodic communications audits to monitor adherence to corporate brand identity standards?   ___ ___

Is your brand identity system as simple as possible?   ___ ___

Ultimately, is it immediately clear which brand is the source for all points of contact you have with the consumer?   ___ ___

PART 3
Building the Brand

8

driving the consumer from brand awareness to brand insistence

MY COMPANY believes that the ultimate goal of brand equity building is to move the consumer from brand awareness to brand insistence. Our brand insistence model incorporates five elements that drive consumers to insist upon a particular brand to meet their needs—brand awareness, relevant differentiation, value, accessibility, and emotional connection (see Figure 8–1). We believe that these five areas of emphasis and activity are the primary drivers of consumer brand insistence.

Brand Awareness

Brand building begins with awareness. Consumers first must be aware that there are different brands in the product categories in which your brand operates. Next, they must be aware of *your* brand. Ideally, your brand should be the first one that comes to their minds within specific product categories and also be the first one they associate with key consumer benefits. Consumers should:

- Be able to identify which products and services your brand offers
- Be able to identify which benefits are associated with the brand
- Have some idea of where your brand is sold

Relevant Differentiation

Relevant differentiation is the most important thing a brand can deliver. Relevant differentiation today is a leading-edge indicator of profitability and

Figure 8–1. BrandForward's brand insistence model.

market share tomorrow. Does your brand own consumer-relevant, consumer-compelling benefits that are unique and believable? Today, services and the "total brand experience" often become the differentiators.

CREATING BRANDS OF DISTINCTION:
THE MOST EFFECTIVE SOURCES OF BRAND DIFFERENTIATION

While there are many sources of differentiation, it is my opinion that only a small number of sources have the power to create brands of distinction. Following are the six approaches that I have found to work best.

Self-Image Reinforcement. The brand reinforces the customer's self-image or how the customer intends to be perceived. Using the brand creates a feeling of congruence with self-image. It is also a way to project that image to others. Taking just one product category (motor vehicles) to illustrate this concept, the image might be "I am progressive and I care about the environment." The Toyota Prius brand reinforces this image. Or maybe it is "I am frugal." Hyundai would be a good brand choice to reinforce this image. For someone else the image might be "I am successful and have status." Mercedes is a brand that could reinforce this self-image. Harley-Davidson reinforces the freedom of the open road and the lifestyle that is concurrent with that philosophy. If someone wants to be perceived as unique or different, a Saab, MINI Cooper, or VW Beetle with polka dots might do the trick.

This approach to brand differentiation works in any category. What does going to Reed College, Hampshire College, or St. John's University say about a person? What does attending MIT or Brigham Young University say about a person? One can apply this analysis equally to clothing brands, restaurant brands, food brands, vacation place brands, or residential place brands.

Values Alignment. Closely related to the previous source of differentiation are brands whose values align with their customers' values. Many people buy brands such as Newman's Own, The Body Shop, or Ben & Jerry's because they are socially conscious. Go to Patagonia's website and it will be clear to you that Patagonia promotes a love of the outdoors and outdoor sports and that environmental sensitivity is an important brand value. Some people watch FOX News because it reinforces their view of the world, while others follow MSNBC for the same reason.

PATAGONIA AND SUSTAINABILITY

Patagonia has had an environmental ethos for as long as I have been aware of the brand. (I hiked in their stand-up shorts in my college days, which are long since past.) The company's mantra is "reduce, repair, reuse, recycle, and reimagine." Lately, Patagonia has been urging its customers to "buy less." Patagonia ran an ad telling people "Don't Buy This Jacket." The company has created videos showing people how to repair used clothing and is creating sewing kits for its customers. It also encourages people to buy used clothing and return clothing they no longer want, so Patagonia can find a new use for them. Patagonia donates one percent of its revenues to environmental causes and has set up a fund to invest in start-ups focused on sustainable food, water, and energy. It makes its fleece jackets out of recycled bottles, uses only organic cotton in its cotton products, was one of the first California companies to switch to wind energy, and powers its headquarters with solar panels.

In 2012, the first year of its "buy less" marketing campaign, sales increased almost one-third over the previous year as the company opened fourteen new stores. Patagonia's customers buy into and enthusiastically support its authentic environmental ethic.

Sources: Dale Buss, "Patagonia Enjoys Unique Benefits of Its Authentic Sustainability Ethos," Brandchannel.com, August 29, 2013, www.brandchannel.com/home/post/2013/08/29/Patagonia-Sustainable-Ethos-082913.aspx. Kyle Stock, "Patagonia's 'Buy Less' Plea Spurs More Buying," Bloomberg Businessweek, August 28, 2013, www.businessweek.com/articles/2013-08-28/patagonias-buy-less-plea-spurs-more-buying. Jennifer Elks, "Patagonia Launches 'Responsible Economy' Campaign," SustainableBrands.com, October 1, 2013, www.sustainablebrands.com/news_and_views/communications/patagonia-launches-responsible-economy-campaign.

Customer Segment Focus. Brands that try to be all things to all people eventually fail in being anything important to anyone. Conversely, brands that focus on a specific customer need segment with the intention of becoming customer experts and meeting the specific needs of their customers can achieve uncommon success. I have worked with a wealth management firm that focuses on financially successful entrepreneurs who want to demonstrate to the world that "they have arrived." This firm really knows what is most important to its clients. It constantly designs new touchpoints to deliver on the promise of helping those people feel as if "they have arrived." This source of differentiation relies on customer intimacy and extreme expertise in niche markets. The way organizations with this strategy grow is by getting to know their target customers better and better and by offering more and more products and services to those customers until they become an indispensable partner with their customers.

Unique Purchase or Usage Experience. Starbucks is less about coffee than it is about that "in-between" experience. The people who developed that brand discovered a latent need for a somewhat self-indulgent, pampering space that was neither the "work" space with its job pressures nor the "home" space with its family responsibilities. And now people routinely pay $2 to $4 for a cup of coffee instead of the previous average of 60 cents. Ten Thousand Waves, one of my favorite spas in Santa Fe, New Mexico, is nearly perfect in creating a multisensory experience, from its cedar oil shampoo and coconut soap to the fragrant trees that line its walkways and its numerous hot tubs, all in a very natural environment. I remember reading a Stanford Research Institute (SRI Consulting Business Intelligence) report in the mid-eighties entitled "The Experience Economy." Back then, researchers were predicting a world in which there would be an increased need for services and experiences in lieu of physical products. Another example of this phenomenon is the Build-A-Bear Workshop, in which children can create their own customized teddy bears from scratch (at a hefty price premium). Amazon revolutionized the book-buying experience and Netflix revolutionized the way we watch movies. Apple iPods delivered an intuitively simple approach to downloading and listening to music. They are so user-friendly that their user's manual is probably the least used of any technology-based product.

Outstanding Customer Service. More and more brands deliver an outstanding customer experience. Ritz-Carlton's mantra is "Ladies and gentlemen serving ladies and gentlemen." One can imagine how this promise might play out under different scenarios. The Bangkok Oriental, one of the finest hotels in the world, delivers impeccable, extraordinary service. Midwest Airlines (previously Midwest Express) won every industry award possible (Travel + Leisure, Condé Nast Traveler, Zagat, Air Transport World, etc.) for several years in a row in the 1990s for delivering first-class service. Service included leather seats, great food, glass salt and pepper shakers, real linen napkins, and free champagne. Disney's theme parks are impeccable, and the Disney Institute is available to organizations outside of the Disney family to share their secrets on how to exceed customer expectations. Lazzara Yachts of Fort Lauderdale featured "Imagine Perfection" as its tagline. Many people might argue that this slogan establishes an unreasonably high expectation; however, it is a promise that the company has delivered on for some time, from its custom-designed megayachts to customer-tailored christening ceremonies. Nordstrom's free exchanges, easy returns, and other exemplary customer service policies are legendary. So are Nordstrom prices. Establishing truly extraordinary customer service requires both business process/system components and employee recruiting, training, and evaluation/reward components.

Best Value. Value has a numerator and a denominator. That is, value is not just about price. Often the brands that deliver the best value are not even the lowest-priced brands. Amazon has enabled people to buy books in an entirely different way, 24/7. Amazon's search and browse technology is legendary, and once you have purchased a number of items from the online retailer, its systems get increasingly good at guessing what else might interest you. And, with Amazon's everyday price discounts (often 34 percent to 40 percent) and a membership program that provides free shipping on all orders for a fairly nominal annual fee, the company offers some of the lowest prices around. IKEA is famous for delivering high style to the masses through very reasonably priced furniture and home accessories. Honda and Toyota both make a wide variety of well-built vehicles with consistently good safety ratings, respectable gas mileage, well-researched amenities, few maintenance issues, reasonable prices, long lives, and great resale values. No wonder those brands have made inroads on U.S. automobile manufacturers. They deliver an all-around great value.

Summary. While it is important to deliver on the basic functional benefits of one's product category, that is not sufficient to create a relevant, unique, and compelling brand in today's world. That requires intimate customer knowledge and understanding, which then must be applied to create a unique brand. The most effective ways to create brands of distinction are through some combination of the following:

- Customer self-image reinforcement
- Customer values alignment
- Customer segment focus
- Unique product/service purchase or usage experience
- Outstanding customer service
- Best overall value

DIFFERENTIATING COMMODITIES

An increasing number of brand managers indicate that their brands operate in commodity categories. I first began focusing on this area when I conducted a branding seminar in Dubai, UAE, and was asked by several conference attendees who worked for different energy companies to help them think through how to differentiate their brands so that they could command a price premium.

When marketing true commodities such as petroleum, palm oil, and soybeans, consider the following ways to differentiate your brand:

- Deliver superior product or service consistency (quality control).
- Deliver superior responsiveness (order fulfillment, technical support, customer service).
- Offer a superior range of products and services.
- Consider value chain integration.
- Uniquely bundle or unbundle your products and services.
- Customize your products and services to meet each customer's specific needs.
- Identify your most important or profitable customers. Determine what they value most (through conjoint analysis or a similar technique) and then tailor your products and services to meet their specific needs.

- Add a differentiating "ingredient" to your brand (ingredient branding).

- Add unique packaging to your brand.

- Distribute your brand in a unique or superior way.

- Establish your "brand as a badge," adding psychological value to its products and services.

- Create a superior product purchase or usage experience.

- When all else fails, make superior creative in marketing communication the hero in brand differentiation.

To drive home the point that any commodity can be differentiated, I assign "branding water" as a case study. As you know, water, the odorless, colorless liquid, is the ultimate commodity. Despite its scarcity in certain parts of the world, 70 percent of the earth's surface is water and the amount of water in the human body ranges from 50 percent to 75 percent. Furthermore, in most developed countries, water is readily available from public sources and in every home.

I have assigned this case study to hundreds of teams over the years, and many of the outcomes have been truly impressive and worthy of new business ventures. People have identified the following differentiating elements:

- Target customers

- Suggested/specialized uses

- Ways to drink

- Taste/flavoring/carbonation

- Color

- Bottle/packaging shape, color, and functionality

- Size

- Price

- Source/story

- Health qualities

- Bundling with other products

- Distribution

If you ever run into a brand manager or consultant who indicates that it is impossible to brand something in the "XYZ" category because it is a commodity category, politely thank that person for his or her advice and then apply one or more of these approaches.

BRANDS AND AESTHETICS

Whether one considers the Apple iPod, iPad, or iPhone, or Tỳ Nant bottled water, or the Bugatti Type 57 SC Atlantic automobile, or Giorgio Armani clothing, or the Relais & Châteaux hotels, aesthetics plays an important role in the appeal of those brands. Even the appeal of less upscale brands is often driven at least in part by their aesthetics. Consider Dove soap or the Gillette Fusion ProGlide razor or Hershey's Kisses or the earlier version of the Hyundai Sonata that looked like a Jaguar. My company sometimes helps to brand places, too. Aesthetics-related criteria rate high on residents' reasons for choosing a place to live. Attractive neighborhoods and scenic beauty rate next after good job opportunities, low crime, affordable housing, and good medical care as the top reasons people choose a particular place to live. Consider college and university brands. While many factors, including offering the right major, ranking high in selectivity, and offering a competitive financial aid package, contribute to brand preference, most college admissions offices will admit that once a potential student has visited the campus, the likelihood that he or she will attend that school increases significantly (assuming the experience was a good one). An increasing number of college-ranking sources also rank schools based on campus aesthetics. Elon University has become much more popular in the past decade, at least partially because of its campus aesthetics. And here's one final item of interest on building beauty into brands: Beautiful brands almost always command a price premium, generally making them more profitable than other brands in their categories. You might want to consider how to infuse your brand with increased aesthetic appeal.

TOO MANY BRANDS MAKE HOLLOW CLAIMS (THINK TWICE BEFORE MAKING ONE OF THESE CLAIMS FOR YOUR BRAND)

Increasingly, I have encountered brands that make the following types of claims:

- We are the quality leader in the X category.
- We are the innovation leader in the Y category.
- We are the service leader in the Z category.
- We are the leader in the XYZ category (which is the worst of all claims).

Is quality important? Yes. Is Innovation important? Absolutely.

Is service important? Of course. Is it desirable to be the industry leader? Sure. However, in more and more categories, as I perform brand audits, I find that large numbers of companies in many categories make these claims—so much so that the claims have become hollow. "Leader" means top, number one, not one of many striving to be top and number one. Don't claim an aspiration unless you can uniquely deliver on that aspiration.

Regarding quality, who is the leader in the hotel industry? Is it the Ritz-Carlton with its "Ladies and gentlemen serving ladies and gentlemen" service, or is it the Four Seasons, or Mandarin Oriental, or Peninsula, or Amanresorts, or Shangri-La, or InterContinental? With this list of high-quality hotel chains, should Hyatt or Westin or Marriott or Sheraton or Hilton claim quality leadership? Who makes the highest-quality shoes? Who makes the highest-quality kitchen appliances? How about the highest-quality kitchen knives? Who makes the highest-quality shampoo? Why? Based on what? Is one independent ranking enough to make it so?

Are some companies real innovation leaders? Sure. Who would argue that Apple is not an innovation leader in its category with its introductions of the iPod, iPhone, and iPad? If your company is claiming innovation as its primary point of difference, is it as far ahead of its competition in reality and perception as Apple is in its category? Or is it in a pack of companies, each of which has introduced a comparable number of innovations? In the grocery store business, Wegmans has been widely recognized as the innovation leader over time. Trader Joe's is also innovative, but with a different formula. In the auto industry, which company should claim innovation leadership? Toyota because it was the first with a significant introduction of hybrid cars? GM because of its introduction of OnStar? BMW because of its constant innovations? How about Honda or Porsche?

Do some companies stand out as service leaders? I would contend that Ritz-Carlton and Nordstrom would vie for this position in their respective industries. Who is the service leader in banking? In wealth management? How about in insurance? In restaurants? In hospitals? How does service leadership relate to quality leadership?

And what does it mean to be the overall leader in a category? What is the metric for leadership? Market share? Distribution? Dollar sales? Unit sales? Customer loyalty? Leadership is a fairly vague term. Leadership, but in what? How important is quality to leadership? Service to leadership? Innovation?

I would contend that quality, service, and innovation are critical to most companies in most industries. Every organization should try to continuously improve its delivery of each of these performance areas. However, unless you are the undisputed leader in one of them, you should not claim it as your primary differentiating benefit.

I would never try to claim industry leadership. It is a title that can only be conferred through general consensus by outside observers over time. And I would only claim quality, service, or innovation leadership if the following hurdles were cleared:

- Your brand is the undisputed leader in this area as evidenced by customer research, independent rankings, specific proof points, and truly measurable differences.

- You consistently deliver against this measure across all of your products and services at all of your locations/distribution points.

- You are, at least, perceived/recognized by your primary target audiences as a market leader.

Finally, if I made one of these claims, I would make sure that I had the resources in place to ensure consistent superiority in this area for a very long time. Don't manage a brand that contributes to the hollow claims of quality, service, or innovation leadership. Rather, manage a brand that claims something truly unique, compelling, and believable to its target audiences. The organizations that can convincingly claim leadership in one of these three areas (quality, service, and innovation) are rare indeed.

THE POWER OF BREAKING CONSUMER COMPROMISE

"Breaking consumer compromises" is one of the most powerful concepts in business today. Introduced by George Stalk, Jr., David K. Pecaut, and Benjamin Burnett ("Breaking Compromises, Breakaway Growth," Harvard Business Review, September–October 1996, pp. 131–139), it states that the best way to create breakaway business growth is to identify all the ways in which a business has made compromises with the consumer and then break them all so that that consumer gets exactly what he needs and wants.

For example, consider CarMax and the used-car industry. An industry outsider (Circuit City) carefully analyzed the very large and profitable used-car industry to identify all the consumer compromises—limited variety at any one place, no maintenance records, limited knowledge about the car's history, high-pressure sales tactics, perceived lack of honesty, etc. By breaking all of these compromises, Circuit City gained a substantial market share very quickly with its CarMax business. CarMax became an independent, separately traded public company from Circuit City in 2002 and is thriving today having been named one of the "100 Best Companies to Work For" by FORTUNE magazine for ten consecutive years.

The trick is to constantly reinvent your business even if you think you have something to lose by doing so. That is why it is often difficult for industry insiders to transform their industry by breaking compromises. Consider Kodak. It must have been difficult for Kodak to enter the digital imaging world with a passion when most of its business was based on chemical photography. And, it was very difficult for Hallmark, in the late 1990s, to introduce a very large selection of 99-cent cards (Out of the Blue, Children's Seasonal, and Hallmark Warm Wishes greeting cards) with the very real concern of possible trade down. But, to its credit, Hallmark did it, and broke the consumer compromise.

Value

Does your brand deliver a good value for the price? Do consumers believe it is worth the price? Regardless of whether it is expensive or inexpensive, high-end or low-end, it must deliver at least a good value.

IMPORTANT THINGS TO KNOW ABOUT PRICING[1]

Reference Prices. People often compare a product's price with a "reference price" that they maintain in their minds for the product or product category in question. A reference price is the price that people expect or deem to be reasonable for a certain type of product. Several factors affect reference prices:

- *Memory of Past Prices.*

- *Frame of Reference.* That is, the price as compared with competitive prices, presale prices, manufacturer's suggested prices, channel-specific prices, marked prices before discounts, and substitute product prices, etc. Creating the most advantageous (and believable) competitive frame of reference is essential to achieving a price premium.

- *Prices of Other Products on the Same Shelf, in the Same Catalog, or in the Same Product Line.* The addition of a more premium-priced product typically increases sales of other lower-priced products in the same product line

- *The Way the Price Is Presented.* For instance:
  - Absolute number vs. per quart, per pound, per hour of use, per application
  - Four simple payments of $69.95 vs. $279.80
  - Total purchase price vs. monthly loan payment vs. monthly lease payment (e.g., for automobiles)

- *The Order in Which People See a Range of Prices.* Realtors, for instance, use the trick of showing the poorest value house first.

- *"Rule of 100."* Percentage discounts seem larger if the total amount is less than $100. If it is more than $100, the absolute discount amount in dollars seems larger.[2]

Price Sensitivity. It is extremely important to be able to estimate the impact of price changes on sales and profits. That is, it is important to know how a price change will impact consumer response, competitive response, and unit volume. Many businesspeople erroneously believe that a price increase is *the* most cost-effective revenue-generating marketing tactic. I have heard generally intelligent professionals share their excitement about how a price increase will drop to the "bottom line" dollar-for-dollar. Most of the time, this is simply not true.

People display different price sensitivities to different products in different situations. Often people are relatively price insensitive, but only within a relevant price range. Once a price exceeds that range, people become very sensitive. Raising the price across that threshold is akin to walking off a cliff.

Factors That *Decrease* Price Sensitivity

- Relevant brand/product differentiation.

- Marketing and selling on factors other than price.

- Convincing consumers that quality differs significantly among products and brands in the category.

- Self-expressive or "image" products or brands. (For example, if I wear sports apparel featuring Nike's swoosh logo, it implies I have the "Just do it" attitude of Nike's "authentic athletic performance" essence. If I carry a Gucci handbag or wear a Rolex watch or drive a Mercedes-Benz, it says I have social status. If I wear a Harvard ball cap, it says I am extremely smart and successful; and if I wear a

Harley-Davidson tattoo, it says that I know the freedom of the road, that I am a free spirit.)

- Brand advertising.

- Situations in which price is a signal to quality—usually for relatively new or unknown products or brands.

- When it is difficult to ascertain a "reference price" within the category.

- When there are significant switching costs—in dollars, time, effort, risk, or emotional impact.

- Product categories for which the risk of failure is an important issue.

- When the price is insignificant relative to the total budget or discretionary income.

- When the item does not significantly contribute to the cost of the products and services that a business sells.

- When the price falls within the expected price range for products in the category.

- When offering "value-added services" vs. "price discounts" to motivate purchases.

- New markets.

Factors That *Increase* Price Sensitivity

- Price promotions, especially when people are able to stock up on the price-discounted items

- Mature and declining markets

Price as a Signal to Quality. Often, price is a signal to quality. Generally, people think higher-priced items are worth more. In some categories, if a product's or service's price is too low, people worry that the product or service must be inferior. Conversely, when people pay more for a product they are often more satisfied after their purchase, comforting themselves in the notion that they paid for higher quality.

Price Segmentation. Price segmentation (i.e., offering different prices to different market segments) increases overall revenues and profits, and it is particularly beneficial to industries that have high fixed cost structures. Obviously, price segmentation works better when there are real customer need segments and when you can effectively isolate those segments.

Imagine your business only offers one product priced at $5, but you know some consumers would be willing to pay up to $8. You are leaving $3 on the table with each purchase. Other consumers are more price-sensitive and only willing to pay $3. You do not get any of their business. Figure 8-2 illustrates how much more revenue you can generate by offering three prices—$3, $5, and $8—instead of just one price of $5. Although this is a simplified example, it illustrates the financial advantages of price segmentation.

Figure 8–2. Price segmentation.

Segment	Number of people in segment	Maximum price people in that segment are willing to pay	Maximum possible revenues from that segment if you only offer one item at $5	Maximum possible revenues from that segment if you only offer three —one at $3, one at $5, and one at $8
A	10	$3	0	$30
B	10	$5	$50	$50
C	10	$8	$50	$80
TOTAL	30		$100	$160

Prices can be segmented in the following ways:

- By time (e.g., higher hotel room rates for holidays and other peak tourist seasons)

- By location (e.g., higher prices in locations with less competition or where less price-sensitive shoppers shop; orchestra vs. balcony seats in a theater)

- By volume (volume discounts for large orders)

- By product attribute (e.g., first-class vs. coach section on airplanes; solid brass vs. plastic faucets)

- By product bundling—for example:
  - Selling software in product suites vs. by the program
  - Selling e-learning by library vs. the individual course
  - Fixed price vs. à la carte menus
  - "Fully loaded" models vs. "basic" models with additional options available

- Single admission ticket at theme parks vs. charging per ride

● By customer segment (e.g., brand-loyal vs. price-sensitive vs. convenience-oriented; or image-conscious vs. economy-oriented)

Other Price/Value Considerations:

● In your pricing strategy you should consider these five factors:

1. *Perceived* customer value

2. Competitive response

3. Channels of distribution

4. Cost parameters

5. Congruence with the brand position

● Constantly explore new ways to uniquely add customer value to your products and services.

● In creating greater customer value, always ask, "How can we make it quicker, easier, less risky, or more pleasant to do business with us?" Ask, "What could we do that would favorably surprise and delight our customers?"

● Communicate the value of services that you provide for free.

● Remember that providing value-added products and services at "no charge" is superior to price discounting as a short-term purchase incentive, because it preserves the value of the brand.

● Be careful to price your products and services to reward brand-loyal (vs. brand-switching) behavior.

Pricing is becoming an increasingly sophisticated discipline. The three topics we just discussed—reference prices, price sensitivity, and price segmentation—are just a few of the important considerations when developing pricing strategies and tactics. Other pricing approaches/considerations of note, but beyond the scope of this chapter, are introductory pricing (skimming vs. penetration and trial pricing), product mix pricing, fixed and variable price components, price adjustments (reason, amount, and frequency), pricing to meet buying system requirements, loss-leader pricing, prestige pricing, and even-odd pricing. I would highly recommend that you read *The Strategy and Tactics of Pricing* to better understand how to develop effective pricing strategies and tactics.[3]

MCDONALD'S: THE POWER OF THE ARCHES
In a study of the most recognized symbols across several nations, what was right up there in the top five behind the Olympic rings but ahead of the Christian cross? The McDonald's golden arches, of course. How did this icon get to be so well recognized? To answer this question, you only have to go to a McDonald's restaurant. From the moment you pull into the restaurant parking lot and enter the restaurant until you are finished eating and leave, count the number of times you are exposed to the arches. Also make note of the most unusual places in which you discover the arches. You will have witnessed the power of an effective brand identity system and icon repetition.

Accessibility

Your brand must be available where consumers shop. It's much easier for consumers to insist upon your brand if it is widely available, and slight brand preference goes a long way toward insistence when the brand is widely available. The importance of convenience cannot be overestimated in today's world.

THE POWER OF DISTRIBUTION

Distribution contributes to customer brand insistence in two ways. It increases brand accessibility so that brand preference is more likely to be converted to brand purchase. More important, it increases brand exposure, which increases brand awareness. So distribution affects two of the five customer brand insistence drivers. Brands such as Coca-Cola, KFC, and Starbucks rely on extensive distribution as an important driver of their brands' success.

If you slightly preferred Coca-Cola to Pepsi, and both are available in the same place, you would purchase Coca-Cola every time. However, if Coca-Cola was not available but Pepsi was, you might purchase Pepsi instead.

The only situation in which extensive distribution may not be right for your brand is if it is positioned as an upscale or luxury brand. Limited distribution in limited upscale places can add to the cachet of "exclusive" brands. Certainly, those brands would lose their allure if they were available in the mass channel, especially in discount chains like Wal-Mart. Some brands would even suffer from being in well-known department stores. Consider where Armand de Brignac Champagne, Bugatti, Desvall, Hermès, Rolls-Royce, Savoir, Tesla Motors, or Vilebrequin brands are sold.

Even highly upscale brands can benefit from increased exposure to their target audiences, but the places they are available must scream exclusivity.

THE COCA-COLA COMPANY:
THE POWER OF BRAND ACCESSIBILITY

Brand Asset Value

According to BRANDZ Top 100 most valuable global brands 2013 (methodology and valuation by MillwardBrown Optimor), the Coca-Cola brand was valued at $78.4 billion. For the sake of comparison—the Apple brand was valued at $185.1 billion, Google at $113.7 billion, IBM at $112.5 billion, and McDonald's at $90.3 billion.

What does that really mean? If all Coke's plants were burned to the ground, if every one of its employees were to quit, if all its retail distribution was lost to competitors, if every single remaining tangible asset was sold, the person who owned rights to the Coke name and trademark could go to any bank in the world and, based on the value of that trademark, borrow money to completely rebuild the company. In other words, the **Coke name alone** is worth some $78.4 billion—more than the value of all the company's other assets combined. After all, it's Coke that consumers insist on, not any of the other stuff.

From the Three A's to the Three P's

Coca-Cola used to focus on the three A's: availability, acceptability, affordability. While these factors provided tremendous growth, they also led to lower entry barriers. Today, Coke's mantra is the three P's: preference, pervasive penetration, and price-related value.

The Power of Brand Accessibility

If you were another soft drink company, you might define your competitive frame of reference as the cola market or the soft drink market or even the beverage market. But Coke thinks of its business and its market share in terms of the "share of human liquid consumption." This makes water a competitor. In fact, a Coke executive has said that he won't be satisfied until "there is a Coca-Cola faucet in every home." Coca-Cola's mantra is "within an arm's reach of desire."

Another indication of Coke's drive for accessibility, beyond the ever-present vending machines, is illustrated in this story of a recent trip I took to Peru. We spent several days traveling down Rio Madre de Dios on a riverboat, moving deeper and deeper into the Amazon river basin, jungle, and Manu World Biosphere Reserve. When we finally encountered a riverside village of indigenous people and thatched huts, what was waiting for us? A Coke sign and a fresh Coke.

Coca-Cola Is Serious About Brand Building

Each month, Coca-Cola tests twenty brand attributes with 4,000 consumers to measure movement. The company also compensates *(using bonuses and other compensation components) a large portion of its senior managers based on brand preference.*

One Final Coca-Cola Fact

Coca-Cola reports that the second most recognized expression in the world after "OK?" is "Coca-Cola."

Emotional Connection

As we've discussed, the consumer must first know your brand, then like it, and finally *trust* your brand and feel an emotional connection to it.

If you are aware of a brand and it is relevant to your needs, it will be in your purchase consideration set. If it delivers a good value and is differentiated in ways that matter most to you, you will likely prefer it. As long as your preferred brand is equally accessible to other brands you are considering, you will probably purchase it. If the brand creates an emotional connection with you as you purchase and use it, you will be loyal to it. (See Figure 8–3.)

People become emotionally connected to a brand for a number of reasons:

- The brand stands for something important to them.

- It is intense, vibrant, and it connects on many levels.

Figure 8–3. Hierarchy of effects.

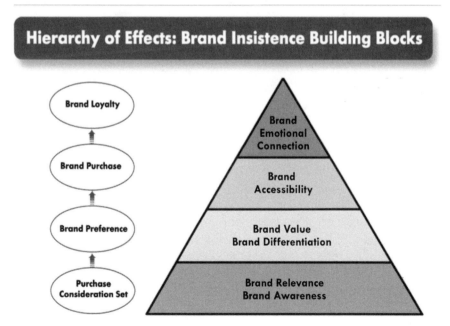

- The brand is unique.
- The brand is admirable.
- The brand consistently interacts with them. It never disappoints them.
- The brand makes them feel good.

There are many innovative ways to achieve this emotional connection—from advertising and the quality of frontline consumer contact to consumer membership organizations and company-sponsored consumer events.

Emotional connection can take your customers beyond brand loyalty to the ultimate measure of a compelling brand: brand advocacy.

Figure 8–4. Brand advocacy.

It is especially important to ensure that all of your employees with front-line customer contact are like Boy Scouts—that is, that they are trustworthy, helpful, friendly, courteous, kind, and cheerful. Add to that list empathetic, good listeners, and reassuring. To have a quality workforce you need to establish the appropriate hiring criteria, training, and organization culture. Remember, good service is all about creating positive feelings, treating people well, and solving people's problems.

Ultimately, emotional connection will come from positive shared experiences with the brand over time. While this trust is built over time, offering an unconditional guarantee is a quick way to reduce the risk posed by a new, unknown brand and to generate some minimum level of trust immediately.

PEDIGREE DOG FOOD: MOVING FROM FUNCTIONAL TO EMOTIONAL MESSAGING

In 2004, Pedigree was the share leader in its category; however, it was losing share to the competition at both the high and low ends of the market. At the time, Pedigree focused its messaging on product attributes. In 2005, Pedigree's advertising agency (TBWA) recommended changing the emphasis from functional attributes to the "love of dogs," appealing to the customers' hearts instead of their heads. TBWA's chairman and chief creative officer, Lee Clow, asked Pedigree to embrace this statement as its new brand mantra: "If you convince me you love dogs, I'll let you feed mine." Today, Pedigree offers its customers a breed gallery, dog age calculator, breed match questionnaire, "adopt a dog" search, free puppy guide, "Dogs Rule" apparel, and an opportunity to donate to the PEDIGREE Foundation, which is dedicated to helping dogs find loving homes.

There are other loyalty-inducing approaches, too. For instance:

- The brand encourages frequent, habit-forming interaction (as long as the interaction is pleasant or beneficial and not against people's wills).

- The brand finds ways to build cumulative value for customers over time, especially if the value is not transferable to the use of competitive products and services.

In his book *The Dream Society*, Rolf Jensen makes the case for a shift from an information society to a dream society in which imagination and storytelling become the primary drivers of value.[4] He identifies six emerging emotion-based markets:

1. Adventure

2. Community (togetherness, friendship, and love)

3. Providing and receiving care

4. Self-expression ("Who am I?")

5. Peace of mind

6. Standing for something (convictions)

Any brand that seeks to create emotional connection should find ways to tap into these and other underlying human motives. See Figure 8–5 for statements taken from real customer feedback on brands with strong emotional connection.

Figure 8–5. Brand emotional connection. You know you have a vital, relevant, compelling brand when customers think or say the following things about your brand.

- It affects you at a gut level.
- It "gets in your blood."
- It evokes strong emotions.
- It speaks from the heart.
- It speaks to the heart.
- It creates a sense of possibility.
- It opens up a new world.
- It is inspiring.
- It is empowering.
- It is invigorating.
- It helps people see that they can make a difference.
- It makes people believe that they can change the world.
- It helps people articulate what they have been trying to say.
- It is the first time people feel they've been heard.
- It is unique.
- It is fresh.
- It is original.
- It is one of a kind.
- It breaks all of the rules.
- It breaks down boundaries.
- It is "a breath of fresh air."
- It defines the category.
- It is quintessential.
- It sets the standard.
- It stands apart from all the rest.
- It is in a class all its own.
- No one does anything like it.
- It is seminal.
- Everything else is derivative.
- It reinvents the category.
- It is genuine.
- It is sincere.
- It is real.

- It is pure.
- It is trustworthy.
- It is approachable.
- It is endearing.
- It stands for something.
- It is passionate.
- It has a distinctive attitude.
- It is powerful.
- It possesses great energy.
- It is entertaining.
- It is elegant, beautiful, and/or haunting.
- It is admirable.
- It is visionary.
- It possesses a timeless quality.
- It is "bigger than life."
- It can't be ignored.

- It demands to be heard.
- It is legendary.
- It is enshrouded in mystery.
- It is profound.
- It is captivating.
- It is otherworldly.
- It is mesmerizing.
- The only way to understand it is to experience it.
- It is unstoppable.
- It is extraordinary.
- It is flawless.
- It is genius.
- It is a "crowning jewel."
- It is "mind blowing."
- It doesn't get any better.

A Quiz: What Brand?

What brand has built enormous equity without huge advertising budgets?

What brand has defined its business not narrowly as a product, but broadly as an experience and a state of mind, despite the fact that the vast majority of its revenues result from one single product category?

What brand has created tremendous brand loyalty by creating a social organization for owners of its products?

What brand sponsors frequent events for owners of its products, which the company's management attends in order to understand the consumer, the consumer's experience, and the consumer's needs firsthand?

What brand proactively leverages publicity as a key component of its marketing plan?

What brand tried to legally protect the sound its product makes as a key element of its brand identity system?

What brand, having been on the brink of bankruptcy twice since the 1960s, has achieved a stunning transformation into a world-class brand?

What brand evokes so much loyalty in its consumers that many of them tattoo its logo on their bodies?

Harley-Davidson, of course.

A CASE STUDY:
Managing Brand Equity

While serving as director of brand management and marketing at Hallmark, I spent the better part of three years developing and refining a brand equity framework and scorecard for Hallmark. As awareness of the Hallmark brand was very high and its image was very positive, we were less interested in measuring and managing these aspects of the brand's equity than we were in identifying the attributes that drove customers to insist upon the brand. This ultimately led to what is now my organization's brand insistence, brand equity model (as addressed earlier in this chapter) with five key drivers: awareness, accessibility, value, relevant differentiation, and emotional connection. Hallmark scored extraordinarily high on awareness, accessibility, and emotional connection. While relevant differentiation was constantly a focus (as it should be for all established brands), we primarily focused on improving value. Although Hallmark's greeting cards were actually less expensive than competitive cards, they were universally thought to be more expensive. People perceived Hallmark cards to be priced between $2.75 and $2.95 (one dollar higher than the actual average price paid), while they perceived mass channel brands to have cards priced at $2 (very near the actual average price paid after in-store discounts). So, people made the following connection in their minds: "Hallmark = The Best = Expensive." (Or "When you care enough to send the very best.") This perception was reinforced in several ways:

• People were especially price conscious in card shops (Hallmark's primary channel at the time) as they assumed products would be more expensive there. Card shops seldom, if ever, offer price discounts. If one shopped in Wal-Mart, with its promise of "Always Low Prices. Always," its prominent "X percent off" displays, and in the case of greeting cards, its generic brands, one was less likely to be on the lookout for high prices. [Note: Wal-Mart's current slogan is "Save Money. Live Better."]

• In a card shop's typical market basket of four greeting cards, card prices were obvious (a total bill of $12 easily translates to $3 a card).

This compares to a typical mass channel market basket, which may be composed of a wide variety of items and cost many times that amount.

Our brand equity measurement system identified this as an issue in two ways: 1) Hallmark received a mediocre score on "value," and 2) the system identified "expensive" as Hallmark's only negative brand association.

Altering price perceptions for a leading premium brand is a tricky exercise. It's kind of like defusing a bomb. The trick is to snip the right wire—the "The Best = Expensive" wire, not the "Hallmark = The Best" wire.

Changing Hallmark price perceptions was also critical to the success of our strategy of launching Expressions from Hallmark into the mass channel (see the Hallmark case study in Part 4, Leveraging the Brand).

After our brand scorecard identified "value" as an issue, we got management's buy-in to develop and test aggressive measures to alter the "expensive" price perception. Here is what we did:

• We developed two lines of 99-cent cards as proof points—children's (occasion and nonoccasion) cards and Out of the Blue, a new line of "any day" friendship cards. We devoted 248 SKUs and eight linear feet of product to this new line, which provided a proof point of (and statement about) our commitment to the new line.

• Because we knew our competitors could not match Hallmark's very high proportion of cards priced below $2, we created pocket identifiers (signs above each card on the display) that highlighted that the cards were priced under $2 (65 percent of what Hallmark's other cards cost, only 11 percent of our competitors' cards).

• We prominently featured "99 cent" signs at appropriate places throughout the card department.

• We advertised the fact that Hallmark now had 99-cent cards.

• Introducing "Expressions from Hallmark" cards to Wal-Mart and other mass channel stores reinforced the point that Hallmark must not be that expensive (to borrow from Wal-Mart's "low price" brand perceptions).

• We implemented this program as a part of a test market in Las Vegas.

• We tested the impact of this action on many brand equity components in that test market, not just "value." For instance, we tested brand preference, quality perceptions, and brand insistence itself to validate that increased "value" led to increased brand equity and insistence. Here is what we found from the Las Vegas test market:

- Greeting card category price perceptions improved significantly.
- All Hallmark brand equity measures increased significantly.
- People gave Hallmark credit for listening to their concerns about price.
- Hallmark sales and market share increased significantly.

Based on the success of this test market, we launched this program nationally, and we achieved the same results nationally. This is a simple example of how a brand equity measurement system led to actions that significantly improved brand perceptions, sales, and market share.

Use the checklist in Figure 8–6 to assess the efficacy of your brand management practices in the area covered by this chapter. The more questions to which you can answer "yes," the better you are doing. The checklist also provides a brief summary of the material covered in the chapter.

Figure 8–6. Checklist: Driving the consumer from brand awareness to brand insistence.

	YES / NO
Was your brand first to market?	__ __
Was it the first to communicate with consumers in significant ways?	__ __
Is your brand the top-of-mind brand in its product/service category?	__ __
Is it the only brand that comes to mind for its primary differentiating benefit?	__ __
Do consumers perceive your brand to be easily accessible and convenient?	__ __
Have you carefully crafted brand pricing strategies and tactics based on a solid understanding of contribution margins, consumer price sensitivities, reference prices, likely competitive responses, and basic pricing principles?	__ __

Does your brand deliver a good value for the price? Do consumers think your brand is worth the price? ____ ____

Is your brand differentiated in at least one highly relevant and compelling way? ____ ____

Does your brand reflect the attitudes and values of its target customers? ____ ____

Does your brand touch people at some deep emotional level? Does it stand for something important to them? ____ ____

Does your brand achieve any of the following? ____ ____

Does it make people feel more in control? ____ ____

Does it make people nostalgic of something from their childhood? ____ ____

Does it make them feel warm and safe? ____ ____

Does it offer a sensual experience? ____ ____

Does it make them feel smart or frugal or important when they use it? ____ ____

Does it make them feel like "masters of the universe"? ____ ____

Does it help them play out unfulfilled fantasies? ____ ____

Does it make them feel as though they have become the people they had always wanted to be? ____ ____

Does it make them feel more connected to the group they most admire? ____ ____

Does it make them feel superior to others? ____ ____

Does your brand invite people into its world? Is it inviting and engaging? ____ ____

Is your brand the most preferred brand in its category? ____ ____

Do your customers perceive your brand to be vital, popular, or leading-edge? ____ ____

Do people like your brand? ____ ____

Do people trust your brand? ____ ____

Is your brand on the short list of most potential customers? Is it typically the only brand that they consider? ____ ____

Are your customers attitudinally loyal to your brand? ____ ____

Do people enthusiastically recommend your brand to others? ____ ____

9

brand advertising

ADVERTISING IS ONE of the most frequently used and powerful communications mediums for brand building. How then does one maximize the effectiveness and efficiency of this medium?

Selecting an Ad Agency*

First, if you don't have an advertising agency, select one. Begin by thoughtfully defining what is most important to you in an agency, and clarify where you need the most help. This decision will be an important touchstone throughout the remainder of the process.

Cut out your favorite magazine ads and record your favorite television commercials. A good place to find great ads is creativity-online.com. Other sources are *One Show* and *Communication Arts* awards books. Also, most cities have ad clubs that judge and recognize the best ads from local agencies. Check with these clubs as well. Once you have selected several ads that you like, find out which agencies created them. Of those agencies, find out which are already working for your competitors. Rule them out. Talk with marketing peers at other companies about their perceptions of the agencies that are left. Ask about the agencies' capabilities in each of the following areas: product, company and marketplace knowledge, creative, strategic insight, media planning, and production. (I have found that the two most important aspects of an

* Much of this section is adapted from an approach David Ogilvy outlines in his book, *Ogilvy on Advertising* (New York: Vintage Books, 1985), pp. 66–69, combined with my personal experience.

effective agency are strategic insight and translating that insight to creative communication.) Contact the top three to four agencies of those that are left.

When you meet with agency representatives, ask to see their best ads. Have the agencies demonstrate how they would address your most pressing strategic issues. You might also ask each agency to create three campaigns to move your brand forward. (Be sure to pay each of the agencies for their work. This protects you if you use an agency's ideas but do not end up hiring that agency.) Look for the agency that you can best work with based on personal chemistry.

Some other tips:

• Don't assume that going with the biggest well-known agency is best. Unless you have an enormous advertising budget, you are likely to be assigned to the agency's "C team" and may not be happy with the work.

• There are significant advantages to choosing an agency that has strengths in multiple areas, such as strategy, creative, media planning and buying, direct marketing, online marketing, website design, and trade shows. It will make it easier to manage your overall marketing budget and, more important, all of your communication is more likely to be consistent and "on brand."

Unfortunately, very few agencies are tops in more than a few aspects of marketing. I prefer to work with a small number of "best in class" agencies, although it requires a strong coordination effort. You need to have well-thought-out and accessible brand identity standards, an accessible brand image library, and frequent (quarterly) "brand champion summits" (in which all agency partners are invited, so they remain informed and aligned with the strategy and key messages). It is particularly important to coordinate the efforts of advertising strategy and creative with that of media planning and buying if performed by separate agencies. The two agencies should meet often and learn to work well together.

• Some agencies are best at (and enjoy most) the development of new breakthrough campaigns. They are critical to your brand's success but also tend to be more expensive. Other agencies don't have a "strategic bone in their bodies" but provide on-spec collateral pieces at a fraction of the cost. I use both types of agencies. Some agencies try to address both needs at different hourly rates, using different individuals and processes. Sometimes that works. Sometimes it doesn't.

• AgencyFinder.com indicates that you may be more successful using an RFI (request for information) or an RFD (request for dialogue) than an RFP (request for proposal) to find the best agency for you.[1]

Figure 9–1 gives additional tips on how to get the most out of your advertising agency.

Figure 9–1. *The care and feeding of advertising agencies, or how to get the most out of your advertising agency.*

- Give them clear assignments with clear deliverables. (See the "agency brief" in Figure 9–2.)
- Tell them that you expect their best work.
- Treat them with respect.
- Expose them to your customers and all of your customer research.
- Get out of their way. Don't micromanage them.
- Run internal "interference" for them. Don't let internal review and approval processes adulterate their product.
- Pay them fairly for their work.
- Praise them when they do good work.

Importance of a Well-Designed Brand to Brand Advertising

As you begin to work with an agency (even during an agency review), you will make greater strides if you have already designed and positioned the brand. Remember, your brand's promise should leverage all three of the following: a) a compelling point of difference in the consumer's mind, b) your organization's unique strengths, and c) your competitors' vulnerabilities. This positioning implies that you have identified the brand's target consumer, essence, promise, archetype, and personality. The brand promise, in turn, implies that you understand your brand's competitive frame of reference and the consumer's benefit structure within that frame of reference. The brand design and positioning will drive brand advertising and every other brand marketing activity. Make sure your ad agency thoroughly understands and embraces your brand's design. (Although you should take the lead in crafting your brand's design, ideally your advertising agency should be actively involved in the process, including immersing itself in the underlying consumer research.)

Specifying the Marketing Objective for Advertising

The next step in advertising development is specifying the marketing objective for the advertising. That is, what do you want the advertising to achieve?

Do you want it to increase brand awareness, attract new customers, increase brand loyalty, encourage add-on purchases, motivate people to switch from competitive brands to your brand, increase frequency of use, reinforce ongoing use, etc.? Make sure the objective is quantifiable and measurable.

As an example, the marketing objective for Hallmark's brand insistence advertising campaign was very simple and tactical: to get consumers to flip the card over and look for the brand name on the back cover.

During your brand positioning work, you should have developed the brand promise, including identification of the brand's relevant differentiating benefit. Next you augment the brand promise with proof points (reasons to believe). Proof points may include the following:

- Product features and attributes (including the design itself or its formula or ingredients)

- Performance features, statistics, and research results

- Performance guarantees

- Service claims

- Side-by-side comparisons

- Third-party endorsements

Writing the Agency Brief

The marketing objective and the brand promise with its proof points are key elements of the agency brief, a document that communicates the strategic direction of a new advertising campaign. Once you have completed the agency brief, your ad agency will use the brief to develop campaign ideas/concepts (e.g., storyboards, print ads). They will likely show you several different campaign ideas.

Figure 9–2 lists the elements of the agency brief.

Figure 9–2. Agency brief.

Background/Overview: (history, context, and a general overview of the competitive environment and the problem)

Marketing Objective: (desired tangible result, usually in target customer's attitude or behavior; intended effect with quantifiable success criteria)

- Current State: (what the customer thinks today)

- Desired State: (what we want them to think and what we want them to do)

Assignment: (deliverable, timing, and budget)

Product or Service: (if product/service-specific)

Target Customer: (be as specific as possible)

Brand Essence: (the "heart and soul" of the brand expressed as "adjective, adjective, noun")

Brand Promise: (only [brand] delivers [relevant differentiated benefit or shared value])

Proof Points: (reasons to believe)

Brand Archetype: (choose and elaborate on one or two archtypes that explain the brand's motivation and drive its behavior)

Brand Personality, Voice, and Visual Style: (from the positioning statement, list adjectives that describe the brand; for instance: *voice:* down-to-earth, assertive, confident, warm, sarcastic, witty, reassuring, eloquent, simple, etc.; *visual style:* bold, bright, energetic, soft, textured, ornate, understated, nostalgic, futuristic, etc.)

Mandatories: (those items that are givens. It is best to provide as few constraints as possible. I usually specify the brand identity standards and system as the only mandatories. There may be legal or regulatory mandatories as well.)

Evaluating Advertising Effectiveness

When evaluating the potential effectiveness of different campaign ideas, I use the following questions:

1. *All Advertising:*
   - Does the ad clearly identify your brand? Does it do so immediately and throughout the ad?
   - Does the ad clearly and forcefully communicate your brand's unique promise?
   - Does the ad feature a tagline that reinforces the brand's promise?
   - Are the ad's tone, voice, and style true to your brand's essence and personality?
   - Does the ad reinforce your brand's identity?
   - Does the ad connect with the reader on an emotional level? Does it win the reader's heart or capture the person's imagination?
   - Is there something about the ad that makes the reader admire the brand?
   - Is your ad significantly different from that of your competitors? Does it look and feel different from anything else featured in the same media?

- Does the ad reinforce the positive value and values of your brand?
- Does the ad seem truly inspired?
- Is your ad so powerful that it has the potential to keep your competitors awake at night worrying about your brand?
- Is the ad persuasive?
- Could another competitor make the same claim? If you inserted a competitor's logo in the ad, would it make no sense or be unbelievable?
- Does the ad lead readers/viewers to believe that they will be better off in some way for having interacted with your brand? Does it create a more favorably perceived end state for your readers? Does it leave a vivid picture in their mind?

DID YOU KNOW?

Psychologist Erich Dichter found that consumers are more apt to relax and accept advertiser recommendations when the tone is that of a friend or an unbiased authority.

(Source: Emanuel Rosen, The Anatomy of Buzz: How to Create Word of Mouth Marketing, *New York: Doubleday, 2000, p. 210.)*

---

2. *Print Advertising.* The benefits of print advertising are good reach and frequency. Print can handle complicated propositions, reaches consumers in a receptive context, and can be very targeted.

- Does the headline immediately "grab" the reader? (In his book *Ogilvy on Advertising*, advertising guru David Ogilvy's states that five times as many people read headlines as read body copy.) Ideally, the headline is nine words or less.
- Does the headline promise an important benefit? (Ogilvy also states that ads with headlines that promise benefits are read by four times more people than those that don't explain a benefit.)
- Is the body copy long enough to provide the reader with useful information and ample proof points for your brand's promise? Long copy is more effective than short copy. This is particularly true for business-to-business advertising. (Alternatively, Roper Starch Worldwide, which maintains a database of more than 2 million print ads, has found that excessive copy reduces the effectiveness of ads and recommends keeping ad copy to fifty words or less. With whole generations having now grown up on "sound bites" of information, some cohort groups will respond better to shorter copy.)

- Increasing white space around the ad or the headline increases the ad's effectiveness.

Figure 9–3 ranks ad placement and size according to impact.

Figure 9–3. *Ranking order of magazine advertising size impact.*

1. Three single-page ads following each other on the right side.
2. Two single-page ads in different sections of the same magazine on the right side.
3. Double-page spread.
4. Single-page ads on right.
5. Single-page ads on left with strip on right.
6. Single-page ads on left.
7. Checkerboard ads on right.
8. Checkerboard ads on left.
9. Half-page ad, upper right.
10. Half-page ad, lower right.
11. Strip on both right and left sides.
12. Half-page ad, upper left.
13. Half-page ad, lower left.
14. Third-page block, lower right.
15. Strip (one column) extreme right.
16. Strip, extreme left.

Source: A study performed by the PreTesting Company and reported by "The MPA Research Newsletter/No. 60" (Magazine Publishers of America).

3. *Television Advertising.* Television advertising benefits are broad reach and the ability to dramatize the brand.

- Do you try to grab people's attention immediately so that they do not become preoccupied with other activities?
- Do you have enough time to tell a story with your commercial? (Two-minute commercials are more powerful than thirty-second commercials.)
- Have you carefully selected the music for your commercial? (Music can make or break a commercial.)
- Have you consistently used a sound or visual mnemonic to reinforce the brand in your commercials?

4. *Radio Advertising.* Benefits are that radio advertising is very efficient, a good frequency medium with coverage flexibility.
- Does the first five seconds of the ad "grab" the listener?
- Have you chosen the right voice?
- Does the dialogue sound natural?

5. *Outdoor Advertising.* Outdoor advertising is a true local medium. Other benefits are very low CPM and the ability to communicate a single "idea" effectively.
- Does the billboard have no more than seven words? Does it have less than five? ("Got Milk?") Remember, motorists often have to "get it" (your message) in a second or less!
- Is the ad "big" in every way? Is it outrageous? Does it turn heads? Does it pique the reader's curiosity? Does it shock the reader? Does it make the reader laugh?

Successful Advertising Approaches

Here is a list of effective general advertising techniques:

- Always dramatize your brand's most important benefit.
- Create simple ads—they are usually more powerful.
- Create copy in smaller chunks (sentences, paragraphs, etc).
- Use natural and "real-life" writing or dialogue.
- *Subtly* tap into people's fears and anxieties.

Here are some print advertising techniques that have proved to be effective:

- Try to evoke the reader's curiosity. Begin by asking a provocative question and/or feature an image that piques the reader's curiosity.
- Put quotes around your headlines.
- Romance/dramatize your product or service.
- Try to trigger multiple senses; use words that help people feel, hear, smell, and taste your product.
- Tell a story.
- Communicate "news."
- Provide information that is useful to the reader.
- Always write in the present tense.

• Be as specific as possible.

• Include customer testimonials (they should seem natural, not scripted or polished).

• Know how readers read (from right to left, top to bottom in the United States) and place your headlines, illustrations, captions, and copy accordingly. (In his book *Secret Formulas of the Wizard of Ads*, Roy H. Williams indicates that savvy photographers and graphic artists have known for some time that there is a spot on a piece of artwork to which the eye is irresistibly drawn, roughly between the middle and upper right corner of the artwork.)

• Use white space to focus the reader's attention on something important.

• Use words that sell: *at last, now, new, introducing, announcing, finally, limited, save, free, win, easy, guarantee, breakthrough, wanted,* etc. (Keep in mind that as consumers become more sophisticated and savvy, there may be instances where these words might be clichés or overused and thus may not be as effective.)

• Avoid metaphors, analogies, puns, double entendres, "insider" references, and other nonstraightforward language. Alliteration is sometimes effective.

• Avoid jargon, dialect, acronyms, and model numbers, especially in headlines.

Here are some successful approaches to television advertisements:[2]

• Company leader as brand spokesperson. Examples are Richard Branson of Virgin Atlantic, Dave Thomas of Wendy's, John Schnatter of Papa John's, and Jim Koch of Boston Beer Company (Samuel Adams brand).

• Interesting character as brand spokesperson (Mr. Whipple for Charmin).

• Customer testimonial.

• Visualization of the brand benefit and/or the "reason why."

• Product demonstration (demonstrating product usage and showing brand benefit).

• Torture test (Timex "Takes a lickin' and keeps on tickin'").

• Problem-solution.

• Before-after. To some large degree, advertising sells the hope of an improved future with the use of a particular brand of product or service. Before-after advertising reinforces this hope.

- Competitive comparison. Although it is usually not wise to identify the competitive brand by name, a special case would be the comparison to premium brand(s). However, this can lead to greater category price sensitivity.[3]

- Slice-of-life vignette (telling a story about the benefits of the brand).

- Presenter/"talking head" (in which a person attempts to persuade the viewer about the benefits of the brand).

In his book, *Cutting Edge Advertising*, Jim Aitchison indicates that every ad must have an idea. He suggests that ideas may come from any of the following: "product name or logo," "packaging," "how the product is made," "where the product is made," "the product's history," "the product's old advertising," "something that is happening around you," "what happens with the product," "what happens without the product," "what happens with and without the product in the same ad," and "where the ad will run."

The following will likely result in bad brand advertising:

- Design by committee.

- Opinionated reviewers and approvers who don't understand marketing.

- Writing ads that appeal to you rather than the target consumer.

- Using flowery language that sounds good but that means nothing. (This is a common ailment of neophyte copywriters. Substance is good. Using an economy of words is good. Simple, persuasive copy is good. Fluff and filler are bad.)

- Squeezing as many features and benefits into the ad as possible (unsophisticated advertising clients often request this information).

- Revising an emotional or metaphorical ad to make it more literal (another common ailment of unsophisticated advertising clients).

- Focusing on reach vs. frequency (as discussed later in this chapter.)

- Assuming that business-to-business advertising is significantly different from consumer advertising (e.g., "it needs to be factual and informative, not emotional"). Don't forget, business decision makers are people, too. And people are ruled as much by their hearts as by their heads. Harding's study of buyers in ten corporations demonstrated that corporate buyers overwhelmingly rely on personal and emotional reasons over rational ones in their purchase choice.

• Jingles. Unless they are very, very good (and most are not very, very good), they will distract from the brand message.

• Celebrity endorsements (because they tend not to be believable).

• Making claims that your brand can't support.

And, although it may not result in bad advertising, for consistency's sake, it is also not a good idea to have a new marketing manager, feeling the need to make his or her mark on the brand, hire a new advertising agency and create a totally new advertising campaign (whether or not the old campaign was working).

When building the brand, the best advertising vehicles to use tend to be radio, television, and with the widespread emergence of broadband, the Internet, due to the auditory elements. These vehicles create a slower build but are more effective in the long run. Trade magazines and shows and direct marketing (regular mail and e-mail) are effective for business-to-business marketing because the target audiences typically are geographically dispersed but highly targeted. Newspapers and the radio are often used to promote brand building events because they can efficiently and effectively deliver a more immediate message. Radio advertising should be scheduled for immediate effect, and radio ads should be scheduled to run just before or during a sale or other event.

The Art of Persuasion

There are certain techniques that advertisers, politicians, salespeople, speechwriters, preachers, and others have long known to be effective in persuading people. Social psychologists have studied many of them in great detail. Anthony Pratkanis and Elliot Aronson, in their book, *Age of Propaganda: The Everyday Use and Abuse of Persuasion*, outline four basic strategies to effectively influence others: 1) defining/structuring how an issue is discussed, which includes setting the agenda and creating the frame of reference, 2) establishing credibility (authority, likability, and trustworthiness), 3) vividly focusing the audience's attention on the key point the communicator intends to make, and 4) arousing emotions in a way that can only be satisfactorily addressed by taking the communicator's desired course of action.

In his book, *Influence: The Psychology of Persuasion*, Robert B. Cialdini, Ph.D., focuses on six principles of persuasion: 1) reciprocation (people try to repay favors out of a sense of obligation); 2) commitment and consistency (people behave in ways that support an earlier action or decision); 3) social proof (seeing other people doing something makes it more acceptable and appealing); 4) liking (people are more likely to say yes to people and brands that they know, like, and trust); 5) authority (people are inclined to yield to authority); and 6) scarcity (people are more motivated by the thought of losing something than by the thought of gaining something).

Cialdini also indicates that many approaches lead to "liking": physical attractiveness (which studies have shown to be a function of body/facial symmetry), similarity (people feel comfortable with you and can relate to you), compliments, familiarity (through contact and cooperation), and direct or indirect association with other likable entities.

Both books are quite interesting and well worth reading, if only to help you better understand how third parties attempt to persuade you on a daily basis.

Other considerations in creating highly persuasive communication:

• Always design the message to play off of the audience's preexisting beliefs, values, and prejudices.

• To be effective, your point of departure must be from a place of agreement.

• Try to define the issue in a way that your brand can't help but "win." This is why it is so important to choose the optimal "frame of reference" in brand positioning.

• Sometimes, just asking the right questions can reorient people's thinking about a topic in your favor.

• Comparisons/contrasts alter perceptions of the items being compared/contrasted. For example, when I moved to Rochester, my Realtor first showed me a number of overpriced houses that required much work. When we got to the houses that she wanted me to buy, they seemed even more appealing than they might have otherwise if she hadn't first shown me the other houses. This concept is also used in establishing reference pricing. Create reference prices that make your price seem more reasonable or even a "bargain."

• Be careful when labeling, categorizing, or describing competing brands or approaches in ways that cast them in a negative light. While it is an effective technique (that is, it usually works), in the long run, it may cast a less favorable light on your brand.

• Making people feel as though they are a part of a group (assigning brand labels, brand-as-a-badge) helps sell products and brands.

• Fear and guilt sell. (Example: "When you care enough to send the very best.")

● Paint vivid pictures of desired or dreaded end states with words or images, or both.

● Let people touch, try, use, and otherwise interact with your product or brand before they buy it. Once they have done so, they are much more likely to want to purchase it. This works for a wide variety of situations: from automobile test-drives and in-home free-trial uses of products, to overnight stays on the campus of a college that you are considering attending (assuming the experience is positive).

● Neurolinguistic programming (NLP) is a well-studied technique that increases persuasion. Through NLP, you can establish a strong rapport with the audience by mirroring the mannerisms and expressions of the audience, which allows you to more easily lead them in the direction of your choice.

● "Largest," "fastest growing," "most popular," "highest rated," and other similar claims provide strong third-party endorsements for a product or brand. (Alternatively, they may be perceived to be puffery by a jaded audience unless you back them up with credible proof points.)

● Repetition increases the effectiveness of communication.

Brands and Storytelling

Recently, I was drawn in again by a street person's story. It is not the first time. A good story tugs on your heartstrings. While, as a marketer, I am always leery of being taken in by total fiction, at the same time, if the story is good enough, it doesn't even matter if it is true. It has entertained me. I give the person some money. Several times a week my wife and I get phone calls from various not-for-profit and political organizations asking for contributions. Again, there are stories. What will happen if they don't get enough money? What will happen if they do? The telephone solicitors are scripted to paint a compelling picture with words. Don't religious leaders do the same thing? How many of Jesus's parables are recounted in the Bible? And there are Hindu, Buddhist, Native American, Taoist, Sufi, and Hebrew parables and stories. I can't think of a religion or a culture that doesn't have its stories. I even hear stories from people who want to sell me investments, stories of people getting rich. They paint a picture of how I will significantly increase my net worth too if I invest in what they are selling. And how about the stories told by places? Come to our country or city or resort and have this type of experience.

Brands tell stories about their history and their heritage and their founders. They also tell stories about their heroic and other admirable deeds.

Many brands like to tell stories that demonstrate their values or their legendary service.

Every brand story requires the following elements:

- Core values that underpin the story
- Moral of the story (central premise)
- Hero (protagonist)
- Villain (antagonist)
- Plot (tension/conflict/resolution)
- "Aha" moment
- Transformation

Here are two other storytelling frameworks that you might find useful.

Mark Lightowler[4] uses a storytelling map that includes the following nine elements:

1. Story setup (the background information the audience needs to know)
2. Protagonist (the hero)
3. Conflict (what stands in the way of the journey's completion)
4. Outer motivation (protagonist's motivation)
5. Deep issues (the deeper issues addressed by the story)
6. Opportunity (the protagonist's inward reward for overcoming the conflict)
7. Arc (how the protagonist grows or changes inwardly over the course of the story)
8. Empathy (what causes the audience to empathize with the protagonist)
9. Tension (the unspoken feeling feeding the conflict)

According to Chris Vogler,[5] the hero's journey consists of the following steps:

1. The ordinary world
2. The call to adventure

3. Refusal of the call

4. Meeting with the mentor

5. Crossing the first threshold

6. Tests, allies, enemies

7. Approach to the inmost cave

8. The ordeal

9. Reward

10. The road back

11. The resurrection

12. Return with the elixir

Furthermore, you should have answered these questions before you write your brand's story:

- What is the brand's archetype?
- What is the brand's personality?
- What is admirable or endearing about the brand?
- What is the context or need that makes this story relevant?
- Where should we tell this story? Using which media?

Storytelling is a strong selling tool. Every brand should have its stories. The stories should be engaging, entertaining, admirable, endearing, and even purchase motivating. Does your brand have a story to tell? If your target customers heard it, would they love your brand even more?

PRECONCEIVED NOTIONS

A person's preconceived notion or expectation can alter his subsequent experience. Recall the Pepsi vs. Coca-Cola challenge in which more people preferred Pepsi in a blind taste test but more people preferred Coca-Cola in the taste test when the brand was identified. Subsequent to the original taste test, a group of neuroscientists conducted their own blind and nonblind taste tests of Coca-Cola and Pepsi. What did they find? They found that when the name of the brand was revealed a different part of the brain was activated, causing a variation in the results. Also, consider how Conservative Republicans interpret the same behavior or event differently than

Liberal Democrats do. Both examples are the result of preconceived notions or expectations. In his book Predictably Irrational, *Dan Ariely cites numerous examples of this biased view of the world that is difficult for anyone to escape. The lesson for marketers is that by linking the brand to positive associations prior to the actual brand experience, it will enhance the experience itself. Robert Graham embroiders "Knowledge Wisdom Truth" into every article of its menswear and women's wear so that people who are familiar with the brand will subconsciously link these noble qualities to their product purchase and usage experiences, enhancing them significantly.*

(Source: Dan Ariely, Predictably Irrational, New York: HarperCollins, 2008, pp. 155–172.)

Advertising Research

Although advertising is part art and part science, there is more science to it than one might realize. There are many "rules of thumb" that ad agencies and advertisers have developed over time, based on experience or research or both. I have found the following types of research to be important to creating strong brand advertising:

• *Qualitative Research.* Focus groups, minigroups, one-on-one research, and anthropological research are useful to better understand the target customer's hopes, needs, desires, aspirations, fears, and concerns.

• *Brand Preference Testing (before and after exposure to the ad).* Asking people what they would tell others about your products and services before and after exposure to the ad is also insightful. (*Ogilvy on Advertising* states that people whose brand preference increases after having seen an ad are three times more likely to purchase the brand than those whose preference does not change.)

• *The Split-Run Technique (a.k.a. A/B Testing).* This technique allows you to test two forms of the ad in the marketplace to determine which one is the most effective.

• *Understanding Customer Response.* Occasionally, you may want to understand how existing loyal customers are responding to your ads, especially if your ad's intent is to attract new customers. For instance, are the ads offering new customers something that you are not offering existing customers? Are the ads promising something that current customers have found not to be true? Are your ads helping existing customers to feel better about your brand? Are they reinforcing the wisdom of having purchased your brand?

When measuring the effectiveness of your ads, increased top-of-mind awareness and purchase intent are the two most important measures. Ad likability, another useful measure, correlates highly with purchase intent.[6] Other measures tend to be specific changes in customer attitude or behaviors based on the specific marketing objective for the ad.

Keep in mind, too, that because advertising's effect is gradual and cumulative (much like the growth of a child), it is difficult to measure the effect of an individual ad on sales or market share. For that reason (and for diagnostic reasons) it is important to measure the effect of advertisements on attitudes. Ad recognition and recall and message takeaways also help diagnose an ad (which is particularly important when an ad is not working).

A word of caution regarding advertising research: It is unwise to delegate this task to your advertising agency. It is best to conduct it yourself or to employ a third party to conduct it. Checks and balances are a good thing. And there is no sense in "hiring the fox to guard the chicken coop."

If you are interested in learning more about advertising research, you should consult the Advertising Research Foundation's website (thearf.org) and consider subscribing to its *Journal of Advertising Research*. Another source is the American Marketing Association's *Journal of Marketing Research* (www.marketingpower.com).

Advertising Rules of Thumb

- Between 8 percent and 12 percent of revenues should be budgeted for advertising and other marketing activities. This amount obviously varies significantly by company and industry. An average company spends approximately 6 percent of sales on advertising alone. Advertising expenditures for computer and office equipment are as low as .09 percent vs. 16.8 percent for toys, dolls, and games.[7] Industrial companies tend to spend less on advertising (one percent to 5 percent typically) than consumer products companies.

- You should spend more on advertising and marketing if the following conditions exist:[8]
  - You are building a new brand.
  - You are launching a new product or service. (Some new businesses and brands spend between 50 percent and 100 percent of revenues the first year of launch.)
  - Your product offering is large and complex.
  - You charge premium prices.

- You sell products and services in a "low involvement" category (typically low-priced items for which there is little risk of failure).
- More than 10 percent of your revenues come from online sales.
- You are selling commodity products (advertising will be the primary differentiator).

• Spend approximately $1 on proactive publicity for every $10 you spend on advertising. (PR budgets are one percent of a company's revenues, on average.[9]) It will multiply the effectiveness of your advertising. (Advertising in trade magazines also gives you a relationship with the publications, alerts you to editorial opportunities, and sometimes impacts your brand's presence in articles.)

• Production costs are usually 10 percent of the media buy.

• You need to know what your brand's "share of voice" is—or the amount of advertising (or consumer communication) dollars your company spends compared to competitors' spending for a given product category. It is a good rough measure, despite its flaws, which include:
- The focus is on traditional advertising spending only.
- Competitors are usually in different portfolios of businesses, so it is difficult to break the spending out for the same categories across all competitors.
- Advertising effectiveness for the same level of spending varies widely.

• It is nearly always more productive to focus on frequency vs. reach. Many people will say that it is more efficient to focus on reach because there are diminishing returns with each new ad exposure. That is, the advertising response curve is usually concave. This is particularly true if your goal is to create an immediate sale of a ubiquitously purchased consumer product. In that situation, reach almost always delivers "more bang for your buck." However, if your funds are limited and your audience is highly targeted, you would do better to focus on a reach schedule of 3+, seeking out media with significant audience overlap.[10] For brand building purposes, I usually focus on advertising frequency targeted at those who are most likely to influence the remainder of the market: primary target opinion leaders and "hard core" users.

• Ads produce better results if they highlight or dramatize the brand's unique compelling benefit.

• The most effective ads combine a subtle emotional appeal with a practical benefit.[11]

• The more an ad can get people to identify with one of its characters, the more powerful its effect will be.

• If the ad is designed so that people hear the message indirectly or through entertainment rather than being told about it directly, they will be less rigorous and defensive in their analysis of the message.[12]

• If a significant portion of your product's sales result from repeat purchases, it may be more important for your advertising to reinforce the purchase than to persuade people to purchase your product for the first time.

• Carrying a particular brand voice and visual style (and mnemonic device) from one ad campaign to another increases the effectiveness of the new ad campaign.

• Scents have the greatest ability to evoke memories. Music has the second greatest ability to do so. Both are mnemonic devices.

WHAT COMES TO MIND WHEN YOU HEAR THE FOLLOWING?

1. You deserve a break today.
2. Be all that you can be.
3. Just do it.
4. It's the real thing.
5. Where's the beef?
6. It takes a tough man to make a tender chicken.
7. We try harder.
8. Oh, what a feeling . . .
9. You've come a long way, baby.
10. Mmm mmm good . . .
11. It's where you want to be.
12. It takes a licking and keeps on ticking.

Answers:

1. McDonald's	7. Avis
2. U.S. Army	8. Toyota
3. Nike	9. Virginia Slims
4. Coca-Cola	10. Campbell's
5. Wendy's	11. VISA
6. Perdue	12. Timex

• Repeatedly featuring a product's packaging in advertising makes its more noticeable at point-of-purchase (and, therefore, more likely to be purchased).[13]

• Fifteen-second commercials are seldom effective, because it is difficult for them to break through the clutter and they are far too short to tell a story. They are best used as reminder commercials (reinforcing messages from previous longer commercials).

• One of the seminal studies on advertising's impact showed that the following factors increase advertising effectiveness:[14]
  - Differentiating brand message
  - Product demonstration (use, result, and benefit)
  - Total time viewed

• The following factors have been shown to decrease advertising effectiveness:[15]
  - Detailed component or ingredient information
  - Multiple propositions

• For manufacturers, advertising can affect sales in two ways: One, it persuades the end consumer to purchase your brand, and two, it persuades the intermediary (retailer) to carry your brand, increasing the brand's accessibility.

• Persuasive ads diminish in their effectiveness over time—a process the industry calls "wearout." This argues for front-loading GRPs (gross ratings points) to maximize the effect.[16]

• There is a strong correlation between how much a company spends on advertising and its share of market.[17]

DID YOU KNOW?

• *There is a direct correlation between advertising spending, brand awareness, and market share (given that the brand's distribution is equal to that of other brands in the category and consumers like the brand's point of difference). In fact, James Gregory and the Corporate Branding Partnership (and others) have linked advertising spending to increases in sales, earnings, market share, and stock price.*

• *A brand's perceived quality increases with increases in advertising impressions, regardless of message.*

• Brand familiarity and popularity increase with increased advertising.[18]

• Advertising influences purchase decisions by affecting the order in which alternatives are evoked (top-of-mind awareness) and the desirability of a particular alternative (positioning). The former is the most important effect. It puts an alternative in people's consideration sets.[19]

• More than 70 percent of the impact of advertising on market share results from increasing brand awareness (vs. creating or building brand image).[20]

• As the number of messages in an advertisement increases, two things happen: Demand increases and recall decreases. The ratio of these effects varies by media and for high- and low-involvement categories.[21]

• Millennials tend to multitask and are more distracted while watching videos, leading to decreased ad recall. Ad duplication and exposure timing across devices could help increase recall.[22]

• It is extraordinarily difficult to try to change the consumer's mind about your brand. You would do best not to try. If you must, link the change in perception to something that consumers currently believe about your brand.

• Often people cannot articulate the brand associations that drive their feelings and decisions because the associations are unconscious or non-declarative.[23]

• Themes and slogans that reinforce the current brand image generate awareness faster than those that support a new positioning.[24]

• In general, the more unique the message, the more successful its communication.[25]

• Highly recalled messages tend to be the result of "well-funded long-standing advertising campaigns."[26]

• The more often a brand repeats a claim, the more likely people are to believe that the claim is true, especially if there is no evidence to the contrary.[27]

• For low involvement categories (in which the alternatives are often virtually identical), advertising can tip the balance in the favor of the advertised brand. For these categories, it is particularly important that the ads break through the clutter and focus on one simple message.[28]

• For high involvement categories, advertising plays less of a role overall. Typically, its role is to put the brand in the consideration set, not to influence the final buying decision.[29]

• People actively seek out information in high involvement categories. Print media, more information, and longer copy work well with this audience.

• It is acceptable, and even preferable, to include a "call to action" in brand advertising. (An impact on short-term sales results will help you justify the expenditure.)

ADVERTISING QUICK ASSESSMENT TOOL

• Does the headline/opening grab people?

• Does the ad clearly and forcefully communicate the intended brand benefit?

• Is the ad distinctive and "ownable"?

• Does the ad feature a strong reason why (proof points)?

• Does the ad communicate something admirable about the company?

• Will this ad resonate with the target audience?

• Does the ad connect with people on an emotional level?

• Does the ad reinforce the brand essence, promise, and personality?

• Does the ad reinforce the brand identity standards?

Media Planning

It is best to leave media planning to media planning professionals. The following are some of the things that they will consider when they develop a media plan for you:

• Reach (percentage of people—or target audience—exposed).

• Frequency (number of times, on average, a person is exposed).

• Impressions (the number of times the target market comes in contact with a media vehicle).

• CPM (cost per thousand exposures), which measures efficiency.

• CPMTM (cost per thousand target market exposures), which measures effective efficiency.

• Most appropriate media vehicles (audience fit with target market, environmental fit with advertising message). For instance:
  - Websites and trade shows provide a high capacity to process information when customer information needs are high, while short TV spots are best used when information processing needs are lower.[30]

- Some media are more appropriate when the purchase decision is based primarily on facts, while others are more appropriate when feelings and emotions are the key influencers.

● Evaluating vehicle effectiveness (clutter, distractions).

● Adjusting potential exposures to actual exposures (e.g., for television, it has been found to vary from 50 percent to 70 percent).

● Developing a media strategy and schedule that maximizes advertising response (against the advertising objective).

With the fast pace at which digital media is evolving, it is advantageous for companies to conduct marketing mix modeling to optimally allocate their marketing investments, especially in a dynamic, real-time way. The following companies are providers of marketing mix modeling services: Analytic Partners, Hudson River Group (HRG), IRI, MarketShare, Marketing Evolution, Marketing Management Analytics (MMA), Nielsen, Ninah, and ThinkVine.

DID YOU KNOW?

● *Research has shown that the media environment affects advertising claims. For instance, quality claims are more effective on elite or prestigious websites because people associate the claim with the media environment.*
(Source: Dean Donaldson, "Location Matters: How Ad Environments Affect Performance," Advertising Age, December 10, 2009, adage.com/article/digitalnext/location-matters-ad-environments-affect-performance/140980/.)

● *Aspirational, upscale, and high-status brands have the potential to alienate customers who lack confidence. While these customers might admire these brands, they don't feel comfortable using them. Building warmth, humor, and less formality into the brands to make them more approachable helps overcome this problem.*
(Source: Max Blackston, "Observations: Building Brand Equity by Managing the Brand's Relationships," Journal of Advertising Research 32, no. 3, May/June 1992, pp. 79–83.)

When we conducted laddering research at Hallmark, we discovered that most product and brand benefits ultimately supported the underlying need to preserve self-esteem. (*Laddering* is a research technique that probes consumers to better understand underlying basic human values the brand addresses. It investigates benefits that underlie product attributes, consequences that result from the benefits, and values that underlie the consequences. The results are often mapped to outline the brand's benefit structure.) Different benefits may have followed different paths to that end, but, ultimately, the need that they fulfilled was the same fundamental one: to preserve self-esteem. We explored certain emotional end benefits—self-affirmations that contribute to different aspects of a person's self-esteem; among them:

- I am frugal.
- I am a good mother.
- I am a good wife.
- I am a good friend.
- I am making a positive difference in the world.

- I am competent.
- I am successful.
- I am unique.
- I am lovable.
- I am in control of my life.

Although the following data is from a study conducted decades ago, it points out that some of the most powerful motives are fundamental ones. Some of the most effective advertising over time has tapped into these motives. I have observed that the most powerful brands and products are those that help people stay healthy physically, mentally, emotionally, and spiritually. In fact, brands and products that can help people with the following (largely spiritual needs) are extraordinarily powerful:

- A sense of purpose
- A sense of self-worth
- Personal empowerment
- A sense of well-being
- Healthy, trusting relationships

- A sense of community
- Peace
- Hope
- Joy

To that list you could also add communication that taps into any of the higher order needs from Maslow's hierarchy of needs: affiliation, esteem, or self-actualization.

Use the checklist in Figure 9–4 to assess the efficacy of your brand management practices in the area covered by this chapter. The more questions to which you can answer "yes," the better you are doing. The checklist also provides a brief summary of the material covered in the chapter.

Figure 9–4. Checklist: Brand advertising.

	YES / NO
Does your ad agency fully understand and embrace your brand design and plans?	___ ___

Do your other external marketing agencies embrace them
as well? ___ ___

Is there centralized management of the client/agency relationship? ___ ___

Do your ads immediately capture people's attention? ___ ___

Does your advertising clearly communicate your brand's promise? Do your ads clearly and forcefully communicate the
intended brand benefit? ___ ___

Are your ads distinctive and "ownable"? ___ ___

Do your ads feature a strong "reasons to believe" (proof points)? ___ ___

Do your ads reinforce your brand's essence, promise, archetype, and personality? ___ ___

Have you kept you ads simple and devoid of meaningless detail? ___ ___

Do your ads connect with people on an emotional level? ___ ___

Are your ads focused on building brand awareness and differentiation? ___ ___

Are your ads clever enough in and of themselves to create
brand buzz? ___ ___

Do you have a way to measure the effectiveness of your ads?
Is your advertising effectiveness measured by a party other
than your ad agency? ___ ___

Have you maximized the frequency of your ads? ___ ___

Have you been consistent in advertising your brand over time?
Have you communicated a consistent brand message over time? ___ ___

Do your brand's successive advertising campaigns share the
same brand identity and mnemonic device (to provide a bridge)? ___ ___

Do you know how your advertising-to-sales ratio compares to
that of your direct competitors? Is it higher? ___ ___

Do you know what your brand's share of voice is? Is it higher
than or equal to its share of market? ___ ___

Does everyone in your organization understand that brand
advertising is an investment leading to increased revenues and
market share over time? ___ ___

Do you realize that maintaining or increasing advertising in a
down market increases brand equity and share of market? ___ ___

10

nontraditional marketing approaches that work

ADVERTISING IS usually the most important element in any brand marketing plan, but many companies are finding that other approaches are also effective. Some have pursued these approaches out of necessity, being unable to support national advertising campaigns, while others are just more innovative than most in developing their marketing repertoires.

Following are some examples of nontraditional marketing techniques:

• *Membership Organizations.* Harley Owners Group (HOG), Hallmark Keepsake Ornament Collectors Club, Pond's Institute.

• *Special Events.* HOG Rallies, BMW Motorcycle Owners International Rally, Jeep Jamboree.

• *Museums and Factory Tours.* World of Coca-Cola Museum in Atlanta and Las Vegas; CNN Factory Tour in Atlanta; Kellogg's Cereal City USA in Battle Creek, Michigan; the American Girl Place in Chicago; the Crayola Factory tour and store in Easton, Pennsylvania; the Hallmark Visitors' Center in Kansas City, Missouri; the Ben & Jerry's factory tour in Waterbury Center, Vermont; Hershey's Chocolate World in Hershey, Pennsylvania; The Vermont Teddy Bear factory tour and store in Shelburne, Vermont; Dewar's World of Whisky in Aberfeldy, Scotland; and MacWorld Expo (85,000 make this pilgrimage!).

• *Theme Parks.* Disney World, Cadbury's Theme Park, Legoland, Busch Garden, Knott's Berry Farm.

• *Flagship Stores.* The Apple Store, Niketown, Warner Brothers Store, and the Disney store at Times Square; ultra-deluxe flagship megastores from fashion designers DKNY, Donna Karan, Gucci, Hermes, Hugo Boss, Hickey Freeman, Louis Vuitton, Prada, and Tommy Hilfiger.[1]

• *Limited Distribution for Product Launches.* Create a sense of scarcity. Focus on those outlets known to be frequented by enthusiasts.

• *Sponsorships.* Rolex and high-end sports events (such as horse shows and races, yacht races, polo); Izod Arena, Allstate Arena, Capital One Bowl.

• *Sponsorship Ambush.* Converse was an official sponsor of the summer Olympics in Los Angeles in 1984. Nike upstaged Converse, however, by creating huge tributes to Nike-sponsored athletes on buildings in downtown L.A. In 2000, Reebok was an official sponsor of the Olympics. Nike upstaged Reebok by contracting with many athletes to wear Nike-branded athletic wear. In both instances, Nike received a much greater "share of mind" than the official sponsors in its category. (Of course, using this technique says something about the brand that uses it. The technique is not compatible with the intended personalities of many brands.)

• *Larger-Than-Life Brand Owners.* At the December 1999 Brand Master Conference, Sixtus Oechsle, the manager of corporate communications and advertising for Shell Oil Company, said that 40 percent of a company's reputation is based on the reputation of its CEO. Examples in more recent years include Richard Branson (of Virgin), Anita Roddick (of The Body Shop), Mark Zuckerberg (of Facebook), Bill Gates (of Microsoft), Ted Turner (of TNT), Jeff Bezos (of Amazon), Steve Jobs (of Apple), and Martha Stewart (of Martha Stewart Omnimedia).

• *Frequency Programs.* Hallmark Gold Crown Card, Starbucks Rewards Card, and any number of frequent traveler reward programs for hotel chains and airlines.

• *Businesses with a Social Conscience.* Ben & Jerry's, The Body Shop, Tom's of Maine, and Newman's Own products.

• *Cleverness That Creates Buzz.* Consider GEICO's Maxwell the pig campaign, Verizon's "Can You Hear Me Now?" and the Dos Equis "Most Interesting Man in the World."

• *Cause-Related Marketing.* McDonald's sponsors the Ronald McDonald House; American Express alleviates world hunger; and Pfizer has donated fluconazole, an AIDS drug, to South Africa.

- *Special Events.* Community-based and grassroots events are especially favored, such as Adidas holding streetball festivals and track-and-field clinics.

- *Proactive Publicity.* This can be one of the most powerful and cost-effective marketing tools. Publicity is free, approximately six times as many people read articles as read ads,[2] and articles are more credible as they are perceived to be third-party endorsements vs. self-promotion. And the average salary of an in-house copywriter is very low compared to the average ad agency fee for creating an ad. Here are some examples of proactive publicity:
    - When Hallmark launched the industry's first personalized, computer-generated cards, they sent cards to talk show hosts.
    - EasyJet invested a large portion of its marketing dollars in a lawsuit against KLM, claiming unfair competitive practices, positioning itself as the underdog on the side of the public.[3]
    - Trivial Pursuit marketers sent games samples to celebrities featured in the game and to radio personalities who had an affinity for trivia.[4]
    - The Peabody Hotel in Memphis has ducks march out of the elevator down a red carpet to its lobby fountain twice a day with great fanfare under the direction of the Peabody Duckmaster. Hundreds of people watch and take pictures, many of which are posted on social media.

HOW TO GET THE NEWS MEDIA TO COVER YOUR STORY

Stories have a better chance of being covered if they:

- *Tie into what people are talking about today*
- *Add to discussions on current "hot" issues or topics*
- *Reference prominent people, places, or things*
- *Have visual impact*
- *Are dramatic*
- *Are unexpected, controversial, or outrageous*
- *Directly impact a publication's readership*
- *Have "human interest"*
- *Educate or entertain a publication's readers*
- *Have a "local" angle*
- *Tie into a holiday or special occasion*
- *Represent a significant milestone or a major honor*

• *Outrageous Marketing Breakthroughs:*
  - A nonprofit organization, whose mission was to encourage woman over age 40 to get mammograms annually, wanted a message that would "break through." I suggested they feature a bare-chested woman with a double mastectomy on outdoor signs along major highways, using shocking copy such as "Over 40? Don't wait until it is too late. Get a mammogram today." Or, "Which pain is worse? Over 40? Get a mammogram today." (Imagine the buzz this billboard campaign would create.)
  - To create buzz about the movie *Frenzy*, Alfred Hitchcock floated a dummy of himself down the Thames River.[5]
  - In the "Will It Blend?" campaign, Blendtec demonstrated the power and durability of its blenders by posting a series of YouTube videos of its blender blending everyday items (an iPhone, marbles, baseball, crowbar, Bic lighters, Super Glue, etc.).
  - Taco Bell quietly conducted nationwide research to find twenty-five men across America named Ronald McDonald, and featured them in television and web ads enjoying items from Taco Bell's breakfast menu.

• *Brand as a Badge.* For this technique to work, the brand must stand for something the consumer wants to say about himself or herself. Examples: the Nike swoosh; Mercedes-Benz; FootJoy: The Mark of a Player; and Tesla Motors.

• *Cobranding.* Kmart and Martha Stewart, Hallmark Confections and Fannie May Celebrated Collection.

• *Ingredient Branding.* Dolby, NutraSweet, Intel, Kevlar, Lycra, Nylon, Gore-Tex, and Culligan.

• *Comarketing with Complementary Products.* Identify organizations with which your target customers are likely to interact at the same time that they might be ready to buy your product or service. Better yet, find a quality branded product that your customers would use in conjunction with your product. Best, find another product that matches these criteria and that provides complementary distribution opportunities. Examples: bundling a free sample of a washing detergent with the purchase of a new washing machine, or accounting firms referring clients to financial service firms and estate planning attorneys, and vice versa.

• *Contests.* Crayola Kids Coloring Contest and new crayon color contest; Mars, Inc.'s "Choose the next M&M color" contest.

• *Being Helpful While Building the Brand.* The Charmin SitOrSquat mobile app helps people find clean public restrooms all over the United States.

• *Brand Magazines and Newsletters.* Crayola Kids, Martha Stewart Living.

• *Network Marketing.* Primerica, Sprint's Framily Plan, Amway, Mary Kay, Avon, Tupperware.

• *Colossal Ads.* The 500-foot-high working Swatch watch draped from the tallest skyscraper in Frankfurt, Germany.[6]

• *Word-of-Mouth, Folklore, Testimonials, and Referrals.* Taco Bell ran a television commercial about dropping a truck from a helicopter in Bethel, Alaska, to bring residents its Doritos Locos tacos.

- In its Global Word-of-Mouth Study, GfK Roper found that consumers worldwide cite people as the most trustworthy source of purchase ideas and information. In fact, it finds that by a very wide margin over advertising, people are the best source of ideas and information for prescription drugs, new meals/dishes, retirement planning, restaurants, saving and investing money, new ways to improve health, places to visit and hotels to stay in. Word-of-mouth tends to be more effective than paid-for marketing communication because it is more persuasive (coming from a third party) and more targeted (only communicated to people who are likely to find the information valuable).

- According to Keller Fay Group research, 93 percent of word-of-mouth occurs offline.[7]

- In his book, *Contagious: Why Things Catch On*, Jonah Berger outlines six things that cause ideas, products, and messages to become contagious: 1) social currency (i.e., people share things to make them look good to others); 2) triggers (it is important to make sure the message is linked to everyday occurrences in the target customer's market; e.g., the Kit Kat + Coffee campaign increased Kit Kat sales by a third in the first twelve months of the campaign); 3) emotion (awe, excitement, amusement, anger, and anxiety—coupled with the message—increase the contagiousness); 4) public availability (making things more observable makes them easier to imitate); 5) practical value (people pass on useful information to others, which tends to be highly targeted and therefore more likely to become viral); and 6) storytelling (make sure the product or brand benefits are integral to the story so that they are not lost with the story's retelling).

- Focus on hard-core users, opinion leaders, and what Emanuel Rosen, in his book *The Anatomy of Buzz*, calls "network hubs": They read, they travel, they attend trade shows and conferences; they serve on committees; they participate in best practices benchmarking studies; they do public speaking and write books, articles, newsletters, and letters to editors; they teach courses, they consult, they advise others.
- Expose people to things that make great "cocktail party talk."
- Give people sneak previews, "inside information," "behind-the-scenes stories," and factory tours. Let them meet the product designers.
- Give new products to the trendsetters (seeding).
- Ask your employees to spread the word to everyone they know. Give them free products as a perk. This technique will attract people who like the product category and brand. It will also familiarize them with your brand's products so that they can make better salespeople.

THE POWER OF WORD-OF-MOUTH

In his book, Eating the Big Fish: How Challenger Brands Can Compete Against Brand Leaders, *2nd edition (New York: John Wiley, 2009), Adam Morgan indicates that people enthusiastically share information for one of four reasons: 1) bragging rights, 2) product enthusiasm, 3) aspirational identification, or 4) news value.*

Stories and anecdotes make a point real to people and embed it in their memories. Brand stories and anecdotes can become legends. As they are told and retold, they can raise the brand to a mythological level. Stories are often told about consumer experiences that far exceed expectations, which could be the result of extraordinary customer service or some other incredible experience with the brand. Going out of your way as an organization to create these experiences will pay huge dividends—word-of-mouth marketing cannot be underestimated. Ideally, you create experiences that reinforce your brand's point of difference.

For instance, a Hallmark card shop owner cared so much for one of her customers that when the customer could not find what she was looking for in the store, the owner drove several miles away to a few other Hallmark stores until she found what the customer was looking for. She hand-delivered it to the customer's house that evening, at no charge, reinforcing Hallmark's essence of "caring shared." Now that is the stuff of legends. Delivering this type of service, even occasionally, generates significant word-of-mouth brand advocacy.

• *Shopping Channel.* Many companies have discovered that the QVC and other home shopping channels is a great way to promote new products.

• *The Neiman Marcus Catalog.* In the catalog, BMW once offered a limited edition of its Z3 Roadster with a "Specially Equipped 007" dash plaque. After BMW sold all 100 cars, there were still approximately 6,000 people on the waiting list![8]

• *Product Placement.* Featuring your brands and products in movies and TV shows.

• *Covert or "Stealth" Marketing.* For example, companies pay a) doormen to stack packages featuring their logos in building lobbies, b) people to sing the praises of a specific brands of alcoholic beverages in bars, c) actors to pose as tourists asking passersby to take their picture with a new camera/cell phone product, and d) models to ride their scooters around town.[9] (When companies are caught doing stealth marketing, it may have a negative effect on brand equity and cause consumers to become even more jaded, especially if the tactic is more deceptive than it is creative.)

• *The Poison Parasite Defense.* Robert Cialdini of Arizona State University discovered that a new way to counter and dilute a competitor's message is by creating ads that offer opposing arguments embedded in visuals that link to the original ads being countered. An example is a successful antismoking campaign that featured mock "Marlboro Man" ads depicting macho cowboys on horses in the same rugged outdoor settings as the original ads; however, in the mock ads, the cowboys are coughing and showing other signs of ill health associated with smoking, thus triggering this new highly negative association with Marlboro.[10]

• *Airline Radio and Television Shows.* Virgin America, JetBlue, Singapore Airlines, Air Canada, and Emirates provide this opportunity on their in-flight entertainment channels.

• *Unusual Advertising Media.* Companies have used everything from sidewalks (ads written in chalk), walls above men's room urinals, and posters on bulletin boards, to the sides of trucks and buses, athlete's clothes, and crop art (images created by plowing fields in certain patterns). A German company is now printing advertising messages on toilet paper. Evian funded the repair of a run-down pool in London in return for featuring its brand's identity in the pool's tile design, which could be seen by people flying into and out of nearby Heathrow Airport. Procter & Gamble placed upscale port-a-potties (air-conditioned, with hardwood floors and aromatherapy candles) at state fairs to reinforce the luxury of its Charmin toilet paper.[11]

• *Scarcity, Exclusivity, and Secrets.* These qualities make people feel like insiders and make things seem more valuable; they may make things more likely to be talked about.[12]

• *The Internet.* Online marketing (and Amazon.com, in particular) is covered in greater detail later in Chapter 11.

Traditional Marketing Techniques "on Steroids"
Here are some traditional techniques taken to an extraordinary level of success:

• *Packaging.* Method's line of ergonomically designed, minimally printed household cleaning products; Mio's "Liquid Water Enhancer" that fits pleasingly into the palm of the hand; Tŷ Nant's use of cobalt-blue bottles to break into the mineral water category, and Voss's use of aesthetically pleasing cylindrical glass bottles to do the same; the use of blue bags for home-delivered papers by the *New York Times.*

• *The Product Itself.* Never underestimate the power of design to differentiate! Think Apple's iPhone, the Smart Car, and MINI Cooper.

• *Vehicles, Uniforms, and Signage.* Coca-Cola, FedEx, and UPS use trucks as billboards. UPS uses its delivery people's distinctive brown uniforms. Lucent displayed large branded signs in front of each of its offices.

• *Point-of-Sale Signs and Merchandising.* Mass displays of Coca-Cola cases at the ends of aisles (in grocery and other mass channel stores) are designed to bring the brand to the top-of-mind. Signs, posters, and coasters featuring a particular brand of alcohol are intended to accomplish the same in bars and taverns.

• *Free Product Trial.* Candy Crush Saga and Words With Friends both offered a free app to attract users to their games, with the option of additional features if the customer purchases a low-cost upgrade. Element K provided e-Learning IDs featuring run-of-site (over 800 courses) for free for three months. This works especially well with low-variable-cost items for which there is some perceived risk of purchase.

Small-Business Marketing Techniques

Many small businesses cannot afford the techniques persued by larger companies. The following techniques are ideal for individuals and smaller businesses.

- Conduct demonstrations, classes, and workshops. A restaurant's chef can teach a cooking class for a continuing education program or for a department store or cooking supply store.

- Speak at conferences and for professional associations. Join your local chapter of the National Speakers Association and register with speakers bureaus. Publicize your speaking engagements.

- Hold contests.

- Write articles for newspapers, periodicals, and professional journals.

- List yourself as an expert (e.g., in *Radio-TV Interview Report*; the *Yearbook of Experts, Authorities, and Spokespersons*; Broadcast Interview Source, Inc.; ProfNet). Connect with journalists (HARO— Help a Reporter Out). Post your press releases on PR distribution sites (PressReleasePoint, PitchEngine, PR Newswire, PRWeb, etc.).

- Host a local radio or television show on your area of expertise, or be a guest on one.

- Network online and offline (in professional associations, conferences, trade shows, benchmarking groups, chambers of commerce and popular social media channels).

- Publish newsletters (online or offline).

- Write a book.

- Hire a publicist.

- Maintain relationships with the press.

- Get involved in civic organizations.

- Donate money to local charities, especially complementary causes.

- Volunteer to judge competitions.

- Wear branded shirts and other clothing.

- Cross-promote with complementary or nearby businesses.

- Give away insignia merchandise (featuring your business's name, logo, tagline, and contact information).

- Write letters to new residents introducing them to your business (perhaps offering them a free or reduced-price trial).

- Script your customer service and tech support people to cross-sell and upsell products and services as appropriate. (Be careful not to over-incent people. They should only cross-sell/upsell in the most helpful way as appropriate.)

Business-to-Business Techniques

Business-to-business organizations are able to draw on a unique set of marketing tactics that are appropriate for business customers but not end consumers.

- Create and actively interact with customer advisory boards. Invite the most influential opinion leaders to participate.

- Create and actively interact with strategic partner boards.

- Create external "expert councils" for all major new products. Invite the most knowledgeable and influential outside experts to participate, and involve them in the product design itself.

- Hold conferences and seminars, inviting current satisfied customers, prospective customers, and internal and external industry experts. Present case studies, discuss the latest innovations, let the experts speak, and allow time for networking.

- For software companies, beta test your software with major influential customers and those that would provide compelling case studies and testimonials.

- Hold product launch parties for important customers.

- Record testimonials from your most supportive customers and subtly interweave them with the background music that plays when people calling your company are put on hold. (Hopefully, incoming callers aren't on hold for long, otherwise this technique could become annoying to some people who are waiting to speak to a customer service or technical support rep regarding a major problem.)

- Develop and disseminate a portfolio of customer case studies to reinforce specific brand benefits to specific target customers.

- Publish and widely disseminate white papers to position your organization and brand as experts in your field.

- Develop a speakers bureau and actively orchestrate speaking engagements at key industry events such as conferences, trade shows, and industry association meetings. At our company, we started a local chapter of Toastmasters and assigned the speakers bureau responsibility to a specific individual.

- Actively seek industry association committee assignments and board positions.

- Constantly keep the following people and organizations aware of your brand and its latest accomplishments:
    - Industry analysts
    - Financial analysts
    - Resellers and other strategic partners
    - Your organization's professional partners (i.e., lawyers, accountants, management consultants, advertising agencies)
    - Trade magazine editors and writers
    - People who write about your industry for the general business press
    - People who write books about your industry
    - Other opinion leaders

B2B MARKETING BUDGET ALLOCATION

Website design, management, and optimization: 13%

Trade shows: 12%

E-mail marketing: 12%

Search engine optimization (SEO): 11%

Paid search/pay per click (PPC): 9%

Direct mail: 8%

Public relations: 7%

Telemarketing: 7%

Social media: 7%

Marketing automation/lead nurturing: 6%

Direct Marketing

Direct marketing is a very specific subdiscipline with its own rules within marketing. It offers several advantages to the marketer:[13]

- It allows you to target specific people.
- It enables you to tailor your message for each person.
- It is action-oriented.
- It is confidential.
- It is economical.
- You can track and measure the response rate and the return on investment.
- You will be able to significantly and continuously improve its effectiveness over time.

The three most important elements of direct mail response are the list, the offer, and the creative. Of the three, the list is by far the most important.

The List

- You will have the most success with your current customer list (typically, it provides two to ten times the response rate of a rented list). Beyond that, always seek out frequently updated lists.
- Use a list broker that you trust.
- Profile your current (or prospective) customer base (by behavioral and demographic characteristics) and compare that with the profiles of the various lists that you are considering.
- Test each of the lists that you are considering (e.g., ask for free names or rent the minimum number of names possible).

The Offer

- Provide an incentive for the recipient to act immediately (i.e., for consumers: free product trials, percent off, premiums, sweepstakes; for B2B: kits, white papers, research reports).

- Maximize the perceived value of the offer.

- Provide an easy way to respond (an 800 number, postage-paid response cards, coupons, or website address).

- Code the response devices to be able to track the effectiveness of the offer.

- Make the offer time-sensitive in some way.

- Specify a response deadline (not too soon, not too far in the future).

- Provide a guarantee if appropriate.

- Avoid offers that are vague, generic, offered by most of your competitors, or that seem too good to be true.

- Test responses to various offers.

Be Creative

- Use the Johnson Box area (top right corner of the letter) to plainly state your offer.

- Start the letter with a powerful, attention-grabbing, benefit-driven statement.

- Talk to the recipient in his or her own language—be conversational.

- Use the word "you" as much as possible.

- Always use the "active voice."

- Write long copy, but use short words, sentences, and paragraphs.

- Maximize subheads to call out important offers, benefits, and points of differentiation.

- Sell benefits, not features.

- Appeal to the "head" and to the "heart."

- Personalize the letter to the extent possible.

- Make your copy sympathetic to the recipient's problems.

- Use words to "paint a picture"; help the recipient to envision a desired or undesired end state.

- Know that the "fear of loss" is more powerful that the "hope of gain."

- Include testimonials and case studies.

- Include a strong and clear call to action.

- Use the problem-solution construct that almost always works; think about the five P's: picture, problem, promise, proof, and push.

- Always use a P.S. (restate your proposition here). After the Johnson Box, this is the most-read portion of the letter.

- Test various versions of the copy.

Other Considerations in Direct Marketing

- Personalize the envelope.

- Design the envelop/packaging to maximize its possibility of being opened.

- Use dimensional packaging—it has a much higher chance of being opened.

- Test envelope solutions.

- Time the mailing for maximum response.

- Carefully time follow-up contacts to substantially increase response rates.

- Always take the opportunity to thank your current customers—again and again.

Customer Relationship Management

Customer relationship management (CRM) is huge. Most companies use it to increase customer loyalty and retention, and it will continue to grow with the accessibility of the Internet and e-mail worldwide. Increasingly, CRM systems are integrating social media sites as a part of the managed customer experience.

Ideation and Creative Problem Solving

The mostly highly admired brands are usually unique, original, fresh, and leading-edge. In fact, many have invented or reinvented entire categories. To be that kind of a brand, an organization must be highly innovative. Element K's former CEO Bruce Barnes likes to talk about the "Virtuous Circle of Investment/Innovation." It is very simple:

- Investing in customer-relevant product/service innovation leads to increased revenues.

• Increased revenues enable continued product/service innovation.

Innovative brands with innovative products, services, and marketing approaches typically make extensive use of creative problem solving and ideation (idea generation) techniques.

Creative problem solving usually requires two distinct phases: divergent thinking (ideation) and convergent thinking (idea analysis and evaluation). The purpose of ideation is to generate as many ideas as possible in as condensed a time frame as possible.

DID YOU KNOW?

• *In general, it is much more important for a brand to focus on gaining the zealous support of its primary customers than it is to try to gain the business of a much broader audience. If the primary customers are "brand fans," others will follow.*

• *Risk taking, innovation, breaking industry rules, products that outperform, and services that exceed customer expectations strongly contribute to brand vitality. "Adequate," "suffice," and "good enough" are not a part of a vital brand's vocabulary.*

• *The products and services that achieve the most "buzz" and that benefit the most from buzz are innovative, leading-edge, and of superior quality—often creating a new standard for customer experience.*

BRAINSTORMING

The most popular ideation technique is brainstorming. It requires the following components to be successful:

• There must be a well-defined problem.

• Two or more people must be together in a room. Ideally, you have a mix of people from different disciplines, including someone who knows nothing about the subject (to offer perspective) and a subject matter expert. Also, participants should be screened for divergent thinkers with diverse experiences, who are willing to actively share their thoughts and ideas.

• Relaxation training, autogenics, psychodrama, sociodrama, and other techniques can help prepare people to ideate effectively. The intent is to break down mental blocks and preconceived notions and to get people to relax and feel confident and safe from criticism. A warm-up exercise also helps to get people to think about things in new ways and encourages "boundary-less" thinking.

- Providing participants with crayons and paper and other activities (e.g., Play-Doh, clay, Tinker Toys) often helps people open up in their thinking.

- The exchange of ideas helps to generate more ideas.

- Session ground rules should be established: no criticism or judgments allowed.

- The facilitator ensures that each person's ideas are drawn out.

- No ideas are filtered out by the session facilitator; rather, all ideas are captured as presented, typically on a flipchart.

- The facilitator keeps the session moving so that people don't have time to make premature judgments.

- The facilitator interjects questions to stimulate additional ideas when ideas are waning. Facilitators should have prepared a set of conceptual blockbusting questions before the session. What if it were bigger? What if it were the opposite of what it is? What if we morphed it? What if it were only one-dimensional? What could we do to solve the problem if we had no money to do so? What could we do if we had unlimited financial resources? What if it were round? What if it were red? What is the high-tech solution? What is the low-tech solution? How would environmentalists solve the problem? How would farmers solve the problem? How would Albert Einstein solve the problem? How would a five-year-old girl solve the problem? How would the Chinese government solve the problem? How would your cat solve the problem? How does nature address this matter? What if you were the problem? What would you do? What if you were the solution? How would you feel?

Other ideation techniques include the following:[14]

- Visualization, guided imagery, fantasizing, and envisioning the future

- Attribute listing and discovering connections between those attributes

- Mind mapping and diagramming relationships

- Questioning the problem and its assumptions, broadening the problem, looking at the problem at a meta level

- Applying ideas from one context to another (metaphorical thinking)

- Creating connections for two previously unconnected items (biso-ciation)

- Free associations ("What is the first word that comes to your mind when I say . . . ?")

- Forced relationships (forcing an association between the problem or solution and random words)

- Conceiving of two unrelated entities occupying the same space (homospatial thinking)

- Stopping to further consider associations that initially make us laugh (laughter results from the unexpected connection between two things)

- Sketching and doodling

- Stream-of-consciousness writing

- Experiencing the problem emotionally, intellectually, spiritually, and physically

- Incubation (walking away from the problem after intensely thinking about it)

- Living a life of diverse experience

Who drives the pace of change in your industry, you or one of your competitors?

Go to www.brandforward.com for a list of online ideation and creative thinking resources.

Use the checklist in Figure 10–1 to assess the efficacy of your brand management practices in the area covered by this chapter. The more questions to which you can answer "yes," the better you are doing. The checklist also provides a brief summary of the material covered in the chapter.

Figure 10–1. *Checklist: Nontraditional marketing approaches that work.*

	YES / NO
Is marketing perceived to be an investment (vs. a cost) at your company?	___ ___
Are there clear objectives and performance targets for each marketing program you initiate?	___ ___

Do you know the payback or return on investment for each of the following marketing strategies: increasing household penetration, increasing capture, increasing conversion, incenting trial, encouraging repeat purchase, increasing share of requirements (or share of wallet or share of dollar, where the concept is to identify the percentage of every unit or dollar sale within a category that goes to the brand in question), increasing price premium, reinforcing purchase (post-purchase), increasing brand loyalty, and increasing brand advocacy?   ___ ___

Have you made a conscious decision regarding how much you should spend on marketing activities in total?   ___ ___

Are you spending more on brand building than you are on trade deals? Do you know the answer to this question (without having to research it first)? If you are not happy with the spending balance, do you have specific, realistic plans to change the balance?   ___ ___

Do you know who your best customers are? Do you know why they are your best customers? Have you designed programs to retain those customers? Are you actively trying to increase share in your high profit, heavy user market segment?   ___ ___

Do you have a database of your best customers?   ___ ___

Have you established a robust customer relationship management (CRM) system?   ___ ___

Do you use an innovative mix of marketing elements tailored to achieve your brand's key objectives, instead of relying primarily on advertising?   ___ ___

Are your consumer and trade marketing efforts integrated across all marketing elements?   ___ ___

Do your marketing plans and programs include the following elements: products, packaging, pricing, sales, advertising, promotion, publicity, distribution, signing, merchandising, point-of-purchase materials, product placement, marketing events, and sponsorships?   ___ ___

Have you carefully designed your promotions to reinforce the brand promise (vs. primarily delivering price incentives)?   ___ ___

Does your packaging reinforce the brand promise and other key brand messages?   ___ ___

Are customer service departments and customer contacts always included in your marketing programs?   ___ ___

Do you know all of the points of contact your brand has with consumers? Are you measuring the quality of contact at all of those points? Are you actively managing what you are communicating at each of those points of contact? ___ ___

Do you have brand training for all people who come in contact with your consumers on behalf of your brands (whether or not they are your employees)? ___ ___

Do you create brand and product scripts for your salespeople, customer and technical service representatives, and other frontline employees? ___ ___

Do you leverage point-of-purchase as a major consumer communication platform? ___ ___

Is your brand available wherever and whenever your consumers want it (vs. being channel-constrained due to internal or trade issues)? ___ ___

Do you use your website to transact business and to communicate key brand values and to create an emotional connection with the consumer? ___ ___

Does your website provide an engaging interactive experience for your consumers? ___ ___

Do you use database marketing? ___ ___

Do you use proactive publicity to build the brand? ___ ___

Do you use event marketing? ___ ___

Do you use cause-related marketing? ___ ___

Do you use word-of-mouth marketing? ___ ___

Have you identified the industry opinion leaders and "network hubs"? Do you communicate with them on a regular basis? ___ ___

Have you created flagship stores to showcase your brand and its promise? ___ ___

Have you created factory tours, a visitor's center, or a company museum to communicate your brand's promises to the public? ___ ___

Have you considered creating consumer membership organizations to increase emotional connection and loyalty to the brand? ___ ___

Have you created other ways (online and offline) for your customers and potential customers to interact with one another on a regular basis? ___ ___

Have you considered establishing your brand as a consumer badge? Do you offer insignia merchandise to increase the brand's badge value? ___ ___

Are there media to which your brand has privileged access, such as magazines, television programming, radio stations, television networks, billboards, theme parks, retail stores, websites, etc.? Are you fully exploiting them? ___ ___

Do you know which of your marketing programs provide the highest return on investment? Do you know which ones provide the lowest? Based on this knowledge, are you constantly adjusting your program mix? ___ ___

Does your organization frequently use creative problem solving and ideation techniques to promote innovation? Does the organization encourage "out-of-the-box" thinking? ___ ___

Do you measure business innovation? Do you have a constant stream of consumer-relevant innovations? ___ ___

Do at least 20 percent of your annual revenues result from new products and services? ___ ___

11

online brand building

TODAY, HAVING an online presence is mandatory for any brand. If people want to find out more about your brand, it is very likely that their first step is to search for it using Google or another search engine. They may search from their laptops or tablet computers, but increasingly they may perform this search from their smartphones.

Key considerations in online brand building:

- When building brands online, content is king. If your brand is not associated with continuous stream of useful or entertaining content, it will be taken far less seriously.

- The online medium invites feedback and engagement. Build this into your brand's online experience.

- Visuals (including videos) are becoming increasingly important to any online brand experience.

- An important benefit of the online medium is that it makes it possible for your brand's messages to go viral. There are specific strategies and tools to help you initiate and accelerate this viral process.

- As with any other brand activity, you must start by defining your target audiences.

● Furthermore, your brand must have a unique value proposition and you must be very clear about your brand's promise.

In this chapter, I will focus on eleven key components of online brand building:

1. The Brand Website

2. The Importance of Content

3. The Power of Blogs

4. Search Engine Optimization (SEO)

5. Online Advertising

6. Using Social Media

7. Web Analytics

8. E-Mail Marketing

9. Online Public Relations

10. Mobile Apps

11. QR Codes

The Brand Website

Following are important considerations for creating a strong brand building website:

● The brand website needs to perfectly reflect your brand's architecture. This is the one place where the architecture will manifest itself completely.

● The URL should be intuitive. Avoid long URLs. They are more likely to result in keystroke errors. Reserve domain names for the brand name itself and for keywords or phrases that best reflect what the brand delivers to its customers. Also reserve domain names for common misspellings of the brand name. Redirect all of these URLs to the main URL.

● The website must not only mirror brand architecture; it also must be designed around the brand's target markets. That is, there should be intuitively simple entry points, navigation, and paths for each target audience.

● Always focus on usability over flash.

● The "About Us" section is one of the most viewed sections on a website and is mandatory. You should adapt your brand's elevator speech for this section. It should include an overview of the category or categories in which your brand operates, what products and services your brand offers, what benefits it delivers to its customers, and how it is unique or superior to its competitors. That is, the "About Us" section should include the brand's promise or unique value proposition.

- It is critical to include "Contact" navigation on each page.

- Including a website search capability and navigation to a site map on each page helps people find their way around your site.

- A website is a good place to tell the brand story. Some websites do this quite well. Patagonia.com does a great job of communicating its history and values, including its love of the outdoors and its social and environmental responsibility ethic. Bowmore.com also does a great job of telling a story about its history. It even features a webcam of its distillery.

- Designing a home page that allows for frequent updating of content will help search engine optimization.

- Integrating social media into the website will make it more engaging and interactive. It will also help you see what people are thinking about the brand.

- If you are selling products or services on the website, creating an affiliate program will greatly increase its reach. Most shopping cart programs support affiliate programs.

- You should always feature your brand's URL in your e-mail signature.

- Finally, you should monitor your website's effectiveness. Websites such as FreeWebsiteScore.com can help you with these metrics.

Amazon.com is perhaps the best example of a website that does most everything right. The site delivers a superior user experience and has addressed each of the five drivers of customer brand insistence—awareness, relevant differentiation, value, accessibility, and emotional connection. Here are just a couple of things that Amazon does right in each of these areas:

- *Awareness.* Amazon established unprecedented buzz when it was first launched, and an affiliate program creates links throughout the World Wide Web.

- *Relevant Differentiation.* Millions of products are available, including Partner Count merchandise, with superior search and browse technology.

- *Value.* Amazon offers low prices and free shipping on orders over a minimum total and helps shoppers find the right product through recommendations based on past purchases, user reviews and ratings, and suggested complementary purchases; it lets customers "look inside" and listen to books.

- *Accessibility.* There is 24/7 access, with one-click ordering and quick-shipping options.

- *Emotional Connection.* Customers can personally connect with Amazon.com through user profiles, reviews, ratings, wish lists, and Listmania lists for recommending favorite products.

Here are examples of two other websites that have brand strengths in different ways—Cellartracker.com (delivers substantial functional value) and Patagonia.com (communicates a strong commitment to a set of values).

Cellartracker.com is an interesting example of a website and brand that adds real value. I first found this website by searching for "free online wine management tool," but it appears near the top of Google's search results for a large number of relevant search terms. It is an amazing site for people who have wine cellars. You can start using it for free and it is easy to populate with your wines. It allows you to indicate storage location (for multiple locations within a house or for those who have multiple houses), place of purchase, price paid, and much more. You can sort by an unlimited number of criteria, including your own wine ratings, professional ratings, and the average ratings of all CellarTracker users. You can find out almost anything about any bottle of wine from any place. The site's database features approximately 49 million different wines. It defines each wine on a number of dimensions—vintage, type, producer, varietal, designation, vineyard, country, region, subregion, and appellation. For each wine, it shows "drink by" windows, professional reviews, the community's tasting notes, related articles, the community's average price paid, and auction prices. It helps you keep track of what you have already drunk and allows you to enter how you disposed of the wine (drank, used for cooking, gifted, dropped or broke, spoiled, etc.). It indicates the total estimated value of the wines in your cellar and of those you have already drunk (a sobering statistic, to be sure). It allows you to keep a wish list and to order wine from that list. You can print a variety of reports, sorting on almost any set of variables from the relational database. I always keep the latest report in my wine cellar. Here is the best part. For a modest voluntary annual payment (the amount of which is scaled to the size of your cellar), you can see quarterly auction prices for your bottles. It is a soft sell, but one to which I was quick to respond. Once a year, CellarTracker e-mails you a gentle reminder that your voluntary payment is due to continue to provide you access to auction prices.

Patagonia is a company that truly lives by a set of values, and its website is masterful at communicating those values. Consider some of the sections on the website: returns, repairs, and recycling; corporate responsibility; becoming a responsible company; "1% for the planet"; environmental grants and support; the responsible economy; or The Footprint Chronicles, where "the goal is to use transparency about our supply chain to help us reduce our adverse social and environmental impacts—and on an industrial scale."[1] Or consider the section on its Common Threads Partnership, which focuses on helping people discover ways to reduce, repair, reuse, recycle, and reimagine. Its visuals and videos communicate Patagonia's love of the wilderness and the activities that can be pursued in the great outdoors. It features surfing, snow-boarding, fly-fishing, and rock climbing, among other sports. And it communicates the meditative and spiritual quality of spending time in the midst of nature and the importance of preserving it. Another section of the site talks about Patagonia's ambassadors as being more than just athletes. "They are field testers for our gear and storytellers for our tribe."[2] I encourage you to take time to poke around Patagonia's website. It will teach you a lot about effectively communicating a strong commitment to a set of values.

The Importance of Content

Content drives everything on the Internet. All content should be informative, educational, or entertaining. Furthermore, all of your content should have a specific marketing purpose. Every blog post I write is designed to attract a specific type of client that has a specific type of branding problem. You should know what purpose each piece of content is intended to achieve. Strong content can establish your organization or brand as a thought leader in its field.

Following are some of the types of content that you can provide online:

- Social media
- Articles
- Blogs
- Case studies
- E-newsletters
- FAQs
- Webinars
- Tutorials
- Videos
- White papers

- E-books
- Podcasts (rich media distributed through RSS)
- Research reports
- Mobile apps

Following are important considerations in using content to build your brand:

- You must create a content plan.

- It is difficult to provide a continuous flow of fresh content for an extended period of time, so identify and cultivate a variety of content sources.

- Images can increase the power of your content. Consider using photographs and infographics.

- Submit your content to marketing directories.

- Consider creating your own Wikipedia entry.

- Newsjacking is tying into breaking news with a new angle on the story. It is a productive source of ongoing content. It needs to be done as a quick response and is a great source of increased exposure and readership. Twitter is a great way to newsjack, as is a timely blog post. When you are newsjacking, just make sure you have the expertise and authority to back your story angle or it could backfire on you.

The Power of Blogs

Our brand consulting business has grown exponentially through the power of blogs. Our persistence in feeding our blog fresh, useful content five days a week for more than eight years has led to outstanding placement in organic search results against every search phrase people would use to find a firm like ours. In fact, 90 percent of our new clients find us through our blog (www.BrandingStrategyInsider.com).

Blogs provide some advantages. Blogging:

- Demonstrates your expertise
- Creates a personal connection to readers
- Drives traffic
- Builds a subscriber base
- Develops communities

- Is a quick and easy way to announce news
- Is a launching pad for online posts that can go viral

Here are some of the characteristics of successful blogs:

- They are targeted at specific audiences.
- They are updated daily or at least a few times a week.
- They integrate the most popular keywords and phrases throughout the posts, including in the titles.
- They add RSS feeds to the content.
- They automatically send posts to Twitter using Twitterfeed.com.
- They submit the blog to online article and social media directories.
- They provide buttons for readers to submit the blog posts to Digg.com and Reddit.com.
- They have Twitter, Facebook, LinkedIn, YouTube, Pinterest, and Google+ social media widgets.
- They feature an e-mail sign-up widget.

In my opinion, blogs are the most important component to an online brand building effort; however, they require persistence and an enormous amount of fresh content over time. One should not start a blog without full commitment to keeping it going over the long haul.

Search Engine Optimization

Other than going directly to bookmarked, frequently visited websites, people almost always use a search engine to find what they need online. According to Lorrie Thomas, natural search is two and a half times more effective than paid search.[3]

Search engines look for keywords and phrases in website copy, page titles, meta title tags, page headlines, content headlines, blog posts, and other content. The Google AdWords Keyword Tool and Ad Preview Tool can help you identify the most powerful words and phrases to use. It helps to repeat these keywords and phrases as many times as possible as seems natural in copy. These words should include your company name, your products and services, your brand, product and service names (including common misspellings), category descriptors, names of key company personnel, and business locations.

Any photos or other images should include alt tags, captions, and file names that include appropriate keywords and phrases.

Link building is also very important in search engine optimization. Google uses links as one measure of your website's popularity. Outbound linking from content establishes expertise. You should also seek inbounding linking and create cross-linking between pages. Linking newer content to older content as appropriate helps the older content with its search engine rankings. Deep linking to internal pages (vs. the home page) is especially helpful.

Businesses should add their listings to free online phone books such as Superpages and Yellow Pages. Your website should also be listed in the Open Directory Project at DMOZ.org. Finally, frequently updating your home page content aids in search engine optimization.

Online Advertising

Online advertising should be a component of the overall brand media plan. That is, online advertising must be integrated/coordinated with offline marketing objectives, strategies, tactics, and campaigns, whether they focus on building brand awareness, changing brand perceptions, creating positive brand associations, encouraging brand trial, increasing brand loyalty, or something else.

Online advertising has evolved quite a bit in the last decade. Google Ads is a good place to start to understand your options. My favorite type of online ad placement is contextual advertising. It shows ads on sites related to the keywords and phrases that you choose. You can also place advertising based on geography, demographics, language, topics, interests, specific websites, and combinations of these. Generally, you can pay per view or per click. Another online advertising vehicle to consider is TrueView in-stream, in-search, and in-display ads on YouTube. Facebook is also a superior venue for targeted advertising. Go here to get started: www.facebook.com/business/products/ads.

Using Social Media

Social media is another way to reach out to brand fans. It helps your brand remain top-of-mind, creates a dialogue with customers, provides useful feedback, and can be the source of brand information and special promotions. At a minimum, you need to be familiar with the following social media sites: Facebook, LinkedIn, Google+, Pinterest, Twitter, Instagram, Tumblr, and YouTube.

According to Millward Brown, a brand's social media fans outspend non-fans four to one. Furthermore, Millward Brown indicates that the following are the top four most valued fan page benefits: 1) latest news about the brand, 2) new product information, 3) contests and giveaways, and 4) sales, discounts, coupons, and special offers.[4]

Social media is a useful source of brand feedback. Listen to people where they are most likely to be talking about your brand and its competitors. Among the popular product/service/brand review sites to monitor:

- Epinions.com
- CNET.com
- ConsumerSearch.com
- AngiesList.com
- ConsumerReports.com
- TripAdvisor.com
- Amazon.com
- UrbanSpoon.com

And the following are just a sampling of current social media monitoring tools:

- Google Alerts
- Socialbakers.com for Facebook
- Followerwonk.com for Twitter
- SproutSocial.com
- HootSuite.com for Twitter
- UnifiedSocial.com

Social media marketing tools include:

- Buddy Media (SalesForceMarketingCloud.com)
- Involver.com and Virtrue (both now a part of Oracle social relationship management)
- Shoutlet.com

MERCKENGAGE: ENGAGING CUSTOMERS ONLINE

This is a fairly comprehensive online resource for health care professionals, their patients, and others. It has tools for eating well, getting fit, and tracking conditions such as asthma, blood pressure, blood sugar, cholesterol, migraine, and weight. In addition to checklists, meal plans, and guides to help patients make healthier choices, there are interactive tools that help people keep track of how many calories they have consumed and burned each day. There is a condition library and information about health insurance and caregiving, and mobile apps for health care providers and patients. Finally, it keeps health care professionals informed on the progress of their patients. MerckEngage is truly a value-added brand building tool for Merck made possible by the Internet.

Web Analytics

To manage something properly, you must measure it. Web analytics help you do just that. Many hosting companies include web analytics as a part of their hosting service. The most popular web analytics source is Google Analytics (www.google.com/analytics/).

At a minimum, you will want to measure the following:

- The most popular pages and content
- Traffic sources (search engines, paid advertising, links)
- Top keywords and phrases that people use to find your site
- Traffic patterns (day of week, time of day, geographic origin)

E-Mail Marketing

Newsletters are a great way to reach out and stay in touch with brand customers and potential customers. Following are the most important considerations in creating effective newsletters:

- Seriously consider using a third-party e-mail service provider for a number of reasons, not the least of which is to avoid the ISP spam designation.
- Provide an easy way for people to opt out in each newsletter, and promptly honor any opt-out request.
- For more information on compliance requirements for newsletters, search for the CAN-SPAM Act of 2003.
- To facilitate subscription, put opt-in forms on every page of your blog or website if possible.
- Offer white papers, e-books, and other incentives for people to opt in to your newsletter.
- The newsletter subject line should compel people to want to read further.
- You would do well to use a spam evaluator to ensure that your newsletters will not be identified as spam.
- Use the newsletter to link to your blog posts. Use short paragraphs to interest people in reading further, followed by links to the online blog content.

Online Public Relations

Journalists go online to find expert sources and to get quotes for the articles that they are writing. The more easily your brand's content can be found online, the more likely it is that a journalist will quote it in an article that they are writing. ProfNet from PRNewswire.com helps journalists find the right experts for their stories. HARO (HelpAReporter.com) solicits sources for specific articles and stories. FlackList.com touts itself as "The Journalist's Little Black Book," but is a proprietary website. MediaKitty.com focuses on uniting tourism and lifestyle marketing journalists, PR professionals, and expert sources.

Post press releases to your brand's website. (It should have a newsroom section that includes a company overview and a file of current and past press releases. The company overview usually includes mission, vision and values, key facts, products and brands, and leadership profiles.) Also, distribute your press releases through several well-known sites: PRWeb.com, PRNewswire.com, PressReleasePoint.com, and PitchEngine.com.

Mobile Apps

By 2016, more than 1.3 billion people are projected to access social media from mobile devices.[5] Location-based marketing is based on geotargeting technology. Geofencing combines location and timing in presenting marketing messages. ScreenScape.com is one source of location-based media and Mobile Marketing Association (MMAGlobal.com) provides detailed information on this topic.

QR Codes

Marketers use QR codes to drive people to specific online content. When a person scans a QR code with a smartphone it takes him to a webpage specified by the QR code. A person typically lands on a page that offers additional information. Sometimes it presents a deal or promotion. One could use QR codes on business cards, coupons, product packaging, retail shelves, print ads, restaurant menus, real estate signs, movie tickets, and other media. QR code generators convert data into QR codes. There are many available online.

WHAT PEOPLE DO ONLINE

According to the Pew Internet and American Life Project, these are the top 20 things people do online:

Activity	% of adult Internet users in the U.S. who do this activity online
Use a search engine to find information	91
Send or read e-mail	88
Look for information on a hobby or interest	84
Search for a map or driving directions	84
Check the weather	81
Look for information online about a service or product you are thinking of buying	78
Get news	78
Go online just for fun or to pass the time	74
Buy a product	71
Watch a video on a video-sharing site like YouTube or Vimeo	71
Visit a local, state, or federal government website	67
Use a social networking site like Facebook, LinkedIn, or Google+	67
Buy or make a reservation for travel	65
Do banking online	61
Look online for news or information about politics	61
Look online for information about a job	56
Look for "how to," "do-it-yourself," or repair information	53
Look for information on Wikipedia	53
Use online classified ads or sites like Craigslist	53
Get news or information about sports	52

Source: Pew Research Center, Internet and American Life Project Tracking surveys (March 2000–December 2012), December 16, 2013, © 2013 Pew Research Center, http://pewinternet.org/Trend-Data-(Adults)/Online-Activites-Total.aspx.

Summary

I wrote the first edition of this book, including this chapter on online brand building, between 1999 and 2001. Since then, blogs (2001), LinkedIn (2003), Facebook (2004), YouTube (2005), Twitter (2006), and Pinterest (2010) were introduced to the market. In 2000, 361 million people used the Internet. In 2010, just under 2 billion people used the Internet.[6] Between 2.5 and 3 billion people—39 percent of the world's population—were estimated to be using the Internet as of the end of 2013.[7] Your brand must have an online presence in today's world. Doing so gives it a global presence and allows it to reach out to customers and potential customers in a myriad of highly targeted ways. Using the Internet to build your brand is cost-effective and typically allows for ROI measurement, something that is much more difficult to do with offline brand building techniques.

The Internet enables customer engagement. It is an ideal place to tell your brand's story. It is a place to monitor customer perceptions of your brand. A fresh stream of highly useful and entertaining content is critical to online brand success, as are blogs, search engine optimization, the use of social media, and creating mobile apps so that people can interact with your brand from their smartphones.

Use the checklist in Figure 11–1 to assess the efficacy of your brand management practices in the area covered by this chapter. The more questions to which you can answer "yes," the better you are doing. The checklist also provides a brief summary of the material covered in the chapter.

Figure 11–1. Checklist. Online brand building.

	YES / NO
Is your domain name (URL) your brand name?	___ ___
Do you own URLs for all variations of your brand name, including common misspellings? Do you redirect people who enter those URLs to your site?	___ ___
Do you own URLs that feature keywords and phrases that are most related to your brand's products and services? Do you redirect people who enter those URLs to your site?	___ ___
Do you contract with someone to protect your brand name and trademark online?	___ ___
Does your website reinforce your brand's essence, promise, archetype, and personality?	___ ___

Does your website accurately reflect your brand architecture? ___ ___

Is your brand's identity consistently presented throughout the site? ___ ___

Does your site weave a story about your brand's history, heritage, character, or attitude? ___ ___

Does your website create an engaging, interactive, interesting, informative, and helpful consumer experience? ___ ___

Do you feature streaming video on your site? ___ ___

Can users get to almost any page on your site in three clicks or less? ___ ___

Is your site's copy concise, factual, and bulletized? ___ ___

Is your site's navigation intuitive and consistent? ___ ___

Does every page on your site have "Home," "About," "Contact," "Search," and "Site Map" buttons? ___ ___

Do you have a site map that is easy to find and use? ___ ___

Do you have a site search engine? ___ ___

Does your site work for a wide variety of technical platforms (e.g. operating systems, browsers, plug-ins, monitor sizes and resolutions, e-mail programs, and especially mobile devices)? ___ ___

Does your site create a sense of community? Does it provide ample opportunities for community members to interact with each other over time? ___ ___

Do you personalize your site to your site visitors' preferences (wallpaper, first page viewed, customized content, etc.)? ___ ___

Do you give consumers reasons to return to your site on a regular basis? ___ ___

Do you offer customer services (e.g., store locator service, checklists, and consultative or diagnostic tools)? ___ ___

Does your site have hypertext links to specific pages on other sites? ___ ___

Does your site have a searchable library of articles by subject matter experts? ___ ___

Does your site include a blog? ___ ___

Do you post fresh content to that blog at least a few times a week? ___ ___

Do you feature simple surveys and reviews on your site? ___ ___

Do you keep personal user lists on your site? ___ ___

Does your site match people with interests (through search and browse techniques)? ___ ___

Does your site feature user opinion postings? ___ ___

Do you sponsor online events on your site? Do you lead forum discussions on your site? ___ ___

Does your site have an extranet section (password-protected area for clients/members with value-added services)? ___ ___

Do you publish a free online newsletter? ___ ___

Do you provide activities to unobtrusively build a database (e.g., games, contests, sweepstakes, surveys, and newsletters)? ___ ___

Do you know which word combinations people most often use in search engines to find websites like yours? Do you know how your site places in search engine rankings for those key phrases? Do you monitor your listings and check your search engine rankings frequently? ___ ___

Have you included keywords and phrases throughout your site as appropriate, from page titles and meta title tags to page headlines, content headlines, and blog posts? ___ ___

Does you site's ranking place it on the first page or two of a search engine's results? If not, are you actively pursuing ways to increase your site's search engine ranking? ___ ___

Have you listed your site in search engine directories? ___ ___

Do you check your competitors' sites to see how they rank using your key words? ___ ___

Do you analyze the pages with the highest search engine rankings using your keywords? ___ ___

Is someone (internal or external) responsible for your site's search engine optimization (SEO)? ___ ___

Is there significant outbound linking from content, cross-linking between pages, and inbound linking to internal pages? ___ ___

Do you advertise online? ___ ___

Do you write bylined articles for other websites? ___ ___

Do you use social media to interact with your brand's customers, potential customers, and fans? ___ ___

Do you monitor social media and product/service/brand review sites to see what people are saying about your brand?

  ___ ___

Has your brand posted YouTube videos? Does it have a YouTube channel?

  ___ ___

Do you maintain good online media relations? Are you (or is someone from your company) listed as a subject matter expert in online expert lists?

  ___ ___

Do you create microsites to feature specific products, services, or events?

  ___ ___

Do you have virtual shelf spaces within stores on other sites?

  ___ ___

If you conduct commerce online, have you implemented an affiliate program to extend your reach?

  ___ ___

Do you include a signature line (brand name/logo, tagline, address, telephone number, URL, etc.) in all of your outgoing e-mail as a standard business practice?

  ___ ___

Do you include your website's URL in *all* external communication (advertising, business cards, letterhead, etc.) as a standard business practice?

  ___ ___

Do you promote your brand's website offline (through advertising, publicity, published articles, word-of-mouth, etc.)?

  ___ ___

Are you a student of the web, constantly noting effective techniques that other sites use?

  ___ ___

Do you visit your competitors' sites often to better understand how they are interacting with their customers?

  ___ ___

Do you carefully track who is on your site, where they came from, what they look at, and how they found your site, including what keywords and phrases they used (through web analytics programs)?

  ___ ___

Do you ask your consumers what they like and what they don't like? Do you change the site experience based on their responses?

  ___ ___

Do you use cookies to capture additional information on site visitors and to provide them with customized content when they return to your site?

  ___ ___

Have you created mobile apps to allow people to access your online content via smartphones?

  ___ ___

Do you use QR codes in media to drive people to your brand's content using their smartphones?

  ___ ___

12

developing a brand
building organization*

ONE OF THE MOST difficult tasks in brand management is transforming the organization from one that does not understand the scope or importance of brand management to one that embraces and actively builds the brand as a critically important source of sustainable competitive advantage. Key to this transformation is the organization's *brand promise.*

The following comment is typical of what I hear from marketing executives at more and more companies these days: "We conducted exhaustive consumer research," they say. "We carefully positioned our brand. We developed and instituted a comprehensive brand identity system and standards. We are running our new advertising campaign. Now what do we do? How do we get the rest of the organization to understand and care about the brand and its promise? How do we get the organization to deliver on the promise? How do we make the brand promise real?"

Brand management guru David Aaker posed the following very important question when he visited Hallmark during my time there:

> Until everyone from your CEO to your receptionist can accurately and consistently articulate your brand's promise, how do you expect your customers to?

* This chapter is an updated version of my article "Developing the Brand Building Organization," *Journal of Brand Management* 7, no. 4 (2001): 281–290 (copyright Henry Stewart Publications).

Certainly, the brand promise drives your marketing communication and your brand identity system and standards. But it must do much more than that. Your products and services, every point of contact your brand makes with consumers, and the total consumer experience your brand creates must reinforce your brand's promise (see Figure 12–1). This has tremendous organizational implications. How can an organization deliver against its promise if its frontline employees don't know (or care about) what its brand stands for?

Figure 12–1. *Reinforcing your brand's promise.*

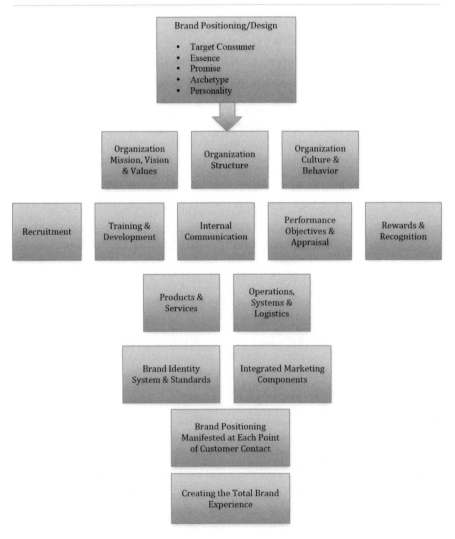

At Hallmark, we did a number of things to incorporate the brand at every level of the organization:

• We worked with our public affairs and communications department to include key brand concepts and messages in all internal and external publications and executive speeches.

• We worked with the training department to build brand strategy modules into all internal training programs, especially new employee orientations.

• We gave Franklin Planner page finders, featuring the brand essence and promise, to all employees.

• We created a brand management and marketing intranet site so that all employees could easily access brand plans, brand research, brand identity standards, and other brand information.

Negative Example: The Toyota Recall

A way to illustrate the importance of developing a brand building organization is through an example of what happens when it is not working. A good example is the Toyota recall crisis, a two-year debacle that resulted in the recall of 7.5 million vehicles and a loss of revenue of $54 million a day. The crisis begain in August 2009, when four people were killed in a Lexus (made by Toyota) because the car accelerated on its own. Over the next several months, Toyota refused to acknowledge a defect in the manufacture of the accelerator, issuing news releases that blamed floor mats. As more cases of out-of-control acceleration came to light and more deaths were reported, Toyota continued to announce minor fixes and was forced into the position of apologizing repeatedly for its lack of a more aggressive response. The crisis could have been averted by an automatic recall when the first few accidents emerged, but Toyota severely damaged its fine reputation and spotless brand identity by refusing to admit to product defects.

United Airlines experienced a similar kind of failure to respond to a customer's injury, made worse by the power of the Internet. The protest song "United Breaks Guitars" (presented as a YouTube video) was written by Canadian musician Dave Carroll after United Airlines broke his guitar in 2008. The song recounts the incident and United's lack of response in resolving it. Within a few days of Carroll posting the YouTube video, United Airlines' stock price decreased by 10 percent, destroying $180 million in company value. As of December 11, 2013, 13,641,538 people have watched the YouTube video.

Critical Support Factors

The Conference Board conducted a study on "Managing the Corporate Brand" that laid the groundwork for brand management during the corporate boom of the late 1990s and early 2000s. In that study, the researchers discovered four organizational support factors were critical to brand strategy success. They are:

1. CEO leadership and support

2. A distinctive corporate culture that serves as a platform for the brand promise

3. The ability to obtain support from a broad spectrum of employees

4. The alignment of brand messages across functions

At the Institute for International Research's Brand Masters Conference in Palm Beach, Florida, Sixtus Oechsle, then manager of corporate communications and advertising for Shell Oil Company, indicated that in a study of sources of brand favorability, Shell Oil found that interaction with company employees had the greatest impact (much greater than brand ads or news) on brand favorability.

Common Organizational Barriers to Brand Building

Here are some of the most common problems that organizations encounter when trying to implement new brand management programs:

- Senior management is not focused on the brand.

- Senior management has a short attention span and fails to provide the support and resources necessary for the branding to occur.

- Some senior leaders do not believe in the brand management concept.

- The organization is highly fragmented and resistant to change.

- The organization is internally focused.

- Difficulties exist in shifting people's focus from their functional "silos" to cross-functional ownership of the brand.

- The organization's culture does not reinforce the brand.

- The organization's operations and systems do not support the brand.

- The brand message is just one of many among a myriad of corporate messages.

Overcoming Obstacles

In my workshops on "Creating a Brand Building Organization," several approaches have been found to be effective in overcoming the obstacles encountered in creating brand building organizations. The main issues and ideas for addressing them are as follows:

• *Issue:* How do you get corporate officers to support brand management initiatives when they don't understand the value of brand management or marketing?

Ideas:

• Use books and speakers to influence the leaders.

• Enlist the help of credible outside brand experts to spend some time with the corporate officer group.

• Provide case studies of how brand management has worked in comparable companies and industries.

• Symbolically "clean house" in the marketing department. Hire some new high-profile marketers with a history of success.

• Invite senior executives to help you solve brand management problems. Appeal to their egos and their propensity to mentor.

• *Issue:* How do you get corporate officers to act as brand champions when they are accountable for other corporate priorities?

Ideas:

• Tie brand performance objectives to their compensation system.

• Give them bonuses based on achievement of brand goals.

• Educate them. Sell them.

• Include "brand passion" as an executive hiring criterion.

• Figure out how the brand helps them.

• Provide them with a quarterly update on progress against key brand objectives.

• *Issue:* Once you have most of the brand pieces in place (e.g., brand promise and positioning, brand identity), how do you translate all of that to a brand building culture?

Ideas:

• "Walk the talk." Challenge others to do so as well.

- Throw it back out to the organization to figure out. You don't have to know all the answers up front.

- Review the brand tenets with various groups. Ask them where your plans are lacking in helping you achieve brand goals.

- Develop a six-month plan, including objectives, obstacles, messages, and vehicles.

- *Issue:* Identify out-of-the-box tactics to ensure continued employee involvement in and support of brand initiatives.

Ideas:

- Hold a poster contest. ("Communicate what the three brand tenets mean to you.")

- Feature twelve of the posters on a twelve-month calendar.

- Hold open houses. (Different areas showcase what they have done to promote brand initiatives.)

- Promote (through internal publications or other means) "the person on the street" who has helped build the brand.

- Name and recognize a "brand champion of the month."

- Create brand "certificates of appreciation." Award them to people who have furthered brand causes.

- *Issue:* If we believe frontline employees are 80 percent of the way there in their understanding of the brand, what else should we ask them to know, say, or do?

Ideas:

- Validate your beliefs with research. Measure your employees' understanding.

- Create an employee "focus group." Run it by the people in the focus group (for ideas on what to do next).

- Ask them how they are going to "live the brand."

- Ask them what actions they are going to take to deliver against the brand promise.

- Instead of focusing on dissemination of information, focus on recognition of the appropriate behavior.

• *Issue:* How do we convince geographically and functionally diverse groups to embrace the brand promise when we have little authority and can only use influencing skills?

Ideas:

- Identify each stakeholder's burning issues and discover ways that your brand initiatives can address them. Relate your brand programs back to their issues.

- Sell your initiatives to top executives in other divisions and departments.

- Set up measures to highlight gaps.

- Identify influencers. Create grassroots support for your initiatives.

Brand Building Requires More Than Advertising and Brand Identity Management

To create the change required to build a brand, all of the following questions must be addressed:

- *Corporate Mission and Vision.* Are they congruent with the brand essence and promise?

- *Business Planning Process.* Is it linked to the brand planning process?

- *Corporate Culture, Values, and Behavior.* Do they support the brand essence, promise, and personality?

- *Recruitment.* Are you screening people for congruence between their beliefs, values, and personality and your brand's essence, promise, and personality?

- *Internal Communication Vehicles.* Are you using them to communicate brand positioning, strategies, and priorities?

- *Training and Development.* Are you using them to increase understanding of brand positioning, strategies, and priorities?

- *Performance Objectives* (especially common objectives). Do they include brand objectives?

- *Performance Appraisal.* Do you provide feedback on how well individuals and groups are delivering against the brand promise?

- *Rewards and Recognition.* Do you reward and recognize people who have furthered important brand goals? Do you compensate people for achievement of brand objectives?

● *Products and Services.* Do they deliver against the brand promise?

● *Operations, Systems, and Logistics.* Do they support delivery of the brand promise?

DID YOU KNOW?

● *The typical No. 1 brand is worth 10 percent more than the No. 2 brand to consumers (range: zero percent to 35 percent).*

● *Home Depot and Ralph Lauren use the same paint formula, but the Home Depot house brand charges $9.94 while Ralph Lauren charges $26.95. (The only differences between the two are packaging, price charged, and the brand name.)*

● *GE receives a 26 percent to 40 percent price premium for its lightbulbs, depending on the SKU.*

(Source: Jim Harmon, "General Electric: Creating a Global Brand Identity," presentation at the Institute for International Research's Brand Masters Conference, December 1997, Atlanta, GA.)

● *In its October 2012 issue,* Consumer Reports *indicates that the store brands they tested cost, on average, 25 percent less than equivelent national brands.*

(Source: Store Brand vs. Name Brand Taste-Off, http://www.consumerreports.org/cro/magazine/2012/10/store-brand-vs-name-brand-taste-off/index.htm, July 7, 2014.)

Brand marketing won't work (at least to its fullest potential) if it is confined to an advertising agency, public affairs department, or even a brand management function. This is especially true when the brand in question is the corporate brand. The CEO is the ultimate brand manager, and everyone throughout the organization must be a brand champion (which implies they all know the brand essence and promise). The corporate culture must support the brand's promise, and indeed, the company should be organized to optimally deliver the brand promise. How can consumers know what your brand stands for if people in your organization don't? Does the person answering your 1-800 number know what the brand stands for? How about the in-store sales associate? The copywriter for your brand catalog? The person developing a brand promotion? The people who design the brand's products?

Hiring employees whose personalities and values match those intended for the brand will ensure that the brand experience is consistently delivered as intended. Hiring employees who are category enthusiasts ensures knowledge, passion, credibility, and the ability to communicate more easily with customers and potential customers. It also helps you tap into customer networks more easily. This is important across functions—from product development, sales, and customer service to marketing research, quality control, and senior management. For example, Oakley looks for employees who have a serious interest in sport. Southwest Airlines hires people for their sense of humor and positive attitude.[1] Virgin Atlantic also hires people based on their congruence with company values.

At the Institute for International Research's Branding Trilogy conference in Santa Barbara, California, Kristine Shattuck, then Los Angeles–area marketing manager for Southwest Airlines, put it well when she said, "Enthusiastic employees spread enthusiasm to customers. Market to your employees as much as your customers. If your employees don't 'get it,' neither will your customers."

You, your executive team, and all your organization's employees should share your passion about your brand each and every day. What story is uniquely your brand's own? Tell that story, and people will pass it on. As you know, "word-of-mouth" marketing is one of the more powerful forms of marketing. The story could spread to a key decision maker or an important influencer.

Also investigate possible organizational misalignments. At Hallmark, a key brand objective was to differentiate the Hallmark brand of greeting cards from the Ambassador brand of greeting cards, but products for both brands were developed in the same business units. Those business units had profit-and-loss responsibility, controlled all the product development resources, and had SKU (stock keeping unit) reduction goals that could not be accomplished except by combining SKUs across brands and removing the brand identity from the affected SKUs. That was a powerful incentive against brand differentiation.

Or consider the Hallmark licensing department. It had a strong incentive to license the Hallmark name out to any organization that was willing to pay the appropriate royalties (whether or not the product category was right for the Hallmark brand). Why? Because it was not managed as a part of a strategic brand development group but rather as a part of an independent division that was driven by revenue- and profit-generation goals. In both of these examples, the organizational design made it more difficult to achieve brand goals.

In both instances, education, persuasion, influencing, and constant communication from the brand group were required to ensure brand goals were not completely compromised. Educating division heads and other executives was a critical component of this approach. If they understand the importance of brand stewardship, it makes the brand manager's job much easier.

Employee morale is a very important element in maintaining a strong brand. It affects everything from quality of frontline service and product defects to word-of-mouth negative comments about the company, some of which will eventually make it into the press (trade and general). It is often true that as you treat your employees, so they will treat your customers. Think about that. *As you treat your employees, so they will treat your customers.*

What are the ramifications of that thought for brand design and organizational design? Only an organization that authentically cares about its employees can demonstrate genuine concern for its customers.

Creating employee goodwill is very much linked to creating customer goodwill. At Element K, we offered our employees special touches, such as paid health club membership fees, Weight Watchers classes, on-site seated massages, company picnics, and holiday parties, as well as ice-cream socials in the warmer months. I have also found that making insignia merchandise available to employees helps them share their pride about the brand and the company. "Learning maps" are increasing used to roll out new or repositioned brands, especially when concurrent cultural changes are required.

A trend in some companies is to include the human resource function as a part (and in support) of the marketing function. Michael Porter's customer value chain concept is based on the thought that every activity a company performs should add to customer value, or it should be eliminated.[2]

If a company has chosen the right promises for its brands, the concept could be adapted to say that all company activities should contribute to the delivery of brand promises or be eliminated—this includes operations, logistics, marketing and sales, human resource management, organization design, technology development, and procurement.

Brands typically are a company's most valuable assets, along with its people. In fact, the value of the brand asset often exceeds a company's annual sales. However, in many companies, people view brand management functions and activities as "overhead," implying they are expendable and do not add value. (In contrast to this view, in the 1950s Peter Drucker stated that "marketing and innovation add value, everything else in the organization adds costs." He assumed marketing was integrated throughout the enterprise.) Accounting systems that categorize brand spending as "nonproduct" or "nondirect" expenses often reinforce the view of brand activities as "overhead." The long-term perspective of brand building also contributes to this view: A brand building (or brand diluting) activity typically does not produce visible results in the current quarter. The results are cumulative and are more visible over time.

If the brand is recognized for what it is—a very important asset that must be built, maintained, and leveraged—then people will begin to view brand activities and spending very differently. This thinking must begin with the CEO and the CFO, but it should be a view shared by all employees. The CFO can become one of the biggest brand supporters if this executive is aware of the financial value of the brand asset, which is why measuring the value of the brand asset is so important.

The New Brand Management Paradigm

The most successful brand building organizations are creating a new brand management paradigm. Increasingly, the brand is becoming the key source of differentiation that guides customer purchase choice. The brand is also the focal point around which an organization defines how it will uniquely deliver value to the customer for a profit. The brand embodies the "heart and soul" of an organization. Its promise is delivered through its products, services, and consumer communication—the total customer relationship and experience. If the brand promise is well conceived and consistently delivered through all business processes and customer contacts, the organization will grow and prosper.

Ultimately, you want to create a company full of brand maniacs, champions, and evangelists. Not until this happens can you be sure that you have developed a brand building organization.

Use the checklist in Figure 12–2 to assess the efficacy of your brand management practices in the area covered by this chapter. The more questions to which you can answer "yes," the better you are doing. The checklist also provides a brief summary of the material covered in the chapter.

Figure 12–2. Checklist: Developing a brand building organization.

	YES / NO
Do the CEO and other corporate officers embrace the brand as a key corporate asset that must be built and leveraged?	___ ___
Is your CEO marketing-oriented?	___ ___
Has your CEO "internalized" your brand's essence? Does your CEO "live" your brand's promise? Does your CEO personally reinforce the brand's intended personality?	___ ___
Does your CEO have a long-term vision for the brand?	___ ___
Have you calculated the value of your brand as a financial asset?	___ ___

Are the CFO and other corporate officers aware of this value? ___ ___

Are there brand evangelists in your organization? Are there brand champions in senior management? Are your employees brand zealots? ___ ___

Have you identified potential allies outside of the brand management function who understand what you are trying to accomplish with the brand? Have you developed a plan to further indoctrinate them and to use them as brand advocates? Have you actively engaged them as brand advocates? ___ ___

Is there a formal process for managing your brands? ___ ___

Is there a person or group responsible for strategic oversight of your brands? Does this oversight include individual subbrands? ___ ___

Is someone held accountable for managing your brand's personality? ___ ___

Do your senior managers own brand strategy (rather than a specific department or an ad agency owning it)? ___ ___

Do you manage your brands as a portfolio vs. allowing (or even encouraging) autonomy in the management of individual brands and subbrands? ___ ___

Are differentiating features reserved for the brands whose promises they best reinforce? Are you confident that there is no pressure to copy one brand's best competitive features for the organization's other brands and subbrands? ___ ___

In recruiting people for jobs in your organization, do you screen people for congruence between their beliefs, values, and personality and your brand's essence, promise, and personality? ___ ___

Do you have a comprehensive internal brand education and communication program? ___ ___

Do you have a published glossary of brand terms to ensure everyone in your organization is using the same nomenclature and the same definitions? ___ ___

Can all employees accurately and consistently articulate your brand's essence and promise? ___ ___

Do you test employees for their knowledge of the brand essence and promise? Do you regularly ask them what they are doing to deliver against the promise? ___ ___

Are your suppliers and other business partners well versed in your brand's essence and promise? ___ ___

Do you have a method in place to indoctrinate new employees on your brand's essence and promise? ___ ___

Do you tell stories to "drive home" your brand's promise and its importance to your company's future (in your internal communication)? ___ ___

Do your brand's essence and promise serve as rallying cries for your employees? Have you used the brand essence to galvanize and focus the activities of your organization's employees? Are your brand's essence and promise stated simply enough so that they are easy to remember? ___ ___

Do you tell your brand's story to as many people as you can each day (in your external communication)? ___ ___

Do you have a brand plan? ___ ___

Do your senior managers and corporate officers understand that designing your corporate brand (e.g., essence, promise, archetype, personality) is inextricably linked with crafting your corporate mission and vision? ___ ___

Is brand planning integrated as a key element of your business planning process? ___ ___

Does the brand promise drive all business decisions within your organization? ___ ___

Is "impact on brand equity" an important criterion in the following decision-making processes: capital investment, budget allocation, business development/acquisition, and cost reduction? ___ ___

Does every decision, action, and communication produced by your organization reinforce your brand's essence, promise, personality, and positioning? If not, can you identify each decision/action/communication that does not reinforce the brand's design and will you do something to correct it? ___ ___

Do your organization's quality standards align with your customer's definition of quality? ___ ___

Is there a process by which all marketing elements are integrated to deliver against the brand promise and key brand priorities? ___ ___

Are there formal processes that enable you to manage the brand across organizational boundaries? ___ ___

Do you constantly benchmark your brand practices against other companies to ensure that you are incorporating best practices into your approach to brand management? ___ ___

Are you personally a student of brand management practices? Do you try to learn from the successes and failures of other brands? ___ ___

Do your organization's common measures include key brand measures? ___ ___

Are your compensation systems and career advancement policies tied to advancing the brand promise and achieving key brand goals? ___ ___

Do you offer special recognition for people who successfully further brand goals? ___ ___

Do you know what functions in your value chain contribute most to your consumer's experience of the brand? Do you have a process to focus organizational resources on those functions (and redirect them from other nonessential functions)? ___ ___

Are you redesigning your business processes and systems, networks of relationships, and customer service functions to better align with and support your brand's promise of differentiated consumer benefits? ___ ___

Does your organization structure support delivery of the brand promise? ___ ___

Does the corporate culture reinforce the brand promise? ___ ___

Is there a spirit of open communication and cooperation between the brand management function and the rest of the organization? ___ ___

Do people in your organization understand that brand building is a long-term exercise with cumulative results? ___ ___

Is your organization as focused on long-term brand building as it is on short-term sales promotion (in contrast to short-term performance goals largely superceding long-term brand building efforts)? ___ ___

Do you have a way of measuring return on marketing investment? ___ ___

Do you know if your brand keeps its promise at each point of contact it makes with consumers? ___ ___

13

integrated brand
marketing

ALTHOUGH BRAND identity management and advertising are two of
the more important and visible components of brand management, I hope
that by the time you have finished reading this book you will agree that brand
management is much more holistic and interdependent than that.

For instance, a typical marketing budget is divided among the following
activities: advertising, promotion, trade shows, lead generation, other sales
support (collateral materials), website, Internet marketing, direct mail, telemarketing, publicity, brand identity management, and market research. Some
companies devote marketing resources to pricing strategy/management,
product marketing, channel marketing, and trade relations. If the company
makes consumer products, add packaging to that. If it has a retail component,
add merchandising and possibly purchasing. Some organizations put sales
under this umbrella as well. Don't forget about communicating with industry
and financial analysts, too. Finally, add internal brand building activities and
brand management legal activities (trademarks, copyrights, etc.), and you
have a very complicated, interdependent set of activities that require skill-
specific subdisciplines and effective integrating mechanisms.

At most companies, not a day goes by that marketers are not trying to
integrate one or more of these activities with others. Consider just one marketing discipline: trade shows. Trade shows support product marketing plans
and help generate sales leads, which go into the marketing database. Trade

shows must also reinforce the brand promise and the most recent brand advertising campaign.

Trade show marketing usually entails a carefully crafted integration of numerous marketing activities, such as:

• Inviting current and potential customers to your trade show booth and events through direct mailings, e-mail blasts, trade magazine ad inserts, and website announcements

• Interacting with the trade press—maintaining relationships, providing company updates, and pitching stories—and also using the shows to maintain relationships with industry analysts and business partners

• Researching product innovations, potential partners, and competitors

• Scheduling sales calls and demo products to potential customers

• Timing new product announcements and press conferences to occur while the show is in session

• Timing any local cause-related marketing activities to occur during the show to gain publicity in local newspapers

• Paying to sponsor the show in return for many items of value to a brand building campaign, such as mailing lists, e-mail lists, a better booth floor position, workshop speaking slots, or having your logos plastered on trade show brochures, convention center banners, cybercafé computers, buses, and a myriad of other things

• Beefing up your advertising and editorial presence in that month's issue of trade magazines

• Placing ads throughout the convention center, such as on hotel room key cards or televisions

Creative marketing may even include buying outdoor advertising along the route between the convention center and the convention center hotels. With all of these activities, however, remember that each trade show must have a simple and coherent set of messages. Also remember that trade shows are just one marketing tactic in a brand building campaign!

Effective Integrating Mechanisms

When integrating your brand marketing efforts, here are some mechanisms you may find useful:

• Create a well-communicated brand positioning statement that includes the target customer and the brand essence, promise, and personality.

• Conduct a workshop on brand positioning with the organization's senior managers, if necessary, to build consensus.

• Place a brand marketing visionary at the top of at least the marketing organization (a marketing VP or chief marketing officer) or better yet (from a marketer's perspective) at the top of the enterprise.

• Provide the chief marketing officer with as broad a span of control as possible (encompassing as many of the aforementioned disciplines as possible) and hold frequent forums to communicate marketing issues and initiatives with other senior leaders of the organization.

• Create a customer brand engagement/experience manager role.

• Set specific brand management and marketing objectives (long term and short term).

• Create a brand marketing plan.

• Integrate brand plans with the organization's strategic plans.

• Establish product, program, and segment marketing plans (driven by, or at least congruent with, brand marketing plans).

• Develop marketing budgets allocated by market segment and subdiscipline (with 10 percent to 20 percent of the overall budget held by the chief marketing officer for unforeseen opportunities).

• Develop integrated media plans.

• Set up an intranet (or extranet) site devoted to brand identity standards and systems (and any other published brand information of use to broad audiences).

• Set up digital brand asset-management systems (to manage organizations with decentralized marketing control).

• Create a brand identity council comprised of brand management personnel, general managers, and creative directors from each of the organization's divisions.

• Hold frequent marketing update meetings for heads of each of the marketing subdisciplines (for people to keep informed about what others are doing).

- Hold quarterly marketing planning sessions.

- Hold brand management forums or summits at least twice a year.

- Situate marketing people as close together as possible.

- Situate marketing people close to salespeople.

- Situate marketing people close to product development people.

- Situate marketing people close to customer service people.

- Provide monthly or quarterly updates on progress against marketing objectives.

- Broadly disseminate brand management and marketing monthly reports.

- Carefully script the sales force on the brand story.

- Send frequent marketing communications to the field sales force.

- Use as few advertising and other marketing agencies as possible. Some organizations will find that a single full-service advertising/marketing agency will help to integrate their marketing effort with a single brand voice and visual style. Others will find that it is best to use multiple agencies with best-in-class services in specific areas, such as brand advertising, collateral materials, direct mail, or public relations. Those that choose to do the latter put a greater burden on internal efforts to integrate brand marketing.

- Designate one internal copywriter and one internal graphic designer as keepers of the brand voice and visual style.

- Designate one brand management person as the ultimate enforcer of the brand identity standards. That person should be widely respected throughout the organization, possess outstanding interpersonal skills, and be very assertive.

- Train every marketer to always ask, "Have I reinforced the brand promise in this decision or activity?"

One other very important consideration is cross-channel integration, especially between online and offline points of brand contact. This type of integration is doubly important for retailers that maintain both online and offline stores. The customer's experience needs to be seamless across these channels, requiring the systems to be totally integrated and designed to accommodate how customers are most likely to gather information and shop across those channels.

The smaller the organization (especially those with fewer than 150 employees), the easier it is to integrate marketing activities across the organization. The larger the organization, the more the integration will need to rely on formal processes and procedures.

Your marketing objectives will dictate the most advantageous mix of marketing and media tactics. For instance, if your primary objective is to build awareness, PR and advertising will be a larger part of your marketing plan. If your primary objective is to generate sales leads, then trade shows, seminars, events, online promotions, and direct marketing will comprise a large part of your marketing plan.

Use the checklist in Figure 13–1 to assess the efficacy of your brand management practices in the area covered by this chapter. The more questions to which you can answer "yes," the better you are doing. The checklist also provides a brief summary of the material covered in the chapter.

Figure 13–1. Checklist: Integrated brand marketing.

	YES / NO
Does your brand always speak with one voice to your customers?	___ ___
Do you routinely integrate multiple marketing disciplines to achieve brand goals?	___ ___
Does everyone in your organization, and do all of your business partners, know your brand's essence, promise, archetype, and personality?	___ ___
When your organization develops brand marketing programs, do you start with the brand marketing objectives and brainstorm the most effective ways to achieve them (vs. immediately applying a particular technique such as advertising or direct mail)?	___ ___
Do marketing people from various disciplines and divisions frequently collaborate and help one another?	___ ___
Are your sales promotions designed to help build the brand (or at least not to diminish it)?	___ ___
Is there a lot of cross-functional teamwork in your organization?	___ ___
Are people in your organization working against common goals?	___ ___
Have you carefully designed the integration of your online and offline brand presence and customer experinece?	___ ___

14

....

creating the total
brand experience

ULTIMATELY, EVERYTHING—products, services, retail environment, corporate culture, frontline employees, marketing, and online presence—must come together to create the total brand experience.

Starbucks

Starbucks does this well. Not only is its product extraordinarily different from and better than a normal cup of coffee, but everything else the company does also adds to the brand experience. The stores feature carefully crafted, aesthetically coordinated components: the smell of fresh-brewed coffee, a wide variety of unusual blends, exotic names (Venti Mocha Frappuccino), fresh pastries, piped-in jazz, comfortable wing chairs, a fireplace (some stores), live music (some stores), functional but stylish lighting, sophisticated sign graphics, stylish merchandising, and so on.

Starbucks store designers must first work behind the counter for a while to better understand the in-store experience. And their employees (called "partners") receive extensive brand and customer service training and stock options to ensure the quality of the customer experience in the store. Each employee receives a document called the Green Apron Book, a booklet that fits into the pocket of a barista's green apron, filled with tips and insights about how "to provide an uplifting experience that enriches people's daily lives."[1] The company's website devotes space to the history and mystique of coffee brewing. Starbucks delivers an affordable indulgent experience. Everything is designed to make you feel sophisticated in a warm and inviting way.[2] (Buy a cup of Starbucks coffee, and you are swept away from the ordinary for a while!)

I wrote the previous paragraphs for the first edition of this book. Since then, Starbucks has experienced a long period of rapid growth through new store openings, geographic expansion, new product development, and selling Starbucks products through new channels (including five airlines) and retail formats (including Express, which caters to the "grab and go" customer). This demontrates the problem of growing successful brands. Starbucks products are now available in environments in which the company can no longer control the brand experience. On an airline, for example, a passenger may get a cup of Starbucks coffee, but its preparation probably does not follow the company's brewing guidelines—and it is served to a passenger in a cramped seat on a crowded plane, one of the least comfortable places anyone can imagine. Does this experience fit with the Starbucks brand? Certainly not. To continue on the growth trajectory, decisions are often made that detract from the intended brand experience.[3] Is Starbucks still about that special "third place" experience, or is it now just another ubiquitous brand with mass appeal?

To answer this question, let's look at an example provided by customer experience expert Marc Gobé in his book *Emotional Branding: The New Paradigm for Connecting Brands to People.* At one point in Starbucks' history, the company's financial managers determined that switching from two-ply to one-ply toilet paper in Starbucks' bathrooms would save the company a significant sum of money annually. Despite the potential cost savings, however, senior management rejected the idea. Why? According to Gobé, "Because Starbucks promises a great coffee experience. And in order to do that, it takes more than a barista and a menu of coffee drinks that will make your head spin. It takes satisfaction at all touch-points."[4]

The question, then, is how Starbucks can continue to create the total customer/brand experience now that it has become the largest coffee shop company in the world. With competing brands like Peet's, Caribou, and Boulder Coffee taking market share away from the coffee behemoth and independent coffee shops appearing in many markets, Starbucks has to work harder than ever to preserve the emotional connection with its customers that made the company the leader it is today.

> **ENGINEERING THE STARBUCKS EXPERIENCE**
>
> • *Starbucks brand is its product, its people, and its in-store experience.*
>
> • *Starbucks' promise: For curious and discerning adults, Starbucks provides the best coffee experience that enriches lives.*
>
> • *Starbucks strives to create an inviting, enriching experience that is stylish and elegant and that provides people with respite, time out, and a personal treat. The experience is designed to enhance sensory signals.*
>
> • *Starbucks romances coffee drinking. It encourages its employees to approach coffee with a wine steward mentality.*
>
> • *Involvement and personal interaction are key to the Starbucks experience. Starbucks strives to be authentic and stand for something through passionate and committed employees. It promotes treating people with respect and dignity.*
>
> *Source: Excerpted from Nancy Barnet's (strategic liaison director, Starbucks Coffee Company) presentation at the Summit on Internal Communications, October 22, 2002, Chicago.*

Saturn

Saturn has not only lost its way; it has gone out of business. Saturn was a company where people carefully thought through the total brand experience. The carmaker extensively reengineered its operations to radically alter the consumer car purchase experience, calling itself a "different kind of (car) company." To make the promise of "salespeople as friends" real, Saturn not only established a "no haggle" pricing policy; it also put in place certain practices to ensure that salespeople would adhere to that policy:[5]

- Restructured compensation packages that emphasized salary over sales commission

- Selling Saturn dealerships in groups by region to eliminate the incentive to use price discounting to pull business away from the Saturn dealership "down the road"

- Extensive salesperson training, with emphasis on commitment to customers' needs and one another's success

- Communicating the approach to external audiences

One of the brand managers who worked for me at Hallmark had previously worked on the Saturn brand. He confided in me that after Saturn had become successful, GM dismantled its separate structure and approach to manage it centrally, as GM did its other divisions. The brand was highly successful but the organization's leadership and the United Automobile Workers ultimately did not allow it to live as a different kind of company and "a different kind of car."

Ten Thousand Waves

Ten Thousand Waves, a spa in Santa Fe, is a case study in creating sensory experience. From its hillside setting, carefully designed layout, architecture, interior design, landscaping, use of water and gardens, fragrant trees, outdoor lanterns, shampoo (scented with real cedar), hand soap (scented with real coconut), in-room fireplaces, hot tubs, and massage sessions, it addresses every human sense in a very sensual and spiritual way.

Ritz-Carlton

Imagine telling your employees that they each had $2,000 to spend on making any customer service issue right—not $2,000 per year, but that much money per incident. For the employees of Ritz-Carlton, this liberty is more than company policy; it's a way of life.

Ritz-Carlton built its reputation by choosing the most desirable locations and investing as much as $1 million per hotel room to create the most comfortable customer experience, but it maintains its position as one of the world's most respected and admired hotel brands through its approach to customer service. The company states its philosophy in a single idea: "Ladies and gentlemen serving ladies and gentlemen." This brand promise instantly creates a sense of well-being and luxury as guests arrive at any Ritz-Carlton hotel—a knowledge that they will be treated not only with respect, but with attention to their needs as honored guests of a well-run establishment.

Every day, every department begins each shift with a fifteen-minute "lineup," in which all employees participate. During the lineup, the manager shares a "wow" story, a tale of one or more of the great things the ladies and gentlemen have done for their guests. This gets every employee on the same page, working toward customer satisfaction by creating an exemplary experience for every guest.

"There are stories about hiring a carpenter to build a shoe tree for a guest; a laundry manager who couldn't get the stain out of a dress after trying twice flying up from Puerto Rico to New York to return the dress personally; or when in Dubai a waiter overhead a gentleman musing with his wife, who was in a wheelchair, that it was a shame he couldn't get her down to the beach. The waiter told maintenance, who passed word, and the next afternoon there was a wooden walkway down the beach to a tent that was set up for them to have dinner in," said Simon Cooper, then CEO of Ritz-Carlton, in an interview with *Forbes* magazine. "That's not out of the ordinary, and the general manager didn't know about it until it was built."[6]

It may seem that the hotel company's growth would be limited by the number of hotels it can build in prime locations around the world, but Ritz-Carlton determined that it was not a hotel brand—it's a lifestyle brand. "Whether you are spending a night, spending a week, buying five weeks of fractional ownership, or buying a lifetime in the Ritz-Carlton with Ritz-Carlton Residence, we feel that we represent lifestyle, that we have moved beyond being just a hotel company," said Cooper.[7] He went on to note that more than 3,000 people have bought into residences at the rate of several million dollars each, making an extraordinary demonstration of their loyalty to a brand that never disappoints them.

Automobile Manufacturers

Automobile manufacturers have gotten much better at creating the total brand experience, from the product to the purchase experience. Automobile designers now consider such factors as ergonomics; textures; the propensity of fabrics and other surfaces to maintain comfortable temperatures throughout the year; the "feel" of knobs, buttons, and other controls; the look of the car itself (consider the Kia Soul, the updated VW Beetle, or the FIAT 500); minimization of road noises; quality of stereo systems and radio reception; road handling; and responsiveness to controls. I test-drove a Tesla Motors Model S. Its advanced tecnology takes the driving experience to a whole new level with features such as remembering each driver's mirror and seat adjustments and providing regenerative braking, steering, and suspension options to make the car feel more like a Mercedes-Benz, Range Rover, or BMW in its road handling, depending on the driver's preference. The process of buying a car has changed significantly as well, in part because of the example set by Saturn and slowly adopted by many other manufacturers.

Musical Groups

Consider another example—musical groups as brands. Have you ever attended a concert that you will never forget? Was the music powerful? Did it speak to you in a way that is difficult to describe? Did the group establish a rapport with the audience that made everything feel completely in sync? Did you find that you could not help but move to the rhythm of the beat? Was the show multisensory? Did they use lights and other special effects? Did their music evoke strong emotions? Did their music make you think about things differently? Did you completely lose track of time? Did you not want the concert to end? What if your brand could accomplish some of these same ends?

JEWISH SENIOR LIFE

Jewish Senior Life offers a full complement of senior services—from a continuing care retirement community, including independent senior living, assisted living, and long-term care, to community-based services that allow people to remain in their own homes.

We were retained by Jewish Senior Life to help them identify a brand position that would help them grow despite a declining Jewish population in their community. After ruling out geographic expansion to adjacent markets, we focused on attracting a greater number of non-Jewish residents. After exploring different angles to attracting non-Jewish residents, we landed on "honoring family" as a value that crossed cultural and religious boundaries. We then ideated a number of additional proof points for this concept, including creating a Jewish Senior Life family cookbook, a directory of residents and their families, hosting family movie nights, and similar ideas. A couple of years later I was contacted by a Jewish Senior Life executive with whom I had worked, who was concerned that the residents had voted to prohibit Christmas trees and red-and-green décor in December. It is not enough to find common values. The brand must also be welcoming to new markets.

Creating the Optimal Brand Experience

How do you create an optimal brand experience? First, ask the following questions:

- Will the experience impact all of the human senses: sight, hearing, smell, taste, and touch?
- How will the experience make people feel?
- Will people want to linger with your brand's products and services?

- Will people want to use the brand often? Will they want to return frequently (for applicable product/service categories)? Will they look forward to using the brand's products and services again?

- Does your brand reinforce something about who your customers are?

- Does your brand have a strong "point of view"? Does it stand for something? Is it clear what it cares about?

- Is your brand exciting, soothing, exhilarating, fun, comforting, relaxing, stimulating, centering, calming, rejuvenating?

- Will your brand conjure up images in your customers' minds? Will it evoke memories?

- Will your brand have the power to take people to "a different place"? Can it put them "in a different state of mind"? Will it have the power to change their mood?

- Will your brand make people feel as though they belong to something important or good or newsworthy?

Use the process, shown in Figure 14–1, as a guide in designing a total brand experience.

Crisis Management

Although all organizations intend to create the best possible customer experiences, occasionally something real or perceived happens that produces just the opposite effect: a crisis. Every brand will experience a crisis at one time or another. The hallmark of a strong brand is how well it handles those crises.

The crisis could come as a result of something the company does (such as the BP oil spill in the Gulf of Mexico—more on this in a moment) or something that is foisted upon it (rumors that McDonald's hamburgers are made of worms). But, when a crisis occurs, it is time to enact a well-rehearsed crisis management plan.

So, think about a crisis management plan now (hopefully, long before any actual crisis), and begin with the following considerations:

- Steadily and consistently build brand goodwill over time.

- Identify and address potential problem areas ahead of any actual crises.

- Have a well-thought-through crisis (or emergency response) plan, including scenarios, step-by-step instructions on how to best address each

Figure 14–1. Designing the total brand experience.

Purchase Cycle Phase	Pre-Purchase		Point of Purchase	Post-Purchase			
Generic Tactics	**Creating Awareness**	**Developing Preference**	**Stimulating the Purchase**	**Reinforcing the Immediately After Purchase**	**Reinforcing the Purchase During Usage**	**Other Post Purchase Reinforcement**	**Nurturing Ongoing Loyalty**
	Advertising	Relevant differentiation supported by strong proof points and "reasons to believe"	Persuasive salesperson	Thank you notes	Superior product performance	Newsletters	Membership clubs
	Publicity	Distinctive/value-added product/service bundling	Persuasive signing	Thank you gifts	Product sensory experience	Customer events	Customer events
	Direct mail	Designing the brand as a badge	Persuasive merchandising	Follow up phone calls soliciting satisfaction feedback	Product itself thanks the customer for using it	Advertising	Ongoing dialogue with customer
	Conferences		Persuasive purchase environment	Coupons for free or reduced price add-ons or upgrades	Account statements used to reinforce brand equity drivers	Publicity	Put customer on your advisory council
	Trade shows		Customer touches/feels/tries product	Coupons for free or reduced price servicing	Superior ongoing customer service and technical support	Product/service awards/rankings	Customer cocreates product enhancements
	Seminars		In-home trials			Product reviews	Customer helps you envision new products
	Articles		Price discounts				Free or reduced price performance upgrades
	Reviews		Value-added products and services				Invite customer to refer your brand to others
	Creating "buzz"		Product customization				
	Heavy user/expert previews		Customer cocreates product				
			Testimonials				
			Guarantees				
			Product layaways				
			Favorable financing/payment terms				

This process is a continuous loop. It is important to generate ideas and develop actions to reinforce the five brand equity drivers—awareness, accessibility, value, relevant differentiation, and emotional connection—in an integrated and cost-efficient fashion throughout the purchase process. The steps include helping the brand to become more emotional, experiential, and self-expressive, and finding ways to stimulate as many senses as possible.

scenario, approved spokespeople, contact information, and key communication documents (e.g., fact sheets, backgrounders, press releases, bios).

● Work with crisis management experts and your legal staff in developing those plans.

  ● Conduct crisis management drills at least once a year.

  ● Conduct a crisis vulnerability audit.

  ● During the crisis itself, follow these general rules:
    - Follow your crisis plan.
    - Identify your spokespeople.
    - Respond quickly.
    - Be honest. Don't deny or cover up things; ultimately, they will be exposed.
    - Accept responsibility as appropriate.
    - Share as much information as is possible and prudent.
    - Let people know what you are doing to manage the situation.
    - Show concern for those affected.
    - Let people know what you are doing to help people who are negatively impacted.
    - Explain what you are doing to cooperate with the authorities.
    - Let people know if neighbors or others are in danger and what they can do about it.
    - Provide the media with telephone and Internet access and the other tools that they need to perform their jobs.
    - Provide frequent updates to keep the communication lines open.
    - Act with integrity, reinforcing the brand's personality.

If not handled well, a crisis can undo years of brand equity building. According to Bob Roemer—who was then responsible for BP-Amoco's public and government affairs worldwide emergency response capabilities—the key to effective crisis management is to offer maximum information with minimum delay. If you don't have a well-rehearsed plan, you should work with your public affairs department and a PR agency to develop one.

When Russian authorities blocked USA Team sponsor Chobani from delivering 5,000 cups of Chobani Greek yogurt to U.S. Olympic athletes and newscasters in Sochi due to Russia's 3-year-old embargo of U.S. dairy products, it became a significant news item in the global press. Chobani received more free publicity when Stephen Colbert mocked the "yogurt blockade" on his television show. As an alternative, Chobani donated the yogurt to food banks in New York and New Jersey, further transforming a minor crisis into a brand building opportunity.

Making and Keeping Brand Promises

Brands make promises and then they must keep those promises. Making the promise is easy. Keeping it is the hard part. One can make a promise with words. But it can only be kept through actions. Consider BP repositioning itself as an environmentally friendly brand with the "Beyond Petroleum" slogan and the bright yellow-and-green sunburst icon. BP supported this rebranding with a $200 million public relations advertising campaign designed by Ogilvy & Mather. It worked well until the massive Gulf of Mexico oil spill in 2010. Then other actions came to light, like the environmentally controversial oil sands project in Alberta, Canada, and a near-identical oil rig blow-out in BP's Caspian Sea platform two years before the Gulf of Mexico blow-out, which BP had been able to successfully cover up. Both disasters were caused by the same cost-saving technique of plugging holes with quick-dry cement, among other factors that favored cost reduction over environmental safety.[8]

A brand's marketing department, often assisted by marketing agencies, can help a brand craft its promise, but who is going to make sure the promise is believable and sustainable with real proof points? Who is going to make sure that the organization can authentically deliver against the promise?

This is why the brand's promise must be crafted at the most senior level of its organization. Delivering on the promise requires alignment with the organization's mission, vision, and business plans. It will affect the allocation of resources including capital expenditures. To deliver on the "Beyond Petroleum" promise, BP needed to invest significantly in alternative energy sources including R&D spending in that area, and it needed to implement tighter environmental standards and controls not only for its own operations, but also for all of its subcontractors. These are not marketing manager decisions. These are CEO decisions.

When we conduct brand positioning workshops for organization brands, we include the organization's CEO (or equivalent) and the CEO's staff, including the CMO. Why? Because this is a strategic exercise that will require total organizational alignment and support. A marketing manager cannot guarantee this alignment. And an external marketing agency certainly cannot guarantee it.

Remember, the most important part of a brand's promise is not the making of the promise, but rather the keeping of the promise. Make sure your brand is able to do that.

Use the checklist in Figure 14–2 to assess the efficacy of your brand management practices in the area covered by this chapter. The more questions to which you can answer "yes," the better you are doing. The checklist also provides a brief summary of the material covered in the chapter.

Figure 14–2. Checklist: Creating the total brand experience.

	YES / NO
Have you designed (and implemented) the "total customer experience" for your brand?	___ ___
Do you draw upon all the human senses in creating your brand's customer experience?	___ ___
Does your brand evoke strong positive emotions?	___ ___
Does your brand make people feel good?	___ ___
Does your brand consistently exceed people's expectations?	___ ___
Does your brand create experiences that are memorable in the most positive sense?	___ ___
Do people want to linger with your brand's products and services?	___ ___
Do people look forward to interacting with your brand again and again?	___ ___
Does your brand steadily and consistently build goodwill over time?	___ ___
If your brand is delivered through third parties, have you put the proper training, control, and feedback mechanisms in place to ensure a consistent and intended brand experience?	___ ___
Do you have a written emergency response plan? Does it include a checklist of key operational and communication steps to be taken? Do you rehearse the plan at least once a year?	___ ___

PART 4
Leveraging the Brand

15

brand extension

A BRAND MAY enter new product categories, new product formats within a category (line extensions), or new markets or market segments. Examples of the latter include taking a brand currently targeted to women and extending it to the male market, or taking a brand that currently appeals to adults and extending it to the teen market.

Another example of extending a brand into new markets is extending it down from its current position to the value segment or up from its current position to the premium segment. Often, to designate a premium version or offering, special words or phrases are used in association with the brand name—words such as gold, platinum, limited edition, signature collection, premier, elite, marquis, reserve, private, professional, or executive class. But, in general, the more subtle the allusion to a brand's premium status, the more effective the approach.

The brand can be extended with or without using another associated brand. If another brand is used, it may be a subbrand or a brand endorsed by the original brand. Another option is cobranding. Hallmark created the "Confections" subbrand to extend into gift candies, but it did so in conjunction with Fannie May Candies Celebrated Collection (premium) subbrand. The product is cobranded with each company's brand and subbrand. Cobranding may be a faster way to enter a new category and gain credibility within it.

Ways to Extend the Brand

Regardless of the branding treatment, extensions can occur in the following ways:

- You manufacture the product (or supply the service) yourself.

- You acquire a company that makes the product (or supplies the service).

- You source the product or service from some other organization but put your name on it.

- You license your name for use by another company that makes the product or supplies the service. Use brand licensing to extend the brand into new categories, expand the meaning of the brand, reinforce key brand associations, build your brand as a badge, or bring your brand to life in new ways. You should avoid licensing your brand where it doesn't make sense just to make a few extra revenue dollars. Where the licensing department resides in your organization structure will have a large impact on how well licensing is used to build (vs. bleed) the brand.

- You form an alliance or joint venture with another company to supply the product or service.

Obviously, the pros and cons of the various methods include speed to market, fit with core competencies, upside revenue and profit potential, asset risk, amount of control over the brand delivery, and the degree to which you are committed to the category in the long term.

> **DID YOU KNOW?**
>
> - *Typically, it costs between $75 million and $100 million to launch a new (mass consumer) brand.*
>   (Source: Brian Wansink, "Making Old Brands New," American Demographics, December 1997, p. 53.)
>
> - *The more extended a brand becomes, the more it needs subbrands to aid with its extensions.*

Benefits of Brand Extension

Launching new products and services under (or linked to) an existing brand, if done properly, significantly decreases perceived customer risk and increases product/service acceptance, all at a fraction of the cost that it would have taken to launch a new brand. In addition to generating incremental revenue and profit for your brand, brand extensions can be beneficial in the following ways:

- Helping to clarify and broaden brand meaning to consumers. (For instance, extending Hallmark into candy and flowers may help redefine the brand, expanding it from "greeting cards" to "ways to show you care.")

- Reinforcing and building on key brand associations.

- Extending the brand's reach and relevance to new consumers.

- Creating brand "news" or "buzz."

- Laying the groundwork for future extensions.

Risks of brand extension include the following:

- Creating confusion regarding brand meaning.

- Tarnishing the quality image.

- Conflicting with or counteracting key brand associations.

- Creating new, undesired brand associations.

- "Turning off" current, key consumer segments.

- Completely diluting brand meaning (if done in great excess with no focus) and overexposing the brand in the marketplace.

Dangers of Extending the Brand into a New Price Segment

One of the biggest dangers is a brand extension that repositions the parent brand in a negative light (like Bayer "aspirin-free" products or Fat-Free Fig Newtons). One of the trickiest extensions is creating a "value" version of the parent brand. Extending your brand up to a premium segment or down to a value segment has the greatest potential for negative impact, as a brand's quality and value perceptions are often central to its positioning. You don't want to create the perception that the original brand was overpriced.

Often the best solution is creating a new brand or subbrand. If the market is moving away from your brand's position, it may be better in the long run, despite the cost, to create a new brand to meet and own the solution to the evolving needs of consumers. This is a more expensive approach with a higher probability of failure *and* is not a brand extension.

Linking Previously Unlinked Brands

If your company has just acquired another company or is considering entering a strategic alliance with another company, research is required to determine how, if at all, the brands should be linked. For instance, do you cobrand, use a parent brand/subbrand, an endorsed brand, have one brand replace the other, or create a new brand?

To decide the best approach to take, it helps to understand the impact of each branding approach on each of the following:

- The essence, promise, archetype, personality, and positioning of each brand involved

- The perceptions of the products and services sold under each brand name

Brand Extensions and Global Branding

If you are in the process of building your brand globally, especially if your brand is in its infancy in some regions or countries, here is something else to watch out for with brand extensions. If a particular extension, especially one less central to the brand's promise, has a strong presence in a marketplace before you have a chance to establish the brand essence, promise, and core meaning in that marketplace, it could be much more difficult to position the brand correctly. It would be better to withhold that extension from the marketplace until the core brand meaning is established there.

Brand Extension Questions

You should answer these questions as you consider each possible brand extension:

- *Business Questions*
  - How "big" is the category or segment?
  - Is the category or segment new?
  - Is it growing?
  - Is there "room" in the category or segment for a new brand?
  - Do you have or can you acquire the assets and competencies necessary to compete successfully in the new category or segment?
  - Have you identified a profitable and robust business model for competing in the new category or segment?

     - What type of competitive reaction might you expect as your brand enters the new category or segment?

- *Brand Questions*
  - What are your brand's primary benefits?
  - Does the brand uniquely own those benefits?
  - Do those benefits matter in the new category?
  - Do they matter enough vis-à-vis other (competitive) brands' benefits to make your brand preferable, at least among some subsegment of the category?
  - What impact would entry into the new category have on your brand's essence, promise, and equity?

Brand Extension Steps

Brand extension work often starts with a brand asset study to identify the most promising avenues for brand extension (see Chapter 17 on Brand Research). This study is often followed by concept development and screening—from a simple "trigger" concept (a brief, several-word concept description, often not even in sentence form) used in focus groups, to "ad form" concepts (more fully developed to look like a full-page print ad, typically with a couple of paragraphs of copy and a visual) tested quantitatively against a normative database. Next steps often include developing business and marketing plans (including pro forma financial statements) for the most promising concepts and then more formal funding reviews and approvals leading to prototyping and eventually market testing.

It is important to pursue brand extensions in a very methodical order so that each extension builds on the previous one. Know where you ultimately want to take the brand, but do it in steps.

Developing Brand Extension Concepts

The concepts must be developed in a standard fashion to allow for comparison. (Do not stack the odds in your favorite concept's favor by reserving score-enhancing adjectives or superlatives only for that concept.) The ideas should be both "close in" and "far out" to determine brand boundaries and associated risks. They can be trigger concepts (i.e., brief concept descriptions) or take a form that resembles a full-page ad. Visuals often help in communicating the idea. Ideally, the concepts are presented in the context of a competitive set to allow for comparison.

CONCEPT SCREENING

You should compare the brand extension concepts to current offerings in the category (and to a normative database of other previously successful concepts) on the following dimensions:

- Purchase intent

- Benefit importance within the category

- Need intensity

- Degree of satisfaction with existing alternatives (category gap)

- Concept uniqueness

- Likes (open-ended question)

- Dislikes (open-ended question)

Many companies offer their own versions of this concept-testing methodology (usually with very large normative databases). At Hallmark, we used methodologies from The Landis Group and Home Testing Institute, but there are many others.

As part of a broader evaluation, there are other important areas to explore when concept screening. They include:

- Concept strengths and weaknesses vis-à-vis competitive concepts

- Benefits/attributes being transferred by the brand to the new category

- Importance/motivational strength of the benefits being transferred

- Impact of the extension on the parent brand

- Ability of the brand extension to draw new consumers to the brand franchise

SUCCESSFUL BRAND EXTENSIONS

Here are some examples of successful brand extensions:

- Jell-O (pudding, pudding snacks)

- Crayola (markers, pens, and paints)

- Dole (pineapple juice, fruit juice, fruit salad, frozen fruit bars)

- Ivory (soap, dishwashing liquid, gentle care detergent)

- Woolite (fabric wash, carpet cleaner spray)

- Arm & Hammer (toothpaste, detergents, household cleaners)

- Febreze (air fresheners, allergen reducers, additive in other detergent brands)

Question: For each brand, what was the transferable core-brand association that made a successful extension possible?

UNSUCCESSFUL BRAND EXTENSIONS: SOME EXAMPLES

- Bic perfume: How do you leverage the "small disposable pocket items" association?
- Levi's tailored classic suits: What is Levi's primary association? (Casual clothes.)
- Campbell spaghetti sauce: Why didn't "tomato sauce" transfer from Campbell's soups to spaghetti sauce?
- McDonald's Arch Deluxe burger (for adults): What is McDonald's primary association? (Fast food for kids.)
- Bayer Aspirin-free: What is Bayer's primary association? (Aspirin.)
- Volvo 850 GLT sports sedan: What is Volvo's primary association? (Safety.) What is a Volvo's primary proof point? (Boxy armored-car styling.)
- Colgate kitchen entrees: What were they thinking?
- Or, my all-time favorite, New Coke: What is Coke? ("It's the real thing"—with a long time secret formula.)

AMERICAN EXPRESS GOLD AND PLATINUM CARDS

While American Express was able to better appeal to premium status segments by creating its gold and platinum cards (basically subbrands), this strategy also transferred some premium status away from American Express itself to the "gold" and "platinum" designations. Visa and MasterCard could not use the American Express brand to connote their own premium status offerings, but with the creation of gold and platinum cards, they could use those two designations as their own subbrands to compete more directly with American Express. Gold and platinum status designations are now common across many industries. So while American Express's creation of gold and platinum cards may have created new higher-status categories for the brand, it also made it easier for its competitors to do the same.

WILL THESE BRAND EXTENSIONS BE SUCCESSFUL?

- Burger King (flame-broiled, "ketchup & fries" flavored) chips

- Cosmopolitan yogurt

- Hot Tamales gum

- Starbucks (cream- and coffee-flavored) liquors

- Diesel wines (limited edition wines from Diesel clothing founder Renzo Rosso's private estate)

- Life Savers soda (in all of the Life Savers flavors and colors)

- Hooters MasterCard

- HUMMER cologne

The Most Common Problems with Brand Extensions

Some of the most common problems associated with brand extension are:

- Extending into a category in which the brand adds nothing but its identity (i.e., its products or services are not significantly different from current products or services in the category)

- Extending through opportunistic brand licensing without regard to its possible impact on the brand

- Extending into lower- (and, sometimes higher-) quality segments

- Not fully understanding brand benefit ownership, transfer, or importance

Evaluating Brand Extension Concepts

Figure15–1 is a rudimentary matrix that I use to focus clients on the most important questions when evaluating opportunities for brand extension. Use each column (category A, B, C, etc.) to evaluate extension of the brand into a different product or service category using the evaluation criteria listed in the first column. The number listed for each criterion is the maximum score for that criterion. The scores for all criteria are additive for each product or service category at the bottom of each column (category A, B, C, etc.) with a maximum possible score of 145. The number of benefits included in the matrix varies by client. For instance, if there are no secondary brand benefits, one can ignore the criteria associated with those benefits, reducing the maximum possible score to 130. Clients can also choose to vary the maximum possible scores for each criterion, altering their relative weightings.

Figure 15–1. *Brand extension evaluation matrix.*

Potential Category for Extension	A	B	C	D	E	F	G
Category size (20)							
Category growth rate (10)							
Category profit potential (20)							
Primary brand benefit meaningful and important in category? (15)							
Uniquely own primary brand benefit in category? (10)							
Secondary brand benefit meaningful and important in category? (10)							
Uniquely own secondary brand benefit in category? (5)							
Other brand associations meaningful and important in category? (10)							
Uniquely own other brand associations in category? (5)							
Extension reinforce brand essence and promise? (20)							
Extension provide flexibility for future growth? (20)							
TOTAL (145)							

Generic New Business Strategies

Whether trying to grow your business through brand extension or by launching new brands, the following are generic approaches to creating new businesses:

- Identifying gaps in your product/service portfolio (for the category as currently defined)
- Identifying current consumers' unsatisfied needs
- Addressing emerging consumer needs

- Expanding the definition of your brand's category

- Exploiting an expanded brand identity

- Exploiting channel opportunities (new distribution)

- Applying new technologies

- Targeting new consumer groups

When developing your growth strategies, you should clarify whether the growth will come primarily from existing customers, competitors' customers, or nonusers. The tactics will vary greatly for each.

Now use the checklist in Figure 15–2 to assess the efficacy of your brand management practices in the area covered by this chapter. The more questions to which you can answer "yes," the better you are doing. The checklist also provides a brief summary of the material covered in the chapter.

Figure 15–2. Checklist: Brand extension.

	YES / NO
Have you identified what your brand owns in the consumer's mind?	___ ___
Have you identified all areas in which the consumer gives your brand permission to operate?	___ ___
Do you have a clear understanding of whether your brand is over- or underextended?	___ ___
Have you identified all the ways your brand and others in its category have made compromises with the consumer? Have you found ways to redefine your business to break those compromises?	___ ___
Have you identified new categories for growth? Can you create new categories that meet previously unmet consumer needs?	___ ___
Have you targeted new market segments to which you would like your brand to appeal?	___ ___
Have you explored ways to make your brand more relevant to the next generation of consumers?	___ ___
Do you know what must be done to ensure the parent brand maintains a relationship with the consumer throughout his or her life (i.e., cradle-to-grave marketing)?	___ ___

Do you have a plan that specifies what categories your brand will enter next, in what order it will enter them, and on what time frame? ___ ___

Have you considered taking your brand global as an alternative growth strategy to brand extension? ___ ___

Do you have a way to screen all new brand extension proposals for their congruence with the brand promise and impact on brand equity? ___ ___

Are you sure that the brand's positive associations will not become negative when associated with a new product category? ___ ___

Have you thoroughly researched how proposed brand extensions might reposition the original brand in consumers' minds? ___ ___

Have you considered acquisition as a way to extend the brand? ___ ___

Do you have a brand licensing department? Does that department have strict guidelines for licensing your brands out to others, in order to ensure brand image is not hurt and brand meaning is not diluted? ___ ___

Have you developed decision criteria to determine whether an extension a) uses an existing brand or b) requires a new brand? And, if you require a new brand, have you decided whether the new brand is c) a subbrand or d) an endorsed brand? ___ ___

Do you have organizational mechanisms to screen, test, and launch brand extensions? ___ ___

Do you test each new product or service for its impact on your brand's equity (i.e., quality, value, reinforcement of brand essence, promise, archetype, and personality)? ___ ___

16

global branding

WHILE MANY consumer-goods markets in the West are stagnating, 65 percent of the world's population lives in societies that are experiencing economic growth of 5 percent or more a year. While the baby boom occurred between 1945 and 1960 in the United States, much of the rest of the world is still experiencing a baby boom that began in 1975. The average person in the rest of the world has seen his or her standard of living double in the past fifteen years, far surpassing that of the United States or Western Europe. Put very simply, today most of the growth potential in consumer markets exists outside the United States and Western Europe.

Benefits of Global Branding

Outstanding growth opportunities are one of the benefits that drive the increasing interest in taking brands global. Other benefits are:

- Economies of scale (production and distribution)
- Lower marketing costs
- Laying the groundwork for future extensions worldwide
- Maintaining consistent brand imagery
- Quicker identification and integration of innovations (discovered worldwide)

- Preempting international competitors from entering domestic markets or locking you out of other geographic markets

- Increasing international media reach (especially with the explosion of the Internet)

- Increasing international business and tourism

When to Leverage a Single Brand Globally

A company is more likely to leverage a single brand globally if:

- It is already operating worldwide (one brand is more efficient).

- The brand is an extension of the owner and this individual's personality.

- The brand's relationship to its country of origin creates positive associations (like a watch brand from Switzerland or a gourmet food brand from France).

GLOBAL BRAND CONSTANTS

At a minimum, when going global, the following elements should remain constant throughout the world:

- Corporate brand

- Brand identity system (especially your logo)

- Brand essence

GLOBAL BRAND VARIABLES

The following elements *may* differ from country to country:

- Corporate slogan

- Products and services

- Product names

- Product features

- Positionings

- Marketing mixes (including pricing, distribution, and media and advertising execution)

These differences will depend on:

- Language differences

- Different styles of communication

- Other cultural differences

- Differences in category and brand development

- Different consumption patterns

- Different competitive sets and marketplace conditions

- Different legal and regulatory environments

- Different national approaches to marketing (e.g., media, pricing, distribution)

LANGUAGE TRANSLATION

A key question in global branding is: Do you translate the brand name into the local language or keep it in the original language? You should probably keep it in the original language if a) there is no intrinsic meaning and it is easy to pronounce or b) global awareness of the brand name is already high. You should consider translating the name into the local language if it is suggestive of a key benefit (that would be lost if the original name were used).

Global Branding Questions

Other key questions when considering global branding are:

- Have you identified the relative attractiveness of each market for your brand (and have you identified consistent criteria for doing so)?

- Have you conducted an attitude and usage study in each country whose market you are considering entering?

- Do you know the category and brand development indices in each country in which you operate?

- Do you have a global branding scorecard that can be applied country by country?

- Do you have agreement on which decisions are made centrally and which ones are made locally?

Here are some other considerations when taking a brand global:

- Because of the extended global baby boom, youth marketing is a huge opportunity. Brand names, designer labels, and other forms of status will play well to the global youth market, in general.

• Global advertising needs to consider the fact that, for much of the world, the economy is booming and the context is unprecedented optimism. Increasing international tensions caused by terrorism and the volatile situations in Iraq and North Korea notwithstanding, the economies of many nations continue this growth.

• The world's consumers are not naïve. Much of the world has access to English-language television programs.

• You should start marketing in countries before their spending power is fully realized. Due to media exposure, people are forming their brand opinions now.

• Representing male/female relationships appropriately will vary from society to society, so be sure that you fully understand the local cultures before attempting to do so.

• Using distributors is frequently a good way to break into foreign markets. It is critically important to choose the right distributor when trying to enter a new market.

Ultimately, there is much to be gained by extending your brand globally. The saying "think globally, act locally" makes much sense in this context. The key is determining what elements you will tailor for local markets. That depends on a thorough understanding of the similarities and differences among the local markets you intend to serve.

Place of Origin

Place of origin often has an impact on the viability of brands that are known to originate from a specific place. That is because the place of origin itself has its own associations and those associations may either enhance or detract from the brand associations.

For instance, any of the following might be associated with these places:

Countries

- Australia: kangaroos, Sydney Opera House, Great Barrier Reef, the Outback, aborigines
- Brazil: Carnival, Rio de Janeiro, beaches, samba music
- Canada: hockey, maple leaf, cold
- China: manufacturing, new cities, economic development, Chinese food and culture

- England: London, Big Ben, royalty, gray skies, fog
- France: Paris, Eiffel Tower, Riviera, wine, food, culture, fashion
- Germany: automobiles, Berlin, castles, Oktoberfest, Hitler
- India: contrasts, exotic (Hindu) religion, bright colors
- Mexico: spicy food, sombreros, siestas, beaches, gang violence
- Spain: Bullfighting, sunny weather, tapas, economic issues
- Switzerland: banks, watches, the Alps, orderliness
- United States of America: New York City, world power, military might, Hollywood, current U.S. president, cowboys

States

- California: diversity, Hollywood, San Francisco, L.A., surfing, Route 1, Napa Valley, liberal, "marches to its own drummer"
- Florida: retirement, alligators, swamps, Orlando, Miami, beaches, fishing
- Maine: lobster, L.L.Bean, rocky coastline, sailing, seaports
- Texas: oil, Dallas, Houston, "everything is bigger," George W. Bush, conservative

Cities

- Bangalore: IT jobs, outsourcing, business hub
- Branson: family entertainment, country music, conservative, tacky
- Dubai: skyscrapers, desert, wealth, Arabs, economic growth, oil money
- Las Vegas: gambling, prostitution, bright lights, shows, adult fun, fantasy
- New York: Wall Street, Broadway, shopping, high energy, nightlife
- Orlando: Disney, theme parks, family vacations
- Paris: The Louvre, Eiffel Tower, cafés, great food, romance
- Singapore: Modern, clean, strict laws, thriving city state
- Vienna: Vienna State Opera, waltzes, Mozart, coffeehouses

Consider which of the preceding places are the most likely to enhance brands in these categories and which are the most likely to make them less credible:

- A new spiritual practice
- Automobiles
- Classical music
- Coffee
- Consumer electronics
- Fashion
- Gourmet food
- Rock groups
- Watches
- Wine
- Yachts

Here is another way to think about places of origin. What comes to your mind when one says Made in China? How about Made in Japan, Made in Mexico, Made in Taiwan, Made in the USA, or Exported from France, Exported from Germany, Exported from New Zealand, or Exported from Patagonia?

DID YOU KNOW?

- *"Purchase intent" tends to be inflated for declining brands and understated for emerging brands.*

- *Advertising is often most effective in increasing share of market when brands are so similar that the advertising message is the primary source of differentiation.*

  (Source: Nigel Hollis, "It Is Not a Choice: Brands Should Seek Differentiation and Distinctiveness," Millward Brown, 2011, www.millwardbrown.com/Libraries/MB_POV_Downloads/MillwardBrown_POV_Brand_Differentiation.sflb.ashx.)

LEVERAGING THE BRAND CASE STUDY:
Hallmark

In the early to mid-1990s, an ever-increasing share of greeting card sales occurred in the mass channels. Wal-Mart alone was projected to achieve a 20 percent share of the total greeting card market by the year 2000. Three brands accounted for the vast majority of sales in these channels: American Greetings, Gibson, and Ambassador—Hallmark's flanker brand. (The sale of Hallmark-branded greeting cards accounted for no more than 20 percent of the overall market. Hallmark-branded products were sold primarily in Hallmark card shops and select chain drugstores. Hallmark's corporate share of greeting card sales was 39 percent, counting all brands, including Ambassador and Shoebox and others).

While Ambassador-brand sales were becoming an ever-increasing proportion of Hallmark's overall corporate sales, Ambassador's margins were eroding because of increased retailer leverage over manufacturers and because of heightened mass channel competition. This trend of a less and less profitable brand becoming a larger and larger share of corporate sales was not acceptable. We knew that more sophisticated contract negotiations and sales term innovations would not be enough to halt or reverse this negative trend. We had to do no less than change the rules of the game itself.

After some thought, we knew our only hope was to unleash the power of the Hallmark brand in the mass channel. But that was tricky and unpopular, because we did not want to undermine the success of the Hallmark card shops and chain drugstores—channels that were our "cash cows" and to which we felt a strong loyalty. We conducted the most extensive research in Hallmark's history to assess the impact of pursuing this strategy on Hallmark card shop and chain drugstore sales—which turned out to be minimal. Nevertheless, prior to the launch of this strategy, we fortified the viability of these two channels through extensive store consolidation, marketing, merchandising, and systems and standards improvements, most notably through the development of the Hallmark Gold Crown program. And we expended great effort to quantify and communicate the equity and power of the Hallmark name to the mass channel retailers. In fact, one mass channel retailer believed in the power of the Hallmark brand so much that it refused to switch to one of our competitor's brands in return for $100 million in sales term.

(Greeting card manufacturers negotiate multiple-year contracts with mass channel retailers in which they receive most or all of a retailer's business for a specified minimum floor space and number of stores for a specified period of time. In return for that privilege, they pay substantial sales terms.)

Here is some salient information to help you understand the strategy: Hallmark's primary competitors had significantly reduced their costs by reducing their internal marketing research and creative development capabilities. They leveraged Hallmark's resources in this area (Hallmark employed over 700 artists and writers and 70 marketing researchers at the time) through well-constructed systems of emulation. All mass channel (non-Hallmark) brands had raised prices faster than inflation for a number of years, as a result of the apparent lack of price sensitivity for greeting cards (until the major price thresholds of $2 and $3 were surpassed) and the pressures applied by retailers for year-over-year sales productivity gains. In fact, more than 65 percent of Hallmark-branded cards were priced *under* $2, whereas 89 percent of competitive mass channel brand's cards were priced *over* $2. Competitors used their lower cost structures and higher product prices to fund ever-accelerating sales terms. They placed their bets that rich sales terms would buy distribution with major mass retail chains, which was in fact what was occurring.

Despite the fact that mass channel share was increasingly based on which brand could write the biggest check, Hallmark was betting on the fact that it could change the rules by introducing the power of brand equity to the mass channel. After all, Hallmark is the only greeting card brand widely recognized by consumers. (It had unaided top-of-mind awareness of nearly 90 percent; and Shoebox—a tiny little division of Hallmark—was the only other greeting card brand with significant top-of-mind awareness or preference.) Hallmark's product also was superior (validated by rigorous market research), and Hallmark products were priced lower than any other major competitive brand.

To rally the internal troops around this strategy, I was fond of saying about Hallmark's primary competitors: "Would you rather be our competitors with overpriced, no name, inferior products?" If Hallmark could align consumer price perceptions with reality (Hallmark was perceived to be "expensive" by consumers), I knew we could win with this strategy. Our competitors (both public companies, one of which consistently touted quarter over quarter revenue and profit increases) were locked into multiple-year retailer contracts with very high sales terms. They would not be able to reduce prices without severely affecting their revenues, profits, and stock prices.

I could devote at least a whole chapter to the nuances of this strategy, but suffice it to say that Hallmark's static 39 percent greeting card market share increased to 42 percent with increased profitability in the first two years after we implemented this strategy. Since then, Hallmark's share has steadily grown to 55 percent in a few short years. Unleashing the power of the Hallmark brand in the mass channel resulted in substantial market share and profitability gains for Hallmark without taking away from the success of the card shop and chain drugstore channels. (Hallmark card shops achieved consistent month-over-month sales increases for at least three years during this period, validating my held belief that the added marketplace exposure to the Hallmark brand would have a positive impact on all channels carrying Hallmark products.)

Use the checklist in Figure 16–1 to assess the efficacy of your brand management practices in the area covered by this chapter. The more questions to which you can answer "yes," the better you are doing. The checklist also provides a brief summary of the material covered in the chapter.

Figure 16–1. Checklist: Global branding.

	YES / NO
Does your company operate as a global enterprise vs. a domestic company that sells its products internationally or that has separate international operations?	___ ___
Do you sell your brand in international markets?	___ ___
Do you believe global expansion of your brand will be a significant source of revenue growth for your organization for the next few years?	___ ___
If you have grown internationally through acquisition, have you either replaced the local brands you purchased with your global brand (if the local brands did not have strong brand awareness or loyalty), or else linked your corporate or parent brand name to the local brand name (if the local brands did have high awareness and loyalty)?	___ ___
Is your brand's market share as large or larger, on average, in international markets than it is in your domestic market?	___ ___
Is your brand's awareness as high, on average, in international markets as it is in your domestic market?	___ ___
Does your brand's essence remain the same throughout the world?	___ ___
Have you investigated the meaning of your brand's name (and other nomenclature), symbols, colors, and other brand identity elements in each country in which your brand is sold?	___ ___
Does your brand's identity system work globally? Is it applied consistently throughout the world?	___ ___

Do you have agreement on which decisions are made centrally and which ones are made locally? Is there sound logic underlying that agreement? ___ ___

Have you identified the relative attractiveness of each market for your brand (and have you identified consistent criteria for doing so)? ___ ___

Have you conducted an attitude and usage study in each country whose market you are considering entering? ___ ___

Have you identified how each of the following vary from country to country (or from region to region): language, culture, consumption patterns, competitive set, marketplace conditions, legal environment, and approaches to marketing? ___ ___

Have you considered how your "country of origin" either helps or hurts your brand? (Often, countries and regions have their own "brand images" that may influence the perceptions of brands from those places.) ___ ___

Do you know the category and brand development indices in each country in which you operate? ___ ___

Have you varied your approach to each of the following, based on the above-mentioned national (or regional) differences: brand slogan, products and services, product names, product features, positionings, marketing mixes (pricing, distribution, media, and advertising)? ___ ___

Have you made a conscious decision to either translate your brand name into the local language or keep it in the original language for each country in which your brand is sold? ___ ___

Do you have a global branding scorecard that can be applied country by country? ___ ___

Are you organized so that your brand and its business are managed globally? If not, is there good communication and cooperation between your domestic and international brand management functions? ___ ___

If you use more than one advertising agency, do you coordinate the agencies' efforts to achieve an adequate level of consistency in communicating the brand's essence globally? ___ ___

Would you describe your brand as a "global power brand"? ___ ___

PART 5
Brand Metrics

17

....

brand research

PREVIOUS CHAPTERS touched upon research that can help with brand positioning and advertising. The next chapter covers brand equity research in depth. In this chapter, I highlight a number of other research techniques that can be helpful to the brand management process, beginning with brand asset research and followed by brand association measurement.

Brand Asset Research

Brand asset research is an important first step in brand extension. Brand asset research identifies and dimensionalizes a brand's meaning to consumers, including its elasticity across product and service categories. It identifies categories within which consumers give the brand permission to operate. (More often than you might expect, consumers will indicate that a brand offers products in a category that it does not. This clearly identifies low-hanging—that is, brand extension—fruit.)

Typically, brand asset studies are conducted qualitatively (i.e., focus groups, minigroups, one-on-one interviews) using the following techniques: word association, qualitative mapping, ranking various brands between contrasting viewpoints, brand extendibility probes, and (often in a second phase) identifying the appeal of various concepts as they relate to the brand in question. I have found that the best way to communicate the result is by mapping the categories, concepts, and attributes as they relate to the core essence of the brand.

Think of a dartboard with the bull's-eye being the brand's core essence. The concepts that are closer to the bull's-eye are less risky brand extension opportunities. The ones farther away risk diluting the brand's essence and have a greater chance of failure (see Figure 17–1).

Figure 17–1. Core essence of a brand.

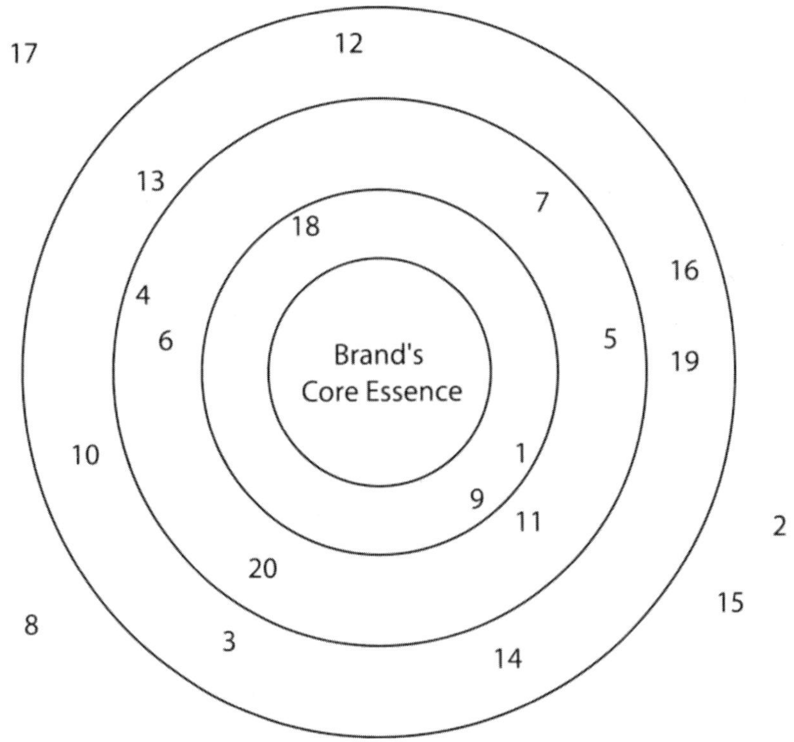

Brand Association Measurement[1]

It is important to measure associations both *from* and *to* the brand. (When I say "Lexus," what comes to mind? What association do you get from the brand? When I say "luxury cars," what comes to mind? You are drawn *to* a brand.) Qualitative research is an effective starting point if little is known. Specific qualitative techniques can be used to solicit associations. The Zaltman Metaphor Elicitation Technique (ZMET) and other projective techniques are covered later in this chapter.

Information gathered by qualitative research must be quantified to lay the groundwork for developing successful brand extension concepts. You should consider using both open-ended and scaled responses. Following are three approaches to quantifying brand associations:

1. *Naming Method* (open-ended). You present consumers with attributes. You then ask them to list the brands that come to mind. With this method, you can measure both the order and frequency of recall.

2. *Latency Method* (close-ended). You show consumers' attributes (or category names) followed by brand names. The consumer answers yes or no for each brand, indicating whether it is associated with each attribute or product category. The computer records the time it took the consumer to respond for each answer. This is particularly effective with broader and more abstract category labels, such as "healthy foods," "outdoor products," or "products to help you manage your relationships."

3. *Scaled Questions.* You can complement the two previous techniques with scaled questions, such as agree/disagree, or opposite pairs on statements regarding attributes, benefits, or personality. Include other brands to mask the brand in question. Choose brands that are key players in categories into which you are considering extending your brand.

Brand Extension Research: Final Steps

After the brand asset study is complete and you have measured brand associations, the next step in brand extension work typically is developing the most promising product concepts and then quantitatively screening them against the following criteria: need/need intensity, uniqueness, market gap/dissatisfaction with current alternatives, and purchase intent.

It is best when the results can be compared to a normative database for the brand and other companies in other industries. The final step, for those concepts that make it through the previous hurdles, is to create one or more test markets (taking the research in phases to reduce investment risk).

Successful brand extensions tend to have three characteristics:[2]

1. *Perceptual Fit.* The consumer must perceive the new item to be consistent with the parent brand.

2. *Benefit Transfer.* A benefit offered by the parent brand must be desired by consumers of products in the new category.

3. *Competitive Leverage.* The new items must stack up favorably to established items in the new category.

Therefore, an actionable, quantitative brand extension research test should incorporate all three components. In particular, incorporating the competitive set for each concept is critical. Consumers evaluate new products in the real world in a competitive context, so they need to do the same in a research test.

Other Useful Research Approaches

At a minimum, in order to understand how consumers perceive your brand, you need to probe in depth their first, most powerful, and most recent experiences with the brand. Following are some useful research approaches.

CUSTOMER SERVICE TESTING

Customer service has a huge impact on brand perceptions. Don't take someone else's word that it is working. As a brand marketer, you should test your customer service approaches at least a couple of times a year by testing online, telephone, and in-person customer and technical support (as applicable). Look for these things:

- How quickly and easily were you able to get your question answered or problem solved?
- Is customer service available 24/7?
- How long you were put on hold, if at all?
- How many steps did you have to go through to get your answer?
- Did you have to communicate the same information more than once (e.g., your name, account number, telephone number)?
- How friendly and helpful was the human interaction?
- Were you treated like an intelligent adult?

BRAND INUNDATION/DEPRIVATION TESTING

Do you want to better understand the benefits that your brand's product or service delivers? Do you want to discover ways to increase use of your brand's products and services? Try this: Identify a group of very light users and ask them to use your product or service as frequently as your heaviest users do for an extended period of time (at least through several usage cycles). Identify a group of heavy users and ask them to refrain from using your product or service for the same period of time. Ask the latter group to articulate what they used in lieu of your product or service to accomplish the same result. Ask both groups to keep a journal of their thoughts and feelings as they use or refrain from using your product or service. Follow up with in-depth, one-on-one interviews to better understand the role your brand's products and services play in their lives. I guarantee you that this exercise will provide profound insight into the full potential for your brand's products and services.

ARCHETYPE DISCOVERIES WORLDWIDE

This research company (www.archetypediscoveriesworldwide.com) was founded by Dr. G. C. Rapaille, the author of *The Seven Secrets of Marketing*. It offers an effective approach to uncovering the unspoken needs of the customer or employees, according to Procter & Gamble, which has commissioned more than thirty-two Archetype Discoveries over the years. In contrast to traditional marketing research firms, Archetype Discoveries does not rely on what people say. Instead these studies use a unique blend of biology, cultural anthropology, psychology, and learning theories to discover the hidden cultural forces that preorganize the way people behave toward a product, service, or concept. Unlike opinions that can change in a minute, cultural archetypes are deeply imprinted in people's minds and strongly rooted in cultural codes. If these "mental highways" and cultural forces change, it is at a glacial pace. The results form a permanent platform for marketing, new product design, innovation, and improvement of products or processes, and for more effective communication strategies. Therefore they are particularly useful for marketing managers, planners, product designers, change agents, advertisers, and public policy makers. Archetype Discoveries has conducted over 200 discoveries, in more than twenty countries, for such diverse products, services, and concepts as perfume, toys, cheese, security, quality improvement, nuclear power, automotives, credit cards, mergers, coffee, teenage pregnancy, and forests.

THE ZALTMAN METAPHOR ELICITATION TECHNIQUE

This interesting technique for discovering how consumers think about brands was developed by Jerry Zaltman of Harvard Business School and Robin Higie Coulter of the University of Connecticut. The technique is largely informed by "neuroscience, semiotics, and the ideas of Carl Jung."[3] ZMET combines neurobiology, psychoanalysis, linguistics, and art theory to try to uncover the mental models that guide brand purchase behavior. This research recognizes that consumers can't easily access or articulate the underlying motivations to their behaviors. They must be drawn out in other ways.

It taps into unconscious thoughts that are believed to be largely visual. Study participants are asked to take photographs or collect pictures that say something about the brand in question. They return for one-on-one personal interviews that include storytelling, sorting the pictures into what will become mental maps, answering a series of probing questions, creating collages that summarize their thoughts, and creating a vignette that highlights important brand issues (among other possible exercises).

OTHER APPROACHES

Other approaches to better understanding consumer behavior include purchase diaries; spending time in participants' homes with them; shopping with participants; asking participants to spend a few weeks collecting photographs of whatever they would like and later discussing the pictures in interviews; checking participants' closets, pantries, and cabinets; and even analyzing their household trash. Another approach is to create detailed identities for each of your target consumers and role-play each one for a day, including shopping for or using products in your category. Much of this is *ethnography*: putting yourself in the consumers' shoes by observing their brand shopping and usage patterns in real-life situations.

USING THE INTERNET

Most companies devote substantial marketing research resources to keeping in touch with their consumers. And yet the Internet provides for a 24/7 interaction with consumers through blogs, social media, and other online forums. Smart companies will embrace these methods to keep in close contact with their consumers. These mechanisms are superior to most traditional research methods in the following ways:

- They provide for ongoing interactive dialogue.
- They allow the company to become aware of and address issues as they emerge.
- They can become a mechanism for creating a stronger bond between the consumer and the company.

GUIDED IMAGERY

In the 1990s, if you to were to ask focus group participants what new features they would like to have integrated into their mobile telephones, do you think they would have said Internet access, e-mail, the ability to purchase music or identify products and their prices from UPC codes, GPS, voice-activated directions, or locating nearby restaurants or gas stations with the lowest gasoline prices? Marketers who are experienced in new product development know that you can't just ask people about their latent needs and expect detailed visionary answers. However, guided imagery is a technique that allows you to help people imagine and experience ideal future states, uncovering many new product, service, and brand attributes and features. You do this by getting people to close their eyes and breath deeply, and once they are very relaxed and comfortable, you guide them through an ideal future state and help them to explore it with each of their senses. When they open their eyes, they write down everything that they experienced. The results can be profound.

PROJECTIVE TECHNIQUES

Projective techniques overcome some of the limitations of direct questioning.[4] Here is why:

- People are not always conscious of their underlying motivations.

- People tell you what they think you want to hear.

- People are sometimes embarrassed to admit their real motivations, thinking that divulging them would reflect negatively on them.

- Most people think of themselves as being completely rational in their decision making, so they discount or dismiss nonrational reasons for their behaviors.

- Some people fear how marketers might use the information "if they were to learn the truth about me," and so they withhold that information to avoid being manipulated.

Projective techniques can help you better understand brand personality. For instance, consider this question: "If the brand was an animal/car/person/sports team/occupation, what animal/car/person/sports team/occupation would it be—and why?" A particularly powerful version of this question is "If this brand were a party, what kind of party would it be and why?" One can then probe on venue, music, food, drinks, people attending, what they are wearing and vehicles they drove to the party, providing deep insight into brand personality.

There are other projective research techniques that help you get below the surface. They include:

- Sentence completion
- Word association
- Consumer letters
- Brand time capsule

- Collages
- Brand obituary/epitaph
- Brand press release/headline
- Brand sorting (on a wide variety of dimensions)

- Stereotypes
- Thought balloons
- Psychodrawing/modeling
- Role-playing and reenactment

I also have used the technique of providing participants with numerous pictures of a wide variety of people in a wide variety of settings. I then ask which of those people would buy, receive as a gift, and use the brand, and which wouldn't. I then ask people to explain their answers.

Another technique explores perceived differences between brands. Ask people to sort products (competitors' products and your products intermixed) into two piles—the "brand in question" and "not the brand in question." (One version of this method disguises the brand mark; the other one doesn't.) Once all the products have been sorted, probe why people thought the product either was or wasn't the brand in question. (If this exercise is done in focus groups, ask participants to write their answers down first so that they are not biased by each other's answers. Collect all of the answer sheets and compare the written responses to the group discussion.)

While at Hallmark, I worked with Dr. Sharon Livingston of The Livingston Group (http://www.tlgonline.com). She and Dr. Glenn Livingston have compiled a list of "43 of the most common emotional self statements" that are based on statistical analyses (factor analyses) of "emotional purchase motivation revealed in focus groups." They have created a projective quantitative technique that:

- Rank orders the importance of the emotional drivers in your category
- Shows the direct link of features and functional benefits to the emotional drivers
- Graphically displays the position of your product or service, each of its features, your competition, the ideal company, and *any* additional advertising stimulus
- Assigns a single number to each product feature that represents the extent to which that feature is associated with all of the most important emotional benefits

You can learn more about this technique at http://www.tlgonline.com/sharon/articles/6.asp.

LOGO RESEARCH

When exploring new logo executions, the research may include any or all of the following components:

● *Logo Imagery.* Imagery evoked by various logo alternatives vs. that evoked by the current logo. (This exercise usually includes the intended brand personality attributes and attributes such as "boring.")

● *Logo Recognition.* A "mock-up" of each variation of the logo is placed in its most likely usage environment (e.g., store marquis, product packaging) and then people at various distances are asked about what they see. This technique measures visibility, recognition, and the ability to break through visual clutter at various distances.

● *Logo Recall.* One at a time, different logo alternatives and the current logo are mixed in with other companies' logos on a panel. People are allowed to view the panel for a few seconds. After that, the panel is covered or taken away and they must write down all of the brands that they remember seeing. Results are compared for each variation of the logo.

● *Logo Preference.* Each variation of the logo is featured on a card. People are given the deck of cards and asked to sort the logos/cards in order of preference. They are then asked to comment on why they ranked each logo variation the way they did.

OTHER RESEARCH TECHNIQUES

Sorting and Discussion. A technique to better understand brand price premium includes exposing different groups of participants to a wide variety of products and brands within the category in question, each time with your brand mark and your competitors' brand marks applied to the products in different combinations. We compare the quality perceptions, associations, intent to purchase, and price that people would be willing to pay for the same products with different brand marks. A variation of this technique is to present the same products but without any brand marks, which highlights product (vs. brand) preference. Often, the first step of this exploration is to sort the products into stacks—for example, product "is brand A" or "is not brand A" or "is high quality" or "is not high quality," etc.

Conjoint Analysis. Traditionally used for pricing research, conjoint analysis is very applicable for brand research as well. Respondents rate their buying intent for products comprised of various combinations of attributes (including product, service, sales terms, price, and brand attributes). Brand name is one of the attributes. Not only is this an excellent approach to measure the overall equity of your brand name vis-à-vis competitors, but it also allows you to measure the interactions/relationships of your brand name with other attributes. Simulation exercises also allow you to project the impact on share of preference for various attribute combinations (what-if exercises).

Corporate Image Tracking. An offshoot of brand image tracking, this technique measures changes in overall brand image on a variety of attributes. Its premise is that consumers have experiences with your company and brands in a variety of ways, and it is important to quantify the frequency and impact of those different experiences on the overall brand/corporate image.

For example, consumers interact with and experience the Hallmark name in many ways: shopping in Hallmark stores, buying and using Hallmark products, seeing television advertising, visiting the website, experiencing sponsorships and other public relations efforts, and viewing the Hallmark Channel on cable/satellite TV. A research-tracking program can measure the frequency of these various points of contact, as well as the satisfaction of those experiences and the subsequent impact on overall brand image.

Electronic Real-Time Research. ERT is qualitative research with some quantification of results. It is most often used for product research but is adaptable to brand research. (Dialsmith is one company that does ERT using its Perception Analyzer system.) ERT is used to:

- Get immediate quantitative feedback on specific benefits or concepts

- Be able to instantaneously see that feedback by any chosen segmentation of the respondents

- Be able to ask the respondents questions based upon that feedback (for additional insights)

Eye Tracking Research. Eye tracking research detects, records, and maps eye positions and movements. In this way, one can see what attracts a person's attention, what the person dwells on, and how his attention flows through a web page, print ad, or other communication. It can be used to assist with web, package, advertising, and retail environment design.

Neuromarketing. Neuromarketing is a relatively new approach to marketing research that uses functional magnetic resonance imaging (fMRI), electroencephalography (EEG), and steady state topography (SST) to measure brain activity/response to specific stimuli, as well as other sensors to measure changes in one's physiological state (e.g., biometrics such as heart rate, respiratory rate, and galvanic skin response) in response to the same. Using these approaches, researchers can measure visceral reactions such as excitement, anger, lust, and disgust.[5]

CBS, Frito-Lay, Google and other brands have used neuromarketing to better understand consumer response to their products and advertising. Political consultants are also starting to use this approach to identify voter reaction to specific messages. Some groups are concerned that this tool will give companies, politicians, and others too much control over people's behaviors.

Big Data Analytics. This is the process of analyzing large amounts of unstructured or semistructured data of various types across different sources to identify patterns and correlations that could provide better targeting, additional revenue opportunities, and other competitive advantages. Some uses of big data include:[6]

- More in-depth and precise business understanding
- Improved customer relationship management (CRM) campaigns
- Optimized segmenting of customers
- Improved market trends and analysis
- Recognition and development of sales and market opportunities
- Improved planning and forecasting

Big data analytics is enabled primarily by substantially improved statistical and computational methods, but also by improved storage and computational capacity. Rather than constructing the experiments first, big data allows one to accumulate vast quantities of data and then identify statistically significant patterns.[7] The largest challenge to big data analytics is an internal skills gap.

Big data can reveal unexpected correlations. My favorite is that the purchase of furniture coasters is a strong indicator of low credit risk and high credit scores.

Jason Frand of UCLA Anderson Graduate School of Management provides these examples of how big data is being used today:[8]

One Midwest grocery chain used the data mining capacity of Oracle software to analyze local buying patterns. They discovered that when men bought diapers on Thursdays and Saturdays, they also tended to buy beer. Further analysis showed that these shoppers typically did their weekly grocery shopping on Saturdays. On Thursdays, however, they only bought a few items. The retailer concluded that they purchased the beer to have it available for the upcoming weekend. The grocery chain could use this newly discovered information in various ways to increase revenue. For example, they could move the beer display closer to the diaper display. And, they could make sure beer and diapers were sold at full price on Thursdays. . . .

American Express can suggest products to its cardholders based on analysis of their monthly expenditures.

Wal-Mart is pioneering massive data mining to transform its supplier relationships. Wal-Mart captures point-of-sale transactions from over 2,900 stores in six countries and continuously transmits this data to its massive 7.5 terabyte Teradata data warehouse. Wal-Mart allows more than 3,500 suppliers to access data on their products and perform data analyses. These suppliers use this data to identify customer buying patterns at the store display level. They use this information to manage local store inventory and identify new merchandising opportunities. In 1995, Wal-Mart computers processed over 1 million complex data queries. In 2010, Wal-Mart processed 1 million customer transactions every hour feeding 2.5 petabyte databases.

The National Basketball Association (NBA) is exploring a data mining application that can be used in conjunction with image recordings of basketball games. The Advanced Scout software analyzes the movements of players to help coaches orchestrate plays and strategies. For example, an analysis of the play-by-play sheet of the game played between the New York Knicks and the Cleveland Cavaliers on January 6, 1995, reveals that when Mark Price played the guard position, John Williams attempted four jump shots and made each one! Advanced Scout not only finds this pattern, but explains that it is interesting because it differs considerably from the average shooting percentage of 49.30 percent for the Cavaliers during that game.

As additional examples:

● Netflix mines its customer digital download database to recommend movies and shows that their customers may like, based on their viewing history.

● Xerox is developing social media analytics software to enable businesses to monitor their brand images. The software will be able to identify specific themes in social media content (tweets, blog posts, etc.) and route them to the appropriate internal people to handle.

Research Mandatories

To ensure that your research is actionable and provides the highest return on investment possible, the first step in any research project should be to define:

- Objectives (both business and research)
- Hypotheses
- Action standards
- A predetermined feedback loop to identify whether the actions resulted in the intended outcome

Use the checklist in Figure 17–2 to assess the efficacy of your brand management practices in the area covered by this chapter. The more questions to which you can answer "yes," the better you are doing. The checklist also provides a brief summary of the material covered in the chapter.

Figure 17–2. Checklist: Brand research.

	YES / NO
Do you conduct research other than focus groups, satisfaction studies, and attitude and usage studies?	___ ___
Have you conducted brand asset research? Have you been able to successfully extend your brand into new products or services based on this research?	___ ___
Have you conducted brand equity research? Have you changed aspects of the brand based on this research? Has it increased your brand's equity?	___ ___
Do you use online methods (chat rooms, discussion boards, social media) to stay in touch with your customers?	___ ___
Have you used a variety of projective research techniques to better understand your brand's associations and those of your competitors' brands?	___ ___
Have you ever used ethnographic research to better understand your customers?	___ ___
Do you measure the effectiveness of your advertising? Have you improved your advertising based on this research?	___ ___
Do you conduct ongoing ad/brand tracker and corporate image studies?	___ ___
Have you researched the effectiveness of your brand's logo?	___ ___

Do you measure the effectiveness of your direct marketing? Do you measure the effectiveness of your online marketing? Have you been able to improve on both, based on this feedback?   ___ ___

Do you keep track of the degree of commoditization within the categories in which your brand operates? (This is determined by increased importance of price in the purchase decision, decreased perceptions of brand differentiation—including greater congruence between competitive brands' perceptual maps—and decreased preference for any brand in the category. Other supporting indicators are lower perceived brand innovation and vitality and higher perceived brand "boringness" in general for all brands across the category.)   ___ ___

Do you create objectives, hypotheses, action standards, and a feedback loop for all of your research?   ___ ___

Do you believe your brand is winning in the marketplace based on your brand research?   ___ ___

$$18$$

brand equity measurement

ACCORDING TO A well-known axiom, *you can't manage what you don't measure*. This is true of brand equity as well. Any strong brand equity measurement system will accomplish the following objectives:

- Measure the brand's equity across a variety of dimensions at different points in time over time.

- Provide diagnostic information on the reasons for the changes in brand equity.

- Gauge and evaluate the brand's progress against goals.

- Provide direction on how to improve brand equity.

- Provide insight into the brand's positioning vis-à-vis its major competitors, including its strengths, weaknesses, opportunities, and threats.

- Provide direction on how to reposition the brand for maximum effect

When I was named director of brand management and marketing at Hallmark, I was given two primary objectives: 1) to increase Hallmark market share and 2) to increase Hallmark brand equity.

Market share is a relatively straightforward objective for which we already had metrics. Brand equity was much less well defined. I spent the better part of the next three years drawing upon the knowledge of various consultants, researchers, and scholars and dozens of different brand equity models to define brand equity in a way that was useful to Hallmark. To be useful to Hallmark, it had to show how to move people from high brand awareness to brand insistence. Since then, this work has resulted in a validated and refined measurement system that is used by scores of organizations across dozens of industries.

Components of a Brand Equity Measurement System

Here are the components that a brand equity measurement system should measure:

- Brand awareness (first mention, or top-of-mind unaided recall, and total unaided recall)

- Brand preference

- Brand importance/rank in consideration set

- Brand accessibility

- Brand value (quality and value perceptions and price sensitivity)

- Brand relevant differentiation (open-ended question and perceptions on key attributes)

- Brand emotional connection

- Brand vitality

- Brand loyalty (multiple behavioral and attitudinal measures, including share of requirements/wallet)

- Brand usage

- Brand imagery (against a standard battery of category-independent brand personality attributes proven to drive brand insistence, and a customized battery of brand personality attributes for the particular organization and its product/service category)

Most Important Brand Equity Measures

The most important brand equity measures are:

- Unaided brand awareness, especially first recall.

- Remembered/recalled brand experience.

- Knowledge of the brand's promise.

- Brand's position in the purchase consideration set.

- Brand's delivery against key benefits. (We have found two separate approaches to be insightful: mapping benefit importance against brand benefit delivery—a scaled response—and an open-ended question, "What makes brand XX different from other brands in the YY category?")

- Emotional connection to the brand.

- Price sensitivity.

- Relative accessibility.

Specific Brand Equity Measures

What follows is a list of specific questions and measures that will help you manage a brand's equity:

- *Brand Awareness:*
  - What is the first brand that comes to mind when thinking about the xxx category?
  - What other brands come to mind for the xxx category?

- *Brand Preference:*
  - Which brand (of product category) do you prefer? (The incidence of those with no brand preference can also provide insights into the importance of brand in the category.)

- *Brand Usage:*
  - Which brand (of product category) do you most often use?

- *Brand Accessibility:*
  - Widely available.
  - Easy to find and purchase.

- *Brand Value:*
  - Quality perception.
  - Value perception.
  - Price sensitivity.

- *Brand Relevant Differentiation:*
  - What makes brand xxx different from other brands in the yyy category?
  - What one or two things make (category) brands different from one another?

- Which brand or brands (of product/service category) do you prefer when you are looking for the (relevant differentiated) benefit?
- Which brand (of category) best meets your needs? Why?
- How well does the xxx brand deliver against the yyy benefit? (Rated on a five-point scale.)

● *Brand Emotional Connection:*
- Your brand is almost like a friend to your customers.
- It stands for something important to them.
- It says something about who they are.
- It has never disappointed them (see Figure 18–1).

Figure 18–1. *Emotional connection.*

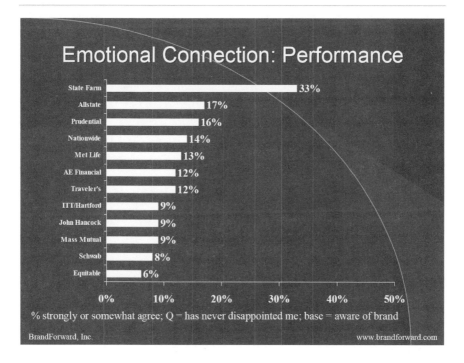

● *Brand Loyalty:*
- Share of requirements/share of wallet.
- Share of last ten purchases. (Constant sum questioning works best. Questions about the "brand most often purchased" or "brands bought in the past six months" almost always overstate purchases for well-known brands and understate purchases for low-price brands.)
- Satisfaction.

- Repurchase intent.
- Willingness to recommend to a friend.
- Deal sensitivity.
- Switching propensity.

A particularly telling question is, "Describe your most memorable recent interaction with [brand]." Such an open-ended question provides insight regarding the source of interaction (touchpoint), quality of interaction, and intensity of interaction.

LADDER OF THE MIND (Consideration Set Continuum: 7-Point Scale)

1. *I would never choose to buy this brand.*

2. *I've never heard of this brand.*

3. *I've heard of this brand but don't know much about it.*

4. *Not one of my preferred brands, but I'd try it under certain circumstances.*

5. *Not one of my preferred brands, but from what I've heard about it recently I'd like to try it/try it again.*

6. *This is one of my preferred brands.*

7. *This is the only brand I would ever consider buying.*

(Source: Transcript Proceedings: "Tracking the Obvious: New Ways of Looking at Old Problems" by Martin Stolzenberg, President, Stolzenberg Consulting, and Peggy Lebenson, Senior Vice President, Data Development Corporation. "Advertising and Brand Tracking: The Power of Today's Advertising and Brand Tracking Studies: An Advertising Research Foundation Key Issues Workshop," November 12-13, 1996, New York, Grand Hyatt Hotel, copyright 1997 by Advertising Research Foundation.)

● *Brand Vitality.* Design marketing campaigns to build perceived brand momentum:
  - Are you hearing more about the brand lately?
  - Is the brand changing for the better?
  - Which brand is reinventing the category?
  - Which brand, in your opinion, will lead the industry four years from now?

● *Brand Consideration Set:*
  - How many other brands are in the consideration set?

● *Brand Personality:*
  - Popular.
  - Trustworthy.

- Unique.
- Other (e.g., innovative, dependable, contemporary, old-fashioned, practical, boring, fun).

A SAD DAY

It is a sad day when a previously meaningful and vibrant brand is taken over by or combined with a new entity that does not share the brand's essence, promise, and values. This happens quite often, with mergers and acquisitions, when a company is taken private or public, or with other changes in ownership or leadership. Sometimes it happens when a financial owner (such as a venture capital firm) replaces the previous management team with its own new team. This is particularly true when people who only understand one thing, ROI (or, more specifically, their personal financial gain), replace the leadership team that had the original brand vision. We saw this happen when General Motors took control of Saturn, losing Saturn's "different kind of company" operating philosophy and forcing it to run like any other GM brand. Likewise, Compaq once owned 20 percent of the personal computer market, but mismanagement of the brand after Hewlett-Packard acquired it eventually resulted in its complete demise.

Such a change is akin to a person's spirit exiting his or her body to allow a new spirit to inhabit it. While the newly combined physical/spiritual entity may seem to be the same entity as before, new attitudes and behaviors will eventually betray the new spirit, but not until after the huge reservoir of brand equity is traded for short-term financial gains for the new owners. This is one reason previously strong brands seem to "lose their way."

What a Robust Brand Equity Measurement System Must Have

A robust brand equity system should include all the measures listed previously. It should be tailored to a particular company and industry. (At a minimum, the competitive set, personality attributes, and category benefit structure will vary by industry. Ways of measuring value and loyalty typically also vary by industry.) The measurement system should also include behavioral and attitudinal measures, especially for brand loyalty. Through regression analysis and other techniques, the system should determine attitudinal measures that best predict brand loyalty and other desired behaviors (predictive modeling). The system should be capable of analyzing brand equity by category or customer segment if required. Comparing results of frequent users, occasional users, and nonusers also provides useful insights. It is important to measure brand vitality because purchase intent is almost always overstated for well-known, well-regarded older brands with waning differentiation (i.e., declining brands) and understated for newer brands with low awareness but high relevance and differentiation (i.e., emerging brands). Brand vitality can help adjust for this variance.

Robust brand equity systems also deliver these beneficial features:

- A visual portrayal of positioning opportunities and vulnerabilities, such as mapping attribute/benefit importance against brand delivery (see Figure 18–2).

- Comparisons to other industries (from a normative database) to identify additional opportunities and vulnerabilities.

- Identification of natural customer clusters.

- Demographic/lifestyle analysis and profiling.

Figure 18–2. Perceptual map.

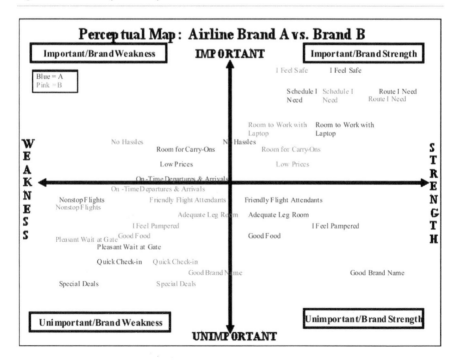

Common Problems with a
Brand Equity Measurement System

The most common problems include the following:

• The system from which to manage brand equity is too simplistic (e.g., those omnibus studies that measure only two to four dimensions of brand equity, such as awareness or favorability).

• No competitive comparisons are included in the measurement. (Many companies measure against themselves by, for instance, measuring customer satisfaction improvements. A brand equity measurement system must include competitive comparisons. By definition, brands are positioned against other brands. And few customers compare you against yourself. Most customers compare you with other companies and brands. Competitive context is not only highly insightful—it is critical to managing your brand's equity.)

• The sample size is too small to provide for valid subgroup analysis.

• The sample size is too small to detect small changes in brand equity in the shorter term.

• Customers are surveyed too frequently. Typically, it is sufficient to measure brand equity once a year, unless one of the following conditions exist:
  - The brand is new.
  - You have repositioned the brand or otherwise altered the brand communication or delivery in a major way.

• You make use of the organization's own customer and/or prospect list so that brand awareness, usage, and other measures are not projectable to the general population.

• The survey is designed in a way that biases the unaided brand awareness question—rendering the results of that question invalid.

• Organizations are unable to identify a primary product category or set of competitors because of the uniqueness of their brand or the lack of a brand unifying principle. This eliminates some of the most important brand equity measures (top-of-mind awareness, brand differentiation, etc.) from the measurement system.

• A tailored set of brand/category benefit statements is not included in the study. These statements must come from a rigorous understanding of the category benefit structure, typically identified by prior qualitative customer research dedicated to the purpose of identifying that structure.

• The organization confuses other studies with a brand equity measurement system. Mostly, people believe that customer satisfaction studies, attitude and usage studies, and corporate image studies are the same as brand equity measurement systems (or viable substitutes for them).

Assessing the Effectiveness of an Organization's Brand Equity Measurement System

Brand equity measurement systems are the most effective when clients can answer each of the following questions affirmatively:

• Do you have a profound understanding of your brand's consumers?

• Do you know what drives your brand's equity?

• Have you established and validated equity measures for your brand?

• Have you set objectives against these measures?

• Do key decision makers regularly see results against these objectives?

• Are people held accountable for achieving brand objectives?

Brand Equity Should Not Be Measured Just for Customers

Businesses should also monitor their brand equity with certain groups (in addition to their customers). These groups include:

• Industry analysts

• Financial analysts

• Employees

• Business partners

A brand's power comes not just from the loyalty that it creates in its customers, but also from the loyalty that it creates in its employees and its investors.

Brand Building and Marketing Are Investments with a Tangible Return

I am tired of hearing some businesspeople say that there is no way to correlate business results with marketing expenditures, implying that marketing is an expense with no corresponding return. Others are slightly more charitable and say that there is no way to measure *direct* results. This is wrong—at least for direct response marketing, including direct response marketing via the Internet. (Many direct marketing websites even offer free direct marketing ROI calculators.) For other types of marketing, this conclusion is partially wrong.

There are a few important components to measuring the results of marketing programs. They include 1) being clear about the program's objectives up front, 2) being sure that there are ways to measure results against the objectives, 3) measuring those results, and 4) evaluating the program's results against the objectives. This is a closed-loop system.

It is also important to keep in mind that there are marketing programs with long-term results, such as brand building, and there are marketing programs with short-term results, such as direct response marketing and sales promotion. You must be clear about which ones each marketing investment is intended to achieve (see Figure 18–3).

Figure 18–3. Long-term vs. short-term marketing investments.

	Long-Term Investment	Short-Term Investment
Type of Marketing Investment	Brand building	Direct response marketing, sales promotion, and other shorter-term marketing expenditures
Primary Result	Creation of leverageable asset	Short-term increase in sales
Indirect Impact on Business	- Decreased price sensitivity - Increased customer loyalty - Increased revenues - Increased share of market - Increased ability to hire and retain quality employees - Increased stock price - Increased company value - Increased ability to grow into new product and service categories - Increased ability to mobilize the organization around a vision	NA
Measurement	*Financial:* asset value *Nonfinancial:* awareness, relevant differentiation, preference, loyalty	Program ROI

Measuring Marketing ROI

There are many useful models for estimating the impact of various revenue drivers on total revenues. One of the more widely used models is based on the following calculation:

The total customer base (number of people)

$\times$ (multiplied times) the average number of purchase transactions per person (per time period)

$\times$ (multiplied times) the average unit sales per transaction

$\times$ (multiplied times) the average price per unit

$\times$ (multiplied times) the percent of those transactions received by your brand

$=$ (equals) your sales (per time period)

You can design your marketing programs to affect any combination of these factors, and you can measure the level of investment required to get the results through each of these levers:

- You can introduce your products to new audiences.

- You can encourage customers to upgrade their products or services or to purchases additional products and services.

- You can entice them to make more frequent purchases.

- You can increase the amount that they pay for the products and services.

- Your can encourage them to rely on your brand for a greater proportion of their purchases.

Given the right data, it becomes trivial to estimate the return to your company from increasing your market share by one share point, gaining one more customer, or retaining a current customer's business for another year.

Take another example: lead generation. If you code ads and direct mail pieces, you will be able to determine which marketing programs resulted in leads, which of those leads were qualified, which of those qualified leads were translated into sales by your sales force, and how much revenue each of those successful leads returned. You can relate this result to the marketing investment required to generate those leads. Now you have calculated return on marketing investment.

Many marketing tactics achieve numerous objectives. For instance, banner ads have been shown to increase brand awareness and reinforce a brand's positioning while also generating sales leads or transactions (depending on what is on the other side of the click-through). Trade shows also achieve multiple ends. Through our postshow research, Element K has found that shows increase brand awareness and preference and the prospect's propensity to purchase our products. They also increase current customer attitudinal loyalty. They generate qualified sales leads as well. Be careful to evaluate marketing tactics that achieve multiple ends against all of those ends—not just one.

On a macro basis, one can measure the effectiveness of marketing expenditures by comparing increases in total marketing expenditures to increases in sales for a specified period of time (e.g., quarter-over-quarter, year-over-year). Two cautions with this approach, however. First, a complex combination of variables affects sales. Not all the credit (positive or negative) can be attributed to marketing actions. The general economy, sales tactics, and other executive-level decisions can also impact sales in significant ways. Second, remember that some of your marketing programs, including most brand building programs, are designed to affect a longer-term cumulative result not measurable in the short term.

Importance of Investing in the Brand Asset

A number of studies have shown that the percentage of a company's value that is unaccounted for by tangible assets has increased significantly. From 50 percent to 90 percent of a company's total value is now attributable to factors other than tangible assets. In a 2013 study, the intellectual capital equity firm Ocean Tomo discovered that nonfinancial assets account for as much as 80 percent of institutional investors' valuation of a company. In 2000, Cap Gemini Ernst & Young joined with *Forbes Magazine* and the Wharton Research Program to develop the Value Creation Index, a method for determining the real value of intangible and nonfinancial assets. In "Measuring the Future: The Value Creation Index," Cap Gemini reported that, after rigorous research, it discovered that 50 percent of a traditional company's value and 90 percent of an e-commerce company's value result from nine factors. The following value drivers seem to be common across most industries:[1]

- Innovation/R&D
- Quality of management
- Employee quality/satisfaction

- Alliances

- Brand investment

- Product/service quality

Neel Foster, a former board member at the Financial Accounting Standards Board, once said:

> As we move into more of an information age and service-based economy, the importance of soft assets is becoming more relevant to valuing some companies than brick and mortar. A lot of companies don't even have brick and mortar.[2]

An increasing number of methods have emerged to measure nonfinancial business drivers, from economic value added and the balanced scorecard to value-based management and the Value Creation Index. Wharton accounting professors conducted a study across 317 companies and discovered that 36 percent of the companies sampled used nonfinancial measures to determine executive incentive compensation.[3]

Building brand awareness, differentiation, and emotional connection together with the appropriate pricing and distribution strategies results in brand preference, purchase, repeat purchase, and, eventually, loyalty. Also, an increasing body of evidence links brand building activities with a wide range of long-term benefits, from decreased price sensitivity and increased customer loyalty to increased stock price and shareholder value.

Sometimes, the results of brand building programs are obvious, especially for new brands. When I arrived at Element K, it was a newly created brand. People in the e-learning industry had not heard of Element K. Our sales force found it difficult to gain the attention of potential buyers: We were not on industry analysts' "radars," we did not receive coverage in trade magazine articles, people passed by our trade show booth, and we got few calls from conference companies. After a year of focused and relentless brand building efforts, prospects started coming to us (we are on their "short lists"). Soon we were in all of the industry analysts' reports, our president writes a column for one of the major trade publications, we sponsor a major user conference in parallel with one of the most important industry trade shows, we receive a continuous stream of invitations to participate in conferences and other industry events, companies approach us about business partnerships, our employees are sought after as industry experts, and our competitors talk about us. In this case, the results of our brand building efforts were obvious and didn't require the validation of formal brand equity measures or the corresponding revenue increases (both of which we also have).

You can measure and manage the nonfinancial impact of your brand through a brand equity measurement system (covered earlier in this chapter). You can also measure the financial value of your brand as an asset.

Brand valuation has been made possible by a number of financial approaches—activity-based costing (ABC), discounted cash flow (DCF), and economic value added (EVA)—and by a myriad of more recent customer purchase tracking techniques.[4] Interbrand (www.interbrand.com) has a depth of experience in brand valuation. Also, Don E. Schultz, Ph.D., professor of integrated marketing communications at Northwestern University and president of Agora, Inc., has studied and applied the concepts of brand valuation and return on marketing investment in depth. Both would be good resources for people with a further interest on this topic.

Brand Building and Marketing as Investments: A Summary

1. Brand building is an investment that results in a significant leverageable asset.

2. Other shorter-term marketing actions exist for the sole purpose of increasing sales.

3. You can measure the asset value of brands.

4. You can also measure the nonfinancial aspects of brands that drive positive financial consequences in the long term—awareness, relevant differentiation, and loyalty, for instance.

5. You can and should measure ROI for other shorter-term marketing programs.

6. Brands are a primary source of value creation for organizations.

7. Although some businesspeople (typically finance and operations types) may view marketing as an expense without significant corresponding benefits, this is untrue. Marketing is one of the most important investments a company can make.

Implication: Don't look first to marketing (and employee training, for that matter) when expenses need to be trimmed to achieve short-term goals. This decision will only hamper value creation and revenue growth in the long term.

Marketing is a fundamental driver of organizational success. Together, brand building, marketing. and sales strategies and tactics create, build, and sustain a company's revenues. To ensure positive results, you must understand and track how each marketing program impacts sales in the short term and the long term. In many instances, you will be able to track and measure the specific short-term impact of specific programs. In others, especially for longer-term brand building programs, you will have to track and measure indirect business drivers (e.g., brand awareness, attitudinal loyalty) and validate how each of these affects revenue gains in the long run. Formal marketing (and brand) plans and metrics will help you achieve this end. And don't forget—a brand is an asset, and one of the most important assets in creating long-term value for organizations. Build the brand, sustain it, *and* leverage it.

Use the checklist in Figure 18–4 to assess the efficacy of your brand management practices in the area covered by this chapter. The more questions to which you can answer "yes," the better you are doing. The checklist also provides a brief summary of the material covered in the chapter.

Figure 18–4. *Checklist: Brand equity measurement.*

	YES / NO
Do you know what drives your brand's equity?	___ ___
Have you established and validated equity measures for your brand?	___ ___
Have you established targets against those brand equity measures? Do you actively manage against those targets?	___ ___
Do you measure your brand's equity at least once a year?	___ ___
Are people held accountable for achieving brand equity objectives and targets?	___ ___
Is senior management regularly updated on performance against brand equity objectives and targets?	___ ___
Do you measure each of the following brand equity dimensions: awareness, accessibility/convenience, value, relevant differentiation, emotional connection, preference, usage, vitality, loyalty, and key associations?	___ ___
Do you also measure your primary competitors against the same brand equity dimensions?	___ ___
Do you know if competitors are making inroads on key associations that you intend your brand to own?	___ ___

Do you measure behavioral and attitudinal aspects of brand loyalty? ___ ___

Do you measure your brand's price premium (with consumers and the trade)? ___ ___

Do you measure "intent to purchase"? ___ ___

Do you measure your brand's rank in the consideration set? ___ ___

Do you measure your brand's share of dollar/share of requirements? ___ ___

Do you measure your brand's share of market? ___ ___

For products sold at retail: Do you measure retail sales productivity/turns for your brand vs. competitive brands? ___ ___

Is your brand equity system sensitive enough to measure changes in your brand's equity over time? ___ ___

Does the system provide diagnostics on why the equity is increasing or decreasing? ___ ___

Does the system provide insights into positioning threats and opportunities? ___ ___

Do you track changes in consumers' ability to accurately play back key brand positioning points? ___ ___

Do you have a plan (and measurement targets) for the brand associations you want to increase and decrease? ___ ___

Has your brand's equity been increasing over time? ___ ___

Is your brand perceived to be authentic? ___ ___

Is your brand likable? ___ ___

Do you know if your brand is perceived to be an up-and-comer (rather than on the decline)? Do you measure brand vitality? ___ ___

If your brand is venerated and dominant in the market, would you be able to tell if it was in danger of becoming generic? If it was, are you aware of the steps that can be taken to avoid that outcome? ___ ___

Have you measured the financial value of your brand asset? Have you shared that information with your organization to reinforce that your brand is an asset that should be actively managed and leveraged? ___ ___

PART 6
Other Brand Management Considerations

19

....

how organization age and size affect brand management issues

BRAND MANAGEMENT issues differ significantly based on the age and size of the organization. A key role of brand management is to create and reinforce an identity that promises relevant points of difference to consumers.

According to Al and Laura Reis's book, *The 22 Immutable Laws of Branding*, the first two laws of branding are as follows:

1. *The Law of Expansion.* The power of a brand is inversely proportional to its scope.

2. *The Law of Contradiction.* A brand becomes stronger when you narrow its focus.

Clearly these first two laws favor smaller, younger organizations.

Brand identity firms will tell you that often they can create much stronger brand identities for smaller, younger companies because those companies have fewer constraints (existing logos, store décor, and signage), more focused businesses, and stronger business visions. They also have a more coordinated marketing function (often a single department with just a few people). Conversely, large organizations usually have separate product development, advertising, promotion, public relations, sales, and marketing research departments (to name a few).

Some people will tell you that the best promise a large organization's brand can make is to be "the quality, innovation leader in (insert the company's business category)." They say that organizational brands of large enterprises offer authority and assurance, *period*. Yet some of the most successful organizational brands have more focused (consumer benefit–based) brand essences. For instance, Disney promises *fun family entertainment*, Nike promises *authentic athletic performance*, and Hallmark promises *caring shared*. All three statements are distinctive yet broad enough to make multiple product categories possible. Consider all the businesses that Disney is in. And Hallmark, too, has much growth left (despite a mature greeting card category) and could offer gift candy, flowers, and even "love boat" cruises.

Brand Problems: Small vs. Large Companies

Figure 19–1 is a summary of the most likely brand problems of small and large organizations.

Figure 19–1. Most likely brand problems in larger vs. smaller organizations.

	Smaller, Younger Organizations	Larger, Older Organizations
Leadership	An entrepreneur with a vision and passion.	A seasoned executive with experience in running large, complex enterprises.
Size	A small number of people who work closely together and often share the entrepreneur's vision and passion.	A large number of people in different divisions and departments with different functional backgrounds and allegiances, often very much decentralized.
Business Scope	Usually focused on one core product or product category.	Usually offering a wide variety of products and product lines, many times in multiple business categories and even in different industries.
Brand Structure	Usually one brand.	Often very complex including multiple brands, subbrands, endorsed brands, etc.
Organization Infrastructure	Rapidly being built to support the entrepreneur's vision.	Many assets, systems, processes, and organizational levels. Very difficult to change.
Corporate Culture	Usually strong, based on the entrepreneur's personality. May evolve as new top managers are added.	May be very strong based on the legacy of a strong founder or a current strong leader. Companies that have long and rich histories often have entrenched cultures.
Marketplace	The business category is often in its infancy with many positioning possibilities for a new company.	Industry is often mature or maturing. Sometimes declining. Competitors are much more entrenched with few, if any, viable marketplace positions not taken. (Recently deregulated industries provide notable exceptions.)
Decision Making	Usually very quick with fewer decision makers.	Depending on the organization design, the decision-making process can be very cumbersome.

Financial Resources	Often scarce as the organization is growing rapidly and reinvesting all available cash flow. May be less scarce after an IPO.	Usually substantial, including cash flow and borrowing capacity.
Primary Marketing Method	Publicity.	Advertising.
Brand Identity	Often evolving, but easier to encode in standards and systems (because the organization is starting with "a clean slate").	Often strong and entrenched, but more difficult to codify due to the scope and complexity of the enterprise and the inconsistencies that have arisen over time.
Brand Awareness and Esteem	Usually low or nonexistent.	Often high.
Brand Differentiation	Often very high, but not always. (If its differentiation is not high, the organization may go out of business or be a takeover target.)	Usually declines over time as more and more competitors enter the market or achieve parity on what were differentiating benefits.

For smaller, younger organizations, key brand activities include developing a strong brand identity, building brand awareness through publicity and other less expensive means, and, sometimes, developing a better understanding of their consumers through marketing research (such as attitude and usage studies and focus groups). Building "trust" through consultative selling, legendary service, customer testimonials, guarantees, and other approaches is also very important.

> ### THE VALUE OF PUBLICITY
> At the Institute for International Research's The Branding Trilogy conference in Santa Barbara, July 17–19, 2000, Jill Vollmer, vice president of brand marketing for Mondera.com (now Mouawad, www.mouawad.com), said, "Publicity has helped us achieve five times the ad value of media placement for every $1 spent. If you consider that the message is coming from a third party—not paid, but endorsed—the additional credibility may result in ten times the value."

Because younger organizations must build their brands quickly with limited funds, they often resort to breakthrough ideas: redefining their categories with out-of-the-box marketing tactics, strong differentiation, and thought leadership; taking bold stands; and using the element of surprise to pierce the marketplace clutter (vs. the steady, consistent leadership messages and other brand building tactics more typically employed by larger, more established brands).[1] In taking these risks, smaller, younger organizations have much more to gain and far less to lose than their larger, older counterparts.

For larger, older organizations, the brand management job is much more complex. The most important task is to get the senior leadership team to agree to a distinctive, compelling marketplace positioning for the brand. Often the brand needs to be repositioned. Often, too, the brand identity standards and systems need to be overhauled (and the brand hierarchy simplified). Frequently, major organizational design changes are required. The necessary changes may be as wide reaching as rethinking the business portfolio itself.

Clearly, brand management needs to vary with organization age and size. Use the checklist in Figure 19–2 to assess the efficacy of your brand management practices in the area covered by this chapter. The more questions to which you can answer "yes," the better you are doing. The checklist also provides a brief summary of the material covered in the chapter.

Figure 19–2. Checklist: How organization age and size affect brand management issues.

	YES / NO
Do you know what your organization's number one brand management priority is?	__ __
Given your organization's age and size, do you know what its most likely brand management issues are?	__ __
If you work for a smaller organization with a relatively young brand, have you addressed the following: a) building brand awareness quickly and aggressively; b) pursuing breakthrough ideas, strategies, and tactics to do so; c) fully understanding your customer's attitudes, needs, and behaviors; d) identifying relevant and compelling points of difference to break through the market place clutter; and e) establishing "trust" through outstanding service, guarantees, customer testimonials, and other vehicles?	__ __
If you work for a larger organization with an older and more established brand, have you addressed the following: a) lack of unifying brand vision, b) lack of innovation, c) lack of compelling differentiating benefits, d) overly complicated brand architecture, and e) inconsistent brand identity and communication?	__ __

20

....

legal issues in
brand management*

ALTHOUGH THE best defense against copycat competitors is to stay
ahead of them with a continuous stream of innovative, highly differentiated,
and superior products and services, it is equally important to seek as much
legal protection as possible for your brand.

Trademark Law

As a brand steward, you must be aware of the laws under which legal protection is available. First, trademark law protects a brand's identity. That is, it
protects names, titles, taglines, slogans, logos, other designs, product shapes,
sounds, smells, colors, or any other features that distinguish one source of
products or services from another. Trademarks that protect services are often
called service marks ("SM"). There are also "collective membership marks"
(e.g., Boy Scouts of America) and "certification marks" (e.g., UL approved).

> ### DID YOU KNOW?
> *TM indicates an unregistered trademark.*
> *SM indicates an unregistered service mark.*

* I am not a lawyer and this chapter is not legal advice, but rather is meant merely to help
you consider the legal issues in brand management. When actually dealing with any specific issues in this area, please consult with lawyers who have expertise in intellectual
property law.

® indicates a registered trademark.

© represents copyrighted material.

Harley-Davidson filed to federally register the sound of its motorcycle engines.

Dirt Devil vacuum cleaners are strongly associated with the color red.

GEICO owns the gecko icon.

Trademarks, like brands, build in strength over time. The test for trademark infringement is "confusing similarity." Put another way, if the average consumer believes both products to have come from the same source, there is infringement. Obviously, the more a consumer is familiar with a particular brand, the more defendable its mark. That's why it behooves a company to do the following:

• Choose a distinctive mark, including a "coined" name. As I mentioned in the chapter on brand identity, brand names range from generic and descriptive to suggestive and arbitrary or fanciful ("coined"). Obviously it takes longer to build meaning for *coined* names, but they are also more distinctive and easiest to protect legally. Kodak, Xerox, and Exxon fall in that category. *Suggestive* marks are the next most protectable. Examples include Coppertone, Duracell, and Lestoil. Even common words can be used as trademarks as long as they are not used descriptively. These common words/phrases are also suggestive marks: Amazon (big), Twitter (brief and chatty), and Apple (different, offbeat). *Descriptive* marks are not protectable unless the brand creates a secondary meaning for the word, such as Weight Watchers, Rollerblade, or Wite-Out. *Generic* marks, such as Shredded Wheat and Super Glue, are not protectable at all.

• Avoid geographic names as a part of your mark—they can be the basis of trademark refusal.

• Register the mark.

• Be consistent in the use of the mark.

• Create strong trade dress (as discussed later in this chapter).

• Widely advertise and distribute its trademarked products.

• Do all of this over a long period of time.

Because the strength of a mark is dependant upon consumers' familiarity with it, it is much easier for a competitor to neutralize your mark soon after it has been introduced than after it has been in use for a long period of time.

Courts use the following tests to determine infringement:

- Strength of the trademark claiming infringement.

- Similarity of the two marks.

- Evidence of consumer confusion.

- Care a consumer takes in comparing products.

- Intent of the organization in using the potentially infringing mark. (Some drugstores and grocery stores use generic brands that emulate a leading brand's package shape, colors, typestyle, formulation, etc., and display the product side by side with the leading brand to imply that there are no differences between the two, encouraging consumers to purchase the lower-priced generic item. In this situation, there is clearly intent to emulate the leading brand and reduce the perceived differentiation and value advantage of that brand, but it is not clear that there is intent to deliberately cause confusion as to source.)

- Relatedness of the two businesses.

- Overlap between communication and distribution channels.

By using the mark in association with your products and services over time, you gain trademark protection. Registering your mark (marks can be registered at the state and federal levels) provides additional protection. Although common law and federal trademark statute protect an unregistered mark, registering your mark transfers the burden of proof to the second comer in challenging a mark's registration. With federal registration, you can sue infringers in federal court. Also, after five years of registration, the mark becomes incontestable. Federal trademark registrations last ten years and can be renewed every ten years ad infinitum.

You can acquire trademark rights in one of two ways. To acquire trademark rights based on use in commerce, you must be the first person or organization that uses the mark in conjunction with the products or services for which trademark protection is sought. To acquire the mark base on intent to use, you must apply to register the mark through the United States Patent and Trademark Office.

Before choosing a trademark, first conduct a simple search to weed out marks that are not available. This search can be done online for free (for a list of online resources, go to www.brandforward.com). After that, for the remaining candidates, conduct a full search through a law firm specializing in trademark law or through an experienced trademark search firm.

Strong brands run the danger of becoming category descriptors. Always use trademarks as adjectives, not verbs or nouns. If your brand is in danger of becoming a category descriptor, consider talking about your brand in the following way that differentiates the brand from the category. For example: "Jell-O® gelatin," "Kleenex® facial tissue," and "Xerox® photocopier."

Trade Dress

Trade dress is a second form of legal protection for a brand. Trade dress is a brand's distinctive aesthetic design features (package or product design). To be protectable, trade dress must be nonfunctional and distinctive (or have acquired a "secondary meaning," that is, source-identifying characteristics). The more nonfunctional differentiating features one can build into a product and its packaging, the more likely it will be that infringement can be proved.

It is easy for a competitor to say, "I developed this very similar product independently" when it is fairly generic (such as a birthday card with a floral design that says simply "happy birthday"). It is more difficult to convince a courtroom of that claim when your product has many of the same random, nonfunctional elements that a competitor's product has (e.g., a line of greeting cards of an unusual size that open from the top with rounded edges printed on green-tinted recycled paper, all at 99 cents, and all addressing the theme of friendship). For a competitor to develop a similar line of cards with similar features independently is highly unlikely. It points to copying.

To protect its trademarks and trade dress, a company must constantly be watchful for and strenuously defend against infringement. For instance, Apple has filed several lawsuits to defend its iPhone against knockoffs, winning a major legal battle against Samsung in summer 2013. Trademark rights can be enforced through lawsuits at a state or federal level. Proving infringement requires proof that the infringer had second use of the mark and that the second user's mark is confusingly similar to the senior party's mark.

When launching brand extensions, companies should be careful to maintain the same brand identity and trade dress in those new items. If the brand's name and logo are the only common elements across all a brand's products, it weakens the power of the other trade dress elements to differentiate and legally protect the mark.

SIGNATURE DESIGN ELEMENTS

Christian Louboutin shoes have red-lacquered soles. Wolf ovens have red knobs. Apple cords are white. My personal favorite: Robert Graham shirts have bright colors, unusual textiles, embroidered elements, and distinctive flip cuffs. And the words "Knowledge Wisdom Truth" are sewn into each garment.

Signature design elements, if executed properly, protected legally, and used consistently can create strong brand recognition while dissuading competitors from imitation and legal infringement.

(Source: Andy Logan, "Defensible Signature Elements [Part 1]," AWOL Company, http://awolcompany
.com/articles/defensible-signature-elements/.)

Copyright Law

Although organizations don't often pursue this protection, logos are typically protectable by copyright law. Make sure your organization, and not an outside person or agency, owns the copyright to your brand's logo. Advertising/marketing agencies will often include an assignment of rights, titles, and interests (including copyright interests) to their clients in their letters of agreement. While trademark infringement requires proof of "confusing similarity," copyright infringement requires proof of "substantial similarity."

Online legal interpretation is evolving, but in general, organizations whose brands are strong and well known ("famous brands") can legally defend their names and other marks against unauthorized use in domain names and meta tags. For example, Playboy (unsuccessfully) and Estee Lauder (successfully) sued other sites for using their brands' names or slogans in their sites' meta tags.

Other online legal issues include the following:

- Cybersquatting, which refers to people who register and warehouse domain names that are other party's marks

- For-pay search engines selling marks as keywords to businesses that don't own the marks

- Spammers who use the e-mail addresses of others as return addresses for their solicitations

SPECIAL PROBLEMS

Organizations that license and franchise their marks encounter added challenges to protecting their marks. License and franchise agreements should be drafted to provide maximum control over the mark and to minimize the mark owner's exposure to liability. Furthermore, every effort should be made to establish processes to review, approve, and monitor use of the mark by licensees and franchisees.

Trade Secrets

Don't overlook trade secrets as a form of protection. Trade secrets are simply information, techniques, procedures, codes, patterns, plans, processes, formula, and prototypes that are developed confidentially and that are kept confidential. Trade secrets even include customer lists and instructional methods. The Coca-Cola syrup formulation is an example of a trade secret. (The added value of this approach from a brand perspective is that it often creates a mystique that has its own cachet.)

Sometimes it is better to keep something a trade secret than to patent it. In some industries, companies routinely watch for competitors' new patents and then try to design around them. Noncompete and nondisclosure agreements are important, but not infallible, in protecting trade secrets. The Economic Espionage Act of 1996 protects trade secrets against theft. Information is legally considered to be a trade secret if an organization can show that it took reasonable measures to keep the information secret and that there is economic value to the information not being made public.

> **DID YOU KNOW?**
> Coca-Cola's syrup formula is kept in a bank vault in Atlanta, and only Coca-Cola's board of directors has the power to request the vault to be opened. Only two anonymous employees know the formula; they have signed nondisclosure agreements, and they are not allowed to fly together on the same plane.
>
> (Source: Stephen Fishman and Rich Stim, Nondisclosure Agreements: Protect Your Trade Secrets and More, Berkeley, CA: Nolo, 2001).

A business can protect its trade secrets in the following ways:

- Share confidential information only on a "need to know" basis.

● Limit the number of employees exposed to trade secrets. Always inform employees exposed to those trade secrets a) that they are being exposed to secrets and b) of the importance of keeping the secrets secret.

● Mark all confidential documents CONFIDENTIAL—NO COPIES ALLOWED. For added security, number each copy and keep a log of which numbered copy was given to which employee.

● Use access logs for trade secrets.

● Require anyone (employees, suppliers, customers, consultants, and other business partners) who might come in contact with trade secrets to sign confidentiality and nondisclosure agreements *before* the relationship begins.

● In consultant contracts, be clear about what intellectual property the consultants are to assign to your company during their assignment.

● Require employees to sign noncompete agreements that prohibit them from working for competitors for a period of time after their employment with you ends. If this is done within an employment contract, present this information to prospective employees well before they commence their employment with you so that the "consideration" is employment.

● Employment contracts can also prohibit moonlighting or consulting for companies in similar lines of business while employed at your company or, less restrictively, while on company time or using company equipment (including computers).

● Educate employees about the treatment of proprietary information during and after their employment with you.

● Carefully orchestrate employee terminations so that employees are not able to take proprietary information with them.

● Schedule exit interviews with departing employees. Use those interviews to remind departing employees of their confidentiality obligations.

● Develop, communicate, and enforce security processes—from physical security for the building to security of paper documents and computers. Secure confidential information with electronic and mechanical locks. (Passwords or codes should be changed regularly.)

● Never store or allow transfer of confidential information outside of your company's firewall.

- Make extensive use of shredders.

- Be especially careful of contract workers. Provide them with a company computer so that they don't have to use their own on the job.

- Conduct trade secret audits.

- Most important, identify all trade secrets and develop formal protection plans for those secrets.

> **DID YOU KNOW?**
> *Perceptions of your product or service's performance have a significant impact on your brand's equity. So says Nigel Hollis, EVP and chief global analyst at Millward Brown International.*
>
> (Source: "They Said My Brand Was Popular—So What?" Presentation to the Advertising Research Foundation.)

False or Deceptive Advertising

False or deceptive advertising is another legal consideration in brand management. Advertising is considered to be false or misleading if it *could* mislead consumers about a product's place of origin, nature, quality, or maker. (It is not necessary to prove actual deception.) Advertisers must be accurate about material aspects of their products or services and those of their competitors (in comparative advertising) to avoid prosecution.[1] The Federal Trade Commission looks for the following when investigating complaints:[2]

- What are the expressed or implied claims? What was said and what was not said?

- Are the claims material? That is, do they say something about the product's functions, features, performance, effectiveness, maker, price, or safety?

- Does the advertiser have evidence to support the claims?

- Could the ad as a whole mislead a consumer acting reasonably under the circumstances?

Note that claims such as "best in the world" or "the world's leader" are considered to be puffery (not false advertising) and that the average consumer is believed to process such claims with some degree of skepticism. False advertising claims can be brought before the following entities for resolution:[3]

- The organization against which the claim is made

- State or local consumer protection offices

- The National Advertising Division of the Better Business Bureau

- The Federal Trade Commission

- Industry self-regulating bodies

- Advertising regulatory bodies

Ethics in Marketing

Related to legal issues is the topic of ethics. Ethics is not a topic that I hear marketers talking about very often, but it is something that I think about frequently because I understand the societal impact of what I do. Marketers can often drive human desires and behaviors, getting people to buy things that they may or may not need, making them feel better or worse about themselves in the process.

So what are some of the ethical issues in marketing? First and foremost, we should not be using marketing to make a product that is clearly harmful more appealing to people—for instance, selling cigarettes by appealing to people at a deep emotional level. This can be achieved by linking the cigarette brand to independence, rebellion, good times, or coming into one's own power.

Next is getting people to buy stuff that they just don't need. How many toys does one child actually need? How many pairs of shoes are enough? Or how many homes are enough?

Then there is using fear to sell something. As we all know, fear works really well as a motivator; however, constantly using fear to market products and services only serves to create a more fearful society, where people are more motivated to avoid potential problems than to embrace that which is beneficial or uplifting.

Making false claims is both unethical and illegal. I am personally not as concerned about what is generally considered to be puffery; for instance, stating that one's brand is "the best in the world," because few people are going to take that statement at face value.

Certainly, an ethical dilemma that most marketing agencies face is whether to do a) what is in the client's best interest or b) what the client wants (if you know that what the client wants is not in its own best interest). In this situation, are you forthright with the client but then ultimately collect your fees for executing what the client desires, or do you walk away from the project or business if what you are being asked to do is not in the client's best interest? Is the client always right or is the client sometimes wrong?

How about getting someone to pay a huge price premium for a product because your brand bestows status on that product? Is this just helping people climb Maslow's hierarchy of needs, or is it getting them stuck on one step in that ladder (at a hefty profit to the brand)?

Knowing that brands can sometimes make people feel more appealing, loved, smart, accomplished, or valued, I want to scream to them, "You are already appealing, loved, smart, accomplished, and valued. You don't need a product or brand to be that."

There is also this question: Does the relentless pursuit of more and better products, services, and experiences lead to improved lives with more leisure time and a higher quality of life, or does it just constantly raise the bar for what will satisfy while depleting natural resources and placing more demands on people's lives?

How about those huge purchases that marketers can get people to make— for instance, luxury cars, luxury boats, fine art, and expensive wines? Some people can easily afford these things and very much appreciate even minutely incremental improvements in quality. Others, however, may be stretching their budgets to "keep up with the Joneses." This second group may experience immediate post-purchase remorse after such a large purchase. Is it ethical to market to these people based on aspiration?

And, related to that, if people experience buyer's remorse immediately after a purchase, is it a good thing or a bad thing to create a post-purchase touchpoint that relieves their anxiety and makes them feel better about the purchase?

And what about selling functional substance, a real solution to a problem, vs. good feelings? Many brands (and salespeople for that matter) are masterful at selling good feelings without really delivering much else. I often feel this way about motivational speakers. Is something tangible really more valuable than something completely intangible?

Is it better to market to and deliver on a need or a desire? Is one better than another? What if people desire something that is not good for them? Is that the marketer's problem? Is it another person's right to judge what is good or bad for you?

So how do I see that marketing can be truly helpful to organizations, brands, and their customers? First and foremost, brands can help organizations focus on how they can best add value in the market, especially in unique ways. A brand's unique value proposition can become the organization's internal rallying cry, energizing employees and mobilizing them to deliver on the brand's promise. Marketing can also highlight a particular brand's unique advantage over competing brands, helping consumers to make more informed decisions. If businesses include marketing research as a part of marketing (as well they should), there is a huge advantage to understanding what customers actually need and want so that the organization can deliver it to them. Identifying and determining the best ways to meet human needs is a noble endeavor

Use the checklist in Figure 20–1 to assess the efficacy of your brand management practices in the area covered by this chapter. The more questions to which you can answer "yes," the better you are doing. The checklist also provides a brief summary of the material covered in the chapter.

Figure 20–1. Checklist: Legal issues in brand management.

	YES / NO
Do you know that coined names and fanciful or arbitrary marks are the most protectable by law?	___ ___
Is your trademark distinctive?	___ ___
Have you completed a full trademark search for any new brand name you are considering using? Have you completed this search in all countries in which the brand might operate?	___ ___
Have you registered your trademark at a federal level and in all countries in which your brand will operate?	___ ___
Have you marketed your brand in all fifty states? (The first organization to use a particular name in a specific geographic area has "priority of use" protection in that area under common law.)	___ ___
Have you searched to ensure that the brand name you are considering is available as an Internet domain name? Have you registered that domain name? Have you registered typical variations of that domain name? Have you registered that domain name as ".com," .org," ".net," etc.?	___ ___
Do you know the difference between trademarks with a ™ and a ® symbol?	___ ___
Do you use the ™ and ® symbols when appropriate?	___ ___

Do you always use your brand name as an adjective (vs. as a noun)? If you are concerned that your brand name may become a category generic descriptor, are you using the following wording in all of your brand communication: "[brand name] brand [product category descriptor]"?   ___ ___

Do you design your brand's trade dress to have as many arbitrary design elements as possible so that you are more likely to win a trademark infringement legal battle with your competitors?   ___ ___

Does your brand identity system include as many elements as possible (beyond name and logo)? Examples are visual style, brand voice, colors, icons, typography, slogan, and mnemonic devices.   ___ ___

Do you retain experts to help you protect your brand mark online?   ___ ___

Did you know that trademark protection is enhanced through proper use and can be lost through improper use?   ___ ___

Did you know you can sue another company for using your brand's name or slogan in their site's meta tags?   ___ ___

Did you know that using another organization's well-known mark as a domain name is also illegal, even if used or associated with an unrelated product or service category?   ___ ___

Do you aggressively pursue those who are using your brand mark improperly or illegally?   ___ ___

Do you have a strong brand identity system and standards that are available to all employees and vendors? Have you trained all people who might use the trademark in its proper use?   ___ ___

Are you very careful about licensing your trademark? Do you have processes in place to monitor the licensees' use of your mark and to immediately stop (or correct) their use of your mark if they are using it improperly?   ___ ___

Are you very cautious about creating registered users of your mark internationally? (They will have rights to your mark forever, even after you have severed a business relationship with them.)   ___ ___

Are you also protecting your intellectual properties through patents, copyrights, and trade secrets?   ___ ___

Have you maintained thorough records of trademark development and use?   ___ ___

Have you kept your website's log files to validate that your brand has been operating in all fifty states and in many foreign countries? ___ ___

Did you know that people can legally use your brand mark if the following three conditions are met: 1) it is a necessary use, 2) the use is limiting, and 3) there was no consumer deception? For instance, a watch repairman that only repairs Timex watches can say in advertising copy (or on the side of his building) that "I repair Timex watches," even if he is not employed or licensed by Timex to do so. This, however, does not give him the right to use the Timex logo improperly. ___ ___

Did you know that under the Trademark Dilution Act of 1995, you can now stop others from using your trademark if it weakens, blurs, or tarnishes the mark? ___ ___

Did you know that you can take action against a competitor for false or misleading advertising claims? Do you know the process you must follow and what you must prove? ___ ___

Did you know that, as a manufacturer, you can lawfully set resale prices? Coach, the maker of luxury leather goods, is one company that does this. (While possible, this is a very complex area of law that should not be pursued without thoughtful legal advice.) ___ ___

Do you know a successful intellectual property attorney? Is that person available to help you with your legal issues? ___ ___

PART 7
Brand Management in Brief

21

common brand problems

AWARENESS OF THE problems and pitfalls that brands can encounter is an important step in maintaining a strong, healthy brand.

Problem 1. *The cumulative result of gradually and incrementally decreasing product or service quality to reduce costs*

    Analysis. There is the old story about each new brand manager of a coffee brand improving brand profitability and his or her promotion potential by slightly reducing the ratio of premium Brazilian coffee beans to the less expensive African beans. Each time, consumer research indicates no discernable difference in taste or preference, but one day the company discovers that its coffee brand share has significantly eroded. Brand quality erosion may not be discernable in the short term, but over time it will negatively affect a brand's market share. Focus cost-cutting on things that are truly invisible to your customers, and most important, *manage brands for the long term.*

Problem 2. *The cumulative effect of raising product or service prices at a rate greater than inflation over time (inviting low-end market segments and competitors)*

    Analysis. This is the other side of a brand's value equation: price. Consider what has happened in several industries in which companies have raised prices faster than inflation over time. Remember Marlboro's Black Friday? Would Malt-o-Meal exist if cereal companies had not raised their prices as much as they had? Would discount card stores like Factory Card

Outlet have grown from zero share of the greeting card market to over 20 percent within a few years if greeting card companies hadn't raised card prices to well over two or three dollars in the same time period? Online universities are burgeoning not only due to technology advances, but also the rate at which college tuition and fee increases had, until recently, exceeded inflation and financial aid. *Make sure your brand delivers a good value to the consumer.* Even if price sensitivity studies show that you can raise prices more, consider the long-term consequences. If you "push the envelope" on price, you will invite two outcomes: 1) consumers leaving your category and 2) new competition.

Problem 3. *Focusing on short-term profitability at the expense of long-term revenue growth*

Analysis. This may be the underlying cause of the previous two problems. This problem is driven by the organization's reward systems. If brand managers and general managers are compensated and promoted on delivering quarterly or annual financial results without a focus on longer-term business growth, this situation is sure to occur. This problem is most acute in publicly held companies that are pressured to deliver quarterly financial results. The solution is to *create a balanced scorecard that integrates growth objectives into common and individual performance measures.*

Problem 4. *Reducing or eliminating brand advertising*

Analysis. When it is time to "tighten the organizational belt," advertising is always a likely source of savings. The budget is usually big enough to contribute significantly to cost savings, and it is often difficult to tell advertising's return on investment. Finally, even if there is an ill effect, the brand won't immediately suffer from an equity withdrawal (or so goes the all-too-common logic). But, actually, studies have shown there is a positive correlation between advertising spending and revenues, earnings, market share, and stock price. Tod Johnson of the NPD Group (which has studied customer purchase behavior since 1978) indicates that a decline in brand loyalty has two causes. One is erratic advertising, or advertising that does not keep pace with the competition. The other is cannibalization caused by brand extensions.[1] Set specific objectives for your advertising and track results against those objectives. Copy test all of your ads to make sure they are effective. And, finally, constantly and vigilantly sell the importance of advertising to key internal decision makers.

Problem 5. *Applying branding and marketing decisions at the end of the product development process ("Now, what will we name this?") vs. including brand management and marketing at the front end of product development activities*

Analysis. You are probably working for a manufacturing company that really doesn't understand brand management and marketing. The company designs, manufactures, and sells products and services. It doesn't market brands, or if it does, the company leaves that function to the advertising or communications department or to the advertising agency. A brand is a source of a promise to the consumer. Everything a company does should support that promise. *Start with the target consumer and the brand design (essence, promise, archetype, and personality) and then decide what the products and services will be.* Design a marketing function or process that identifies and evaluates product concepts against customer needs and competitive alternatives prior to product development.

Problem 6. *Defining your brand too narrowly, especially as a product category (e.g., "greeting cards" vs. "caring shared")*

Analysis. One of the key advantages of a strong brand is its ability to be extended into new product and service categories. It is a growth engine for your organization. It helps you transcend specific product categories and formats that may become obsolete. *Define your brand's essence and promise in terms of what key benefits your brand delivers to consumers (independent of the specific product or service).* Then continue to find new ways to deliver against that essence and promise. GE successfully broadened its frame of reference by moving from "General Electric: Better living through electricity" to "GE: We brings good things to life" and most recently to "GE: Imagination at Work."

One of my most important successes as the "brand guy" at Hallmark was changing our leaders' perceptions of Hallmark from a greeting card company/brand to a "caring shared" company/brand. This change in perception paved the way for us to launch gift candy, flowers, and other products to sustain our growth into the next decade. I did not want to see us make the same mistake that Smith-Corona made (defining itself in terms of its product, typewriters, vs. a consumer benefit, word processing).

Problem 7. *Failure to extend the brand into new product categories when the core category is in decline*

Analysis. "It is our core category. It is our cash cow. We must focus all of our resources on preserving it." Sound familiar? It is one thing to prematurely walk away from your core category. It is yet another to myopically focus all of your organizational resources on a flat or declining category in the misguided hope that you may be able to revive it, especially if you are not trying to radically redefine or reengineer it. Try and try again, but also *know when it is time to "quit"* (that is, when it is time to do no more than maintain and "milk" the core category and reinvest the profits in new, more promising ventures). Often, realistic financial projections are the best wake-up call in these situations.

ONE REASON GREAT BRANDS GET OFF TRACK

It has been my experience that brand decline often stems from the "change of guard" at the top the brand's organization. I have witnessed this firsthand more than once (and have heard many other stories of it from friends that have led other brands). The original top manager knew what the brand stood for "in his gut," perhaps because he was the organization's founder with the original vision or perhaps because he was a visionary leader by nature. Then someone else took over the helm (to mix metaphors), someone with little vision. Perhaps someone who only understands business models or numbers or operational excellence, but not the brand's customers and not the brand's essence and key point(s) of difference. Costs are cut in "unnecessary" areas of employee and customer satisfaction. Actions that preserve the "soft stuff" (such as corporate culture, brand vitality, emotional connection, "unnecessary" services, relationship building "gestures," and experiential elements) are eliminated in the name of efficiency and cost-effectiveness. How does one get through to individuals who only see the world as cash flow, balance sheets, and income statements? Who can only think linearly? Who do not seem to exercise their "right brains" and who are only interested in their own personal power and wealth? Who are unable to empathize with their employees or their customers? Who do not seem to be in touch with their own "souls"? Strong, intuitive, visionary, service-based leadership seems to lie at the core of strong brands.

Problem 8. *Overextending your brand into different categories and markets so as to completely blur the brand's meaning and points of distinction*

    Analysis. You can always make more money in the short term by licensing your brand out for use on a variety of products or by extending your brand into a myriad of new categories. The long-term effect, however, is detrimental. People no longer will be able to tell what your brand stands for. It will lose its meaning and its point of difference. *Extend your brand based on a clear understanding of its essence, promise, archetype, and personality.* And make sure your consumers "get it."

Problem 9. *Frequently changing your brand's positioning and message*

Analysis. New brand managers and marketing executives often feel as though they need to make a name for themselves to continue the climb up the corporate ladder. Don't succumb to this temptation by changing the advertising campaign or the brand slogan, especially if the current ones are working well or haven't been in place long enough for you to assess their effectiveness. *Consistent communication over time is what builds a brand.* After all, Hallmark has used its "When You Care Enough to Send the Very Best" slogan since 1944; the Marlboro Man has been Marlboro's icon since 1955; Absolut Vodka has featured its bottle's shape in consumer communication since 1978. Since 1921, General Mills has used Betty Crocker as its face to the public. Her portait has changed in subltle ways eight times since then. If you do make changes, make them gradually in an integrated fashion, based on sound consumer research.

Problem 10. *Creating brands or subbrands for internal or trade reasons, rather than to address distinct consumer needs*

Analysis. There is nothing more inefficient or wasteful than creating a new brand or subbrand for a purpose other than meeting a different consumer need. *Brands and subbrands exist to address different consumers and consumer-need segments.* It is expensive to launch a new brand (and very expensive to maintain multiple brands that meet similar consumer needs; it also adds unnecessary complexity to your organization). Worst of all, it dilutes the position of your original brand. This problem often results from egos and organization structure. People head up divisions or business units that deliver specific products or services. They create a name and identity to put on business cards and to rally their employees around, without considering whether the products or services are similar to products or services other divisions create. (This tendency has resulted in Hewlett-Packard having multiple printer lines: DeskJet, OfficeJet, OfficeJet Pro, LaserJet, DesignJet, DeskWriter, and PhotoSmart. It is unlikely that consumers understand many of these distinctions. They are likely to think of them all as HP printers.)

Sometimes, companies create separate brands or subbrands for trade reasons—for instance, to offer something different for specialty stores vs. mass channels of distribution. (Hallmark created the Expressions from Hallmark brand to offer mass channel stores while specialty stores continued to carry the Hallmark brand. These two brands don't meet different consumer needs, and I'm not sure consumers perceive differences between the two.) This problem can also result from mergers and acquisitions in which the brands are neither rationalized nor strategically managed after the enterprises are combined.

Problem 11. *Launching subbrands that inadvertently reposition the parent brand in a negative light*

    Analysis. What does Miller Lite say about Miller High Life? What do Bayer aspirin-free products say about Bayer aspirin? What do Fat-Free Fig Newtons say about Fig Newtons? *Make sure you know what you are doing when you create a new subbrand;* be sure to test its impact on the parent brand.

Problem 12. *Well-known, high-profile brands are often targeted by special interest groups who want to make public statements about their causes*

    Analysis. High-profile brands are prone to being knocked off their pedestals by environmental, human rights, and equal rights activists and other groups that are anti–big business. Nike, Wal-Mart, McDonald's, as well as the Boy Scouts of America have all struggled with this issue. Nike has had to deal with opposition to its campus sponsorships and concerns about its alleged use of third-world "sweatshops." Wal-Mart is seen as all-powerful, and is often accused of putting long-standing local mom-and-pop stores out of business through monopolistic practices. People are concerned about Wal-Mart's alleged use of third-world "sweatshops," too. McDonald's faced a number of revelations from the book *Fast Food Nation: The Dark Side of the All-American Meal*, and the high-profile documentary *Supersize Me.* The Boy Scouts of America is a target because of its squeaky-clean, wholesome image, and its incresingly highlighted position on homosexuality.

    Lessons: If your brand is well known, (a) identify possible exposures (through internal muckraking) and rectify them, and (b) develop public relations and crisis management plans to address the exposures.

Problem 13. *Treating brand management primarily as "logo cops"*

    Analysis. Often the current power structure within an organization will try to put a new brand management function in this box, either out of ignorance or as a way to minimize or negate a power shift. As I hope you have discovered by now, the brand management function has responsibilities far beyond brand identity management. It is multifaceted, affecting all of marketing and much of the rest of the enterprise. For this reason, *make sure that the brand management function exists at a high level in the organization structure.* It is also important that the organization's senior executives understand and support this scope of responsibility.

Problem 14. *Viewing brand equity management as a communications exercise, but ignoring it in other business processes and points of contact with the consumer*

Analysis. Too often, organizations relegate brand management to a specific department (e.g., advertising, marketing) or agency. Brand management is an organization-wide process, especially when the brand is a corporate brand. The brand promise must be delivered at each point of contact with the consumer, including customer service lines and retail sales associates. *For the brand promise to be clear to your consumers, it must be well understood by everyone in your organization, from the CEO to the receptionist.* It must be manifest not only in consumer communication, but also when and wherever the brand name and logo are used. Increasingly, organizations are designing the total enterprise in support of the brand promise, including putting mechanisms in place to develop a brand building culture.

DID YOU KNOW?

In his white paper, "Communication as Value Builder," Dr. David Jensen, senior vice president with Ketchum in Atlanta, cites a study by the Wirthlin Group, which concludes that companies with good reputations are:

- *7 times more likely to command premium prices for their products and services*
- *5 times more likely to have their stock recommended*
- *4 times more likely to be recommended as a good place to work*
- *3 times more likely to be recommended as a joint venture partner*
- *1.5 times more likely to receive the benefit of the doubt*

Problem 15. *Not delivering against the communicated brand promise*

Analysis. Again, this is a symptom of viewing brand management as a communications exercise. A 1997 advertising campaign, "United Airlines Rising," backfired on the company. While the airline was trying to communicate that its service was rising to meet consumers' expectations, the flight attendants were involved in a labor dispute and threatening CHAOS

(Creating Havoc Around Our System). The customer relations department was so unresponsive to complaints that it prompted a disgruntled customer to create the website www.untied.com, featuring complaints from United Airlines passengers.

The lesson here: *The communicated promise must be delivered in product, service, and the total customer experience.* Internal brand strategy education and communication may be necessary to ensure that all employees are helping the brand deliver its promise. Tying employee compensation to delivery against the brand promise also will help ensure the promise is delivered.

Problem 16. *Not linking brand planning to the business's strategic planning process*

Analysis. A brand plan is useless if it is not an integral part of the organization's business planning process. And if you aspire to be a market-driven organization, the brand plan should drive or at least provide signifiant input to the business planning process. *Redesign your processes to ensure the two are integrally linked.*

Problem 17. *Licensing the brand name out to whomever will pay for it*

Analysis. Although licensing will generate additional revenues and profits in the short term, it is an unwise practice in the long term. You should use brand licensing to:

- Extend the brand into new categories
- Expand the meaning of the brand
- Reinforce key brand associations
- Build your brand as a badge
- Bring your brand to life in new ways

Lesson: Avoid licensing your brand just for short-term gain where it doesn't make sense. *Where the licensing department resides in your organization and what its objectives are will have a large impact on how well licensing is used to build (vs. bleed) the brand.*

Problem 18. *Trying to be the best at something, especially core category benefits, rather than owning something different*

Analysis. Being the best is not a point of difference if being good is "good enough" for consumers. In industries that have focused on customer satisfaction (such as the automobile industry), standards have risen to the point where all options satisfactorily meet customer needs. In those industries, brands must find new points of difference if they are to maintain consumer loyalty. To truly succeed, *brands need to be unique in highly relevant and compelling ways.*

Problem 19. *Trying to own what have become cost-of-entry benefits—and not owning any differentiating benefits*

Analysis. It is not sufficient to claim leadership of a benefit that consumers expect of all brands in the category. For example, an airline can't win in the marketplace by trying to own "safety." A very high level of safety is a given in that industry. An airline might win, however, by exclusively guaranteeing on-time departures and arrivals (if that were possible) or by offering first-class service throughout the plane.

Interestingly, from airline industry laddering studies, we find that consumers want a few key things from airlines: safety, the desired routing, desired departure and arrival times, and, given these things, the lowest price. It is not surprising that most airlines serve only peanuts, pretzels, or other snacks (and are largely undifferentiated in any substantive ways), but a few highly successful airlines have emerged based on further differentiation: Southwest Airlines (offering an inexpensive but highly reliable trip with a casual, fun atmosphere) and JetBlue (featuring a fleet of brand-new planes with roomy leather seats and free individual television viewing—twenty-four channels—at each seat). Brands must promise and deliver on unique value propositions.

Problem 20. *Focusing too much on product attributes and not enough on brand benefits in consumer communication*

Analysis. You will have to *decide the right combination of attributes, benefits, consequences, and basic human values your brand claims to possess or address.* Typically, the farther up the need hierarchy your brand climbs, the more emotionally compelling it is to customers and the more difficult it is for competitors to make similar claims (or to emulate what your brand delivers).

Problem 21. *Trying to make too many points in your brand communication rather than focusing on the one or two most compelling points of difference*

Analysis. Regarding brand communication: More is not better. *The effectiveness of brand communication diminishes in direct proportion to the number of points you attempt to make in your communication.* I see this problem most often in companies with a very junior marketing staff or in companies where marketing is practiced by nonmarketers (e.g., engineers, doctors, lawyers). Ask these two questions of each marketing piece you produce:

1. Does it quickly and clearly communicate the most compelling reasons to choose our brand over the competitive alternatives?

2. Is it convincing?

Problem 22. *Following challengers because it's easier and produces more immediate results, rather than creating new ways to meet consumer needs*
  Analysis. If you are the market leader, this is an easy trap to fall into. If you are ahead, just match the competition to stay ahead—that way they can never catch up. That is a fairly common sailboat-racing tactic. The problem with this strategy is that you begin to play by your competitor's rules. *It is easier to win at your own game than at someone else's.* It may be a more natural reaction to match competitive moves, but as you are doing that, you are distracted from doing what you do best—playing your own game. And, remember, other competitors that *are* playing by different rules may not be far behind.

Problem 23. *Not applying the latest product and service innovations to your flagship brand because it is getting too old and stodgy (a self-fulfilling prophecy)*
  Analysis. It is a tragedy to walk away from a brand you have invested in— and that might be an investment of millions of dollars, over time. *It is better to reposition, revitalize, and extend an aging brand than to ignore it.* You should carefully monitor consumer opinion to ensure the brand is perceived as relevant and vital. Also, track the brand's consumers to make sure they are not a shrinking or aging group. Often, new subbrands can make the parent brand more relevant to new consumer segments.

Problem 24. *No central control of the brand portfolio (so that each brand team is free to apply the best differentiating features of one brand to each of the others in the portfolio)*
  Analysis. Certain attributes, features, and benefits should be off-limits to certain brands within your portfolio. When the business is organized and run by product category or channel of trade (as opposed to brand), there is more pressure to apply the best ideas to all brands regardless of each brand's positioning or intended point of difference. If the business is organized by brand and most people understand brand concepts, this is less likely to happen.

P&G might offer several different brands of detergent, but each has a distinct point of difference. One might make clothes whiter, one might work best in cold water, one might take out tough stains, one might be gentle on the clothes, yet another might be hypoallergenic, etc. Since P&G manages by brand, the company really understands that points of difference are central to a brand's success, whereas somewhere else (for example, in a company organized around product development or run by engineers), people might feel more pressured to add the best features they come up with to all their products.

A highly placed brand management group or council should have the authority to ensure that brand teams, product development teams, business units, divisions, and subsidiaries don't blur the lines between your organization's brands. *This council should guard against a "silo" or short-term approach to the business.*

Problem 25. *No brand identity system and standards*

Analysis. A brand should be presented consistently across all applications: name, logo, personality, visual style, icons, etc. *Ensure consistency with a comprehensive brand identity system and standards that are well understood and easy to use.* Standards manuals are a minimum requirement. With today's digital technology, consider using an intranet or cloud-based site with a downloadable manual as a PDF file. Think of your brand as a person. Does it present itself consistently in all situations or does it seem to have "multiple personalities"?

Problem 26. *Defining your target consumer too broadly (for instance, women age 18 to 65)*

Analysis. By definition, a brand cannot be all things to all people. A brand promises relevant differentiated benefits to a *target* consumer. Increasingly, companies are focusing on brand usage over penetration. That is, they are getting a larger portion of a smaller group's business by offering more products and services that deliver against the brand promise. This helps to build loyalty, but in lieu of trying to attract additional consumers to the brand. It is a well-known fact that it costs seven times more to gain a new consumer that it does to get a current consumer to make an incremental purchase. *Corporate parent brands can achieve increased targeting through well-targeted subbrands.*

Problem 27. *Not really understanding consumer needs and motivations*

Analysis. This is the "kiss of death" for a brand. A brand only exists to uniquely meet consumer needs. An important part of any business is being able to *stay in touch with consumers, to understand what they need and why they are buying the business's products and services.* Your research should include ongoing market research (of consumers and competitors) and ongoing brand equity monitoring. In-depth qualitative research will give you a better understanding of consumer needs and motivations. Use ethnography (putting yourself in consumers' shoes by observing their brand shopping and usage patterns in real-life situations) and projective techniques ("If the brand were an animal/car/person, what animal/car/person would it be?"), among other types of research. Very successful companies, such as Harley-Davidson, experience the brand right along with their consumers.

THE COCA-COLA COMPANY:
Creating the Total Brand Experience Through Customer Participation

According to Katherine Stone, during her tenure as director of experiential marketing at Coca-Cola, the company's then chairman and CEO, Douglas Daft, had established a goal for the Coca-Cola Company: "to become the world's premier relationship company." According to Stone (who spoke at the Brand Masters conference in Coconut Grove, Florida, on December 13, 2002), "Coca-Cola intends to deliver richly textured, deeply resonating consumer brand experiences." More specifically, Coca-Cola intended to integrate the following into its brand experiences:

- *Meaning—memorable connections to consumers' lives*
- *Participation/control—the consumer is respected*
- *Adaptability—customization*
- *Identity—self-expression*
- *Immersion/sensory experience*
- *Distinction—different, better, special*

As one of its first proof points, Coca-Cola tested its new Shrink Tank. The Shrink Tank allows consumers to apply their own customized labels to Coca-Cola bottles at the point of purchase. The customized labels primarily feature affinity designs, such as local sports team logos. The Shrink Tank resulted in a 375 percent dollar volume increase in Malaysia (vs. control stores) and a 900 percent increase in Singapore.

Problem 28. *Unsuccessfully extending the brand up to a premium segment or down to a value segment*

Analysis. While some companies have successfully used brand extension to grow (for example, Honda slowly extended from lawn-mower engines to

Honda Accords, while creating the Acura brand for its highest-end cars), it can be very tricky to execute successfully. *Know what impact price segment extensions will have on your core brand.* Conduct extensive consumer research before and throughout the process. There are many subbrand and message subtleties that may be required to support such a move. Price affects quality perceptions and is an important brand positioning cue.

Problem 29. *Choosing generic (nonproprietary) brand names*

Analysis. Although it might be tempting to choose a name that describes your product or service, it's a mistake. The name can soon become confused with that of every other brand that takes a similar approach, or, worse yet, it can link the brand to an outdated product or technology. Consider brands with "sys" or "tech" in their names. Is it easy to tell them apart? In retrospect, how about the wisdom of the "Cellular One" name now that PCS and other technologies have emerged? *Own a name that is suggestive of a timeless consumer benefit or one that is "coined" and whose meaning you can define through consumer communication.* An example of the first approach is DieHard (for long-lasting batteries); examples of coined names are Kodak or Xerox.

Problem 30. *Not keeping up with the industry on product or service innovation*

Analysis. The marketplace is too competitive for you not to constantly reinvent your business. *No matter how much of a market share advantage or leadership legacy you have, you should not rest on your laurels.* Maintain a large pool of resources to invest in new ideas. Award the resources based on projected incremental sales and return on investment. Even pursue new business approaches that could make your current core business obsolete. If you don't, someone else will. Think about the impact of digital photography (invented at Kodak) and smartphones on Kodak's chemical-based photography business. Consider Encyclopedia Britannica's entry into interactive software (which sells for a fraction of the cost of its traditional hardcover bound volumes, whose final edition was published in 2010).

Problem 31. *Spending too much money on trade deals and sales promotion at the expense of brand building*

Analysis. Brands shift some leverage back to the manufacturer from the retailer. (This is one relationship the manufacturer can own with the consumer.) Brands also combat category commoditization and the resulting downward pressure on price. Is your sales organization bigger and more powerful than your brand management and marketing organization? Do you know how much you are spending on trade deals and price promotions? Is it more than you are spending on brand building? *It is difficult, but essential, to move from a sales "push" to a marketing "pull" organization if you are to maintain a competitive differential and a price premium.*

Problem 32. *A lack of internal mindshare, supervision, and management for the brand when no person or department has responsibility for it*

Analysis. After having read this book, you should know that *the complexity of the brand management task makes it very difficult to develop a powerful brand in the absence of a brand management mindset and function.* Fortunately, fewer and fewer organizations experience this problem these days. At a minimum, most companies have assigned a brand manager or a brand management department.

Problem 33. *Allowing decisions that adversely affect the brand to be made outside of the brand management context*

Analysis. When making decisions—decisions that may range from mergers and acquisitions, product extensions, and cost-cutting to outsourcing critical customer services, producing private label products to fill production capacity, and offering price discounts to meet quarterly revenue goals— *always consider the decision's impact on the brand.* Corporate executives, general managers, engineers, production managers, salespeople, and others frequently don't consider the impact on brand strategy or equity in such decision making. This highlights the importance of the CEO assuming the role of chief brand champion. It also underlines the importance of having a strong brand management function and creating a brand building organization.

Problem 34. *Senior managers who do not understand what the brand stands for*

Analysis. This could well be the most pervasive and detrimental problem of all. The consumer will never be able to understand what the brand stands for, and what its points of difference are, if your management team doesn't. It would behoove you to gain the CEO's support to involve the management team in a process of defining what the brand stands for, including its target consumer, essence, promise, personality, and marketplace positioning. A particularly important part of that exercise is to gain insight and consensus on the brand's most compelling point of difference. *Managing the transformation of your entire management team into well-informed brand champions may be difficult, but the investment of time and effort will be well worth it.*

Problem 35. *Quarter-over-quarter revenue and profit pressures that gradually cause the brand to become overextended*

Analysis. Constant pressures from Wall Street to increase revenues and profits cause a myriad of problems (see also problems 1, 2, 3, 4, 8, 17, and 31). One of the biggest problems is putting pressure on the brand to extend into more and more market segments in order to broaden its appeal and to provide additional revenue growth. This eventually comes at the expense of the meaning of the brand itself. Witness Volvo. It had a very clear point of difference—family safety—until it created the 850 GLT, which was intended to extend the brand into younger and older markets where the car buyers are childless. Volvo promoted this car as a fun car to drive—not necessarily a safe car for the family. From that point on, Volvo's success has been underwhelming. (See the Volvo case study in Chapter 6.) The degree to which Volvo is successful with vehicles that do not reinforce its safety message is the degree to which its primary point of difference in the marketplace becomes diluted. *If a company must grow to keep Wall Street happy (as all public companies must do), then it should carefully consider its approach.* One of two approaches is recommended:

1. Introduce *new* products and services that deliver against the brand's essence and promise (a family-safe ride in Volvo's case).

2. Bite the marketing bullet and launch new brands.

22

keys to success in brand
building: a summary

BRANDING IS THE concept of imbuing organizations and their products and services with human qualities and identities so that they can stand for something, share values with their customers, make promises to their customers, create emotional bonds with their customers, and generally add value beyond the product or service itself.

After having spent thirty years as a marketer and having helped more than 150 brands craft their strategies, here is what I have come to understand creates strong brands:

1. First and foremost, *the brand must stand for something*. Its mission, vision, and values must be clearly articulated. Furthermore, its promise must have been crafted with much forethought. And the promise must be relevant, compelling, and unique. That is, the brand must offer and deliver on a "unique value proposition" that matters to its target markets.

2. To support this value proposition, *the brand must know whom it is serving*. It must know this customer in great depth. What motivates that person? What are the customer's hopes and fears? What are his attitudes? What does she value? How does the person purchase and use the products and services in the categories within which the brand operates? This requires in-depth research and strong intuition about human behavior and motivation.

3. Next, *the brand's identity must **consistently** support its value proposition*—that is, its intended essence, archetype, personality, mission, vision,

values, and promise. The brand identity refers to the name, logo, colors, tagline, brand voice, and visual style, and other visual, auditory, kinesthetic, olfactory, and gustatory cues associated with the brand.

4. *Aesthetics* matter more than most people realize. Establishing a refined or otherwise compelling brand design aesthetic will have a positive impact on the brand. Witness Apple, Jaguar, and Tỷ Nant.

5. One should put adequate controls in place to ensure this *brand identity consistency* over time and across all customer touchpoints.

6. Brands that have strongly held *values that align with their customer's values* create strong emotional connections with their customers.

7. Furthermore, those brands can become the *source of community* for people who share their values.

8. And they *can serve as a "badge" for people* to signal to the world who they are (or who they want to be) and what they value (self-expressive benefits).

9. These types of brands *have ongoing dialogues with their customers* and engage their customers in a myriad of other ways.

10. One of the ways in which brands engage their customers is by continuously *cocreating* themselves and their products and services *with their customers.*

DID YOU KNOW?

● *Generating brand trial is frequently the focus of smaller brands while large brands tend to focus on maintaining (and building) brand loyalty.*
(Source: Allan L. Baldinger and Joel Robinson, "Brand Loyalty: The Link Between Attitude and Behavior," The NPD Group.)

● *For a new brand, it is important to track the number of stores deciding to sell the product, while for a mature brand, it is more important to look at the number of stores delisting the product.*
(Source: Lars Finskud, "Bringing Discipline to Brand Value Management," Financial Times Retail & Consumer Publishing, Brand Valuations, 1998.)

● *"For a fast-growing brand, the number of new loyal customers is important, but for an established brand it is the number of lost loyal customers that is the telling indicator."*
(Source: Finskud, "Bringing Discipline to Brand Value Management.")

> • *In a major brand loyalty study, the researchers found that two-thirds of the time, when people who were more attitudinally loyal than behaviorally loyal to the brand ("prospects") outnumbered those who were less attitudinally loyal than behaviorally loyal to the brand ("vulnerables"), the brand's market share increased. Market share decreased when the opposite was true. That is why it is important to measure both attitudinal and behavioral loyalty.*
> *(Source: Baldinger and Robinson, "Brand Loyalty," http://www.npd.com/corp/newsletters/product_brandbbldrjar.htm.)*

11. *Storytelling is central to brand building.* Tell stories about the brand's heritage and history and founder. Tell stories about heroic or admirable acts performed by the brand. Tell stories about the brand's legendary service.

12. Whether the CEO, president, executive director, director general, or managing partner, *the brand's leader must understand the importance of building a strong brand* and must share the brand's beliefs and values.

13. *The brand's leader must drive brand understanding and support throughout the organization,* by working with HR, communications, and other functions, and by transforming the organization's employees into brand champions and evangelists.

14. This effort may include *redesigning the organization* structure, recruiting criteria, common measures, rewards and recognition, and even internal systems and processes.

15. *Customer touchpoint design* (delivering on the brand promise at each point of customer contact) can be a starting point for this redesign.

> **ON RELATIONSHIPS**
>
> *People develop relationships with other people. Brands exist so that organizations can do the same. So, what maximizes a brand's appeal? The same things that maximize a person's appeal—authenticity, honesty, integrity (that is, a congruence between thoughts, words, and deeds), charisma, warmth, assertiveness, approachability, passion, reliability, and originality. And here is the thing that makes people and brands the most interesting: Each possesses a different combination of qualities that appeals to different people at different times.*
>
> *The best brands will challenge and comfort and inspire and draw out one's best and help one grow, just as the best human relationships do.*

> *Branding, at its best, transforms organizations so that they are capable of creating, nurturing, and sustaining mutually profitable relationships with people. And that is a very good thing.*

16. Anything you can do to *make your brand more authentic, trustworthy, reliable, likable, and admirable* will strengthen its emotional connection to its customers.

17. *Linking the brand to noble qualities*—"truth, justice, and the American Way," compassion, grace, beauty, freedom, and the like—will enhance people's emotional connection to the brand.

18. *Linking the brand to cultural icons, symbols, and other references* can also enhance people's emotional connection to the brand.

19. It is important that a brand makes a unique and compelling promise, but it is *more important that it keeps that promise.*

THE QUICK BRAND HEALTH ASSESSMENT
You know your brand is winning in the marketplace when:
- *The brand is mentioned to customers and potential customers, and they brim with enthusiasm in their response.*
- *Your brand' s external messages "ring true" with all employees.*
- *Employees are enthusiastic and consistent in recounting what makes their brand special.*
- *The brand's market share is increasing.*
- *Competitors always mention your brand as a point of reference.*
- *The press can't seem to write enough about your brand.*
- *Your CEO has a strong vision for the organization and its brand and talks more about the vision than financial targets.*
- *Your organization's leaders always seem to "talk the brand" and "walk the brand talk."*

---

20. *Anticipating customer needs* (e.g., smartphones), *innovating* products and services (e.g., Amazon.com, Toyota Prius, Tesla Motors), and providing *outstanding customer* service (e.g., Zappos, Nordstrom) all lead to strong brands.

21. Brands that *help people solve their problems* create stronger customer loyalty.

THE FUTURE OF BRAND MANAGEMENT: MY PROGNOSTICATIONS

- *Building emotional connection will be key.*
- *Brands will focus more on creating/engineering the total customer experience.*
- *Customer-relevant innovation will be a key success factor.*
- *Outstanding customer service will also be a key success factor.*
- *Hiring the right employees and creating the appropriate culture will be essential.*
- *More and more, brands will cocreate the customer experience with the customer.*
- *More and more, brands will need to "stand for something" to survive.*
- *Strong brands will not only "stand for something." They will also provide forums for people who believe in what the brands stand for.*
- *Organizations whose employees become consultants to and friends and partners with their customers will be the most successful.*
- *One-on-one marketing will become more and more important.*
- *The Internet will also become increasingly important as a brand building vehicle.*
- *For larger organizations, customer relationship management (CRM) will become a critical success factor.*
- *Fast, flexible, and agile organizations will increasingly "win" in the digital age.*
- *With the explosion of virtual and morphing organizations and ever-changing business alliances, the brand essence and promise and the organizational culture and values may increasingly be the only elements that create a sense of "entity" for organizations.*
- *The viral spread of information will increasingly expose organizations for what they really are—therefore integrity and consistency will be key.*
- *Managing "buzz" will be an essential brand management activity.*
- *"High tech" and "high touch" will both become increasingly important.*

Waning Philosophical— Brand Management at Its Best

At its worst, the organizational brand is a name and a logo that is inconsistently applied to an unrelated set of products and services. It is overused and means nothing, and it reminds people of the worst of an overly commercial and consumptive society. It feels cold and seems exploitative. It is perceived to be a vestige of a past era.

At its best, brand management aligns organizations with value-adding activities. It keeps organizations focused on meeting real human needs in compelling new ways. And, at its best, the organizational brand defines how the organization best meets its customers' needs in unique and compelling ways. It serves as the organization's unifying principle and rallying cry, it infuses the organization with a set of values and a personality, and it holds an organization's employees to a consistent set of behaviors. The organizational brand stands for something. It establishes trust and a certain level of assurance, it makes it possible for people to establish relationships with the organization, and it creates expectations that must be fulfilled. The brand can bring an organization to life in a very real way. Other specific benefits of a strong brand are shown in Figure 22–1.

Figure 22–1. The benefits of building a strong brand.

Brand Equity Drivers

- Awareness
- Relevant Differentiation
- Value
- Accessibility
- Emotional Connection

Business Results

- Decreased price sensitivity
- Increased customer loyalty
- Increased bargaining power with business partners
- Independence from a particular product category
- Increased flexibility for future growth
- Increased ability to hire and retain talented employees
- Increased ability to focus the organization's activities and resources
- Increased market share
- Increased stock price
- Increased shareholder value

In the end, brand management is all about meeting people's physical, emotional, spiritual, intellectual, and other needs in unique ways. It is the application of free enterprise to the timely and timeless needs of mankind.

I wish you a brand at its best. May you unleash your brand's power and transform your organization through branding.

APPENDIX A
Brand Audits

A brand audit provides an analysis of an organization's brand and its brand management and marketing effectiveness. It assesses a brand's strengths, weaknesses, opportunities, and threats. It identifies brand growth opportunities, including those achieved by brand repositioning and brand extension. The audit should result in recommendations to improve brand equity, brand positioning, and brand management and marketing effectiveness.

Brand Audit Components

The following are typical components of a brand audit:

- *Strategy Review:*
  - Business plans
  - Marketing plans
  - Brand positioning statement
  - Brand plans
  - Creative (or agency) briefs
  - Media plans

- *Marketing Research Review:*
  - Brand positioning research
  - Brand asset studies
  - Brand equity measurement system (to gauge awareness, preference, usage, value, accessibility, relevance, differentiation, vitality, emotional connection, loyalty, associations, personality)
  - Brand extension research
  - Product/service concept testing
  - Logo recall and recognition testing

- *Communications Review:*
  - Advertising and promotion materials

- Other brand marketing elements, including pricing, packaging, merchandising, distribution, direct marketing, sponsorships, and flagship stores
- Press kit
- Press releases
- Sales collateral materials
- Internal communications
- Business cards and letterheads
- Website
- Intranet site
- Other online presence
- Employee training programs
- Employee orientation
- Manager training
- Sales force training

● *External Information Source Review:*
  - Competitors' press releases, advertising, and promotion
  - Industry analyst reports
  - Customer comments
  - Business partner comments
  - Marketing vendor interviews

● *Employee Interviews:*
  - Corporate officer interviews
  - Marketing employee interviews
  - Sales force interviews
  - Customer service employee interviews
  - Frontline customer contact interviews
  - General employee interviews

● *Human Resource Systems Review:*
  - Organization charts
  - Department mission/vision statements
  - Department objectives
  - Common objectives
  - Recruiting criteria
  - Individual competency dictionary
  - Succession planning criteria
  - Planning and resource allocation systems/processes

- *Proprietary Brand Research* (conducted by the company performing the brand audit, if required):
  - Brand asset research
  - Brand equity research
  - Brand positioning research (qualitative and quantitative)

Brand Management Audit

A qualified brand audit company will investigate the following areas of brand management:

- *Brand Research:*
  - Does this company have a deep understanding of its consumers' values, attitudes, needs, desires, hopes, aspirations, fears, and concerns?
  - Has this company rigorously analyzed its competition?
  - Which of the following types of brand research has the company conducted: qualitative and quantitative brand positioning, brand asset studies, brand equity measurement and monitoring, brand extension, logo recall and recognition?
  - How robust is each of these research studies?
  - How are the company and each of its competitors positioned in the marketplace?

- *Brand Strategy:*
  - Is there a marketing plan?
  - Is there a brand plan?
  - Are those plans aligned with and integrated into company business plans?
  - Does the company have a future vision and a well-thought-out plan to get there?
  - Is it clear which marketing objectives, actions, and vehicles will provide the greatest leverage in achieving the long-term vision?

- *Brand Positioning:*
  - Is there a brand positioning statement? Does it include the target consumer, differentiating brand benefit, brand essence, brand archetype, and brand personality?
  - Do most employees know the brand's positioning (verbatim or paraphrased)?

- Was the brand's key differentiating benefit based on an analysis of consumer needs, organizational strengths (core competencies), and competitive weaknesses?
- Does the brand own a benefit that is highly differentiated, compelling, and believable?
- What are the brand's strengths, weaknesses, opportunities, and threats?

● *Brand Identity System and Standards:*
- How robust is the company's brand identity system?
- How easy is it for the company's employees and business partners to use?
- What brand identity controls does the company have in place?
- Is the company's brand architecture simple and understandable?
- Which of the following brand identity components does the company use in its system: name, logo, icon, tagline, typestyle, colors, shapes, symbols, visual style, mnemonic (sound) device, brand voice, music, animation?
- Does the company have cobranding standards?
- How accurately and consistently have these standards been applied across all internal and external communications?
- Does the brand's website accurately reflect its architecture?

● *Brand Advertising:*
- Do the ads break through the marketplace clutter?
- Do they powerfully communicate the brand's promise and personality?
- Do they include the "reasons why" (differentiating benefit proof points)?
- Do they connect with the target consumer on an emotional level?
- Do they tap into the consumers' beliefs, values, aspirations, hopes, and fears?
- Do they include components that are "ownable"?

● *Organization Design and Internal Brand Building:*
- Is the company market-driven or does it have a traditional manufacturing company design?
- Does the company's culture support the brand's essence, promise, and personality?
- Is the company's marketing function centralized or distributed?

- What mechanisms has the company put in place to integrate its marketing?
- Are all the required marketing functions present?
- Are brand objectives integrated into company and common objectives?
- Do the company's recruiting, training, performance management, compensation, succession planning, business planning, budgeting, resource allocation, and other systems support brand building? Are they designed to help the company deliver its brand's promise?
- Does the company screen job applicants for their alignment with the brand's essence, promise, and personality?
- Is the organization a "learning organization"?

- *Brand Extension:*
  - What are the brand's assets?
  - Is the brand over- or underextended (or both)?
  - What are the most promising areas for brand extension?
  - What processes does the organization have in place for brand extension? How does it safeguard against inappropriate extension?

- *Marketing Employee Competency:*
  - How competent are the company's marketers?
  - Which skill sets do they possess and which ones are missing?
  - Has the company augmented internal skill sets that it is lacking with external sources?
  - What are its external marketing vendors' strengths and weaknesses?
  - Do the company's marketing employees (and also its senior managers and the rest of its employees) exhibit a marketing mindset? That is, do they profoundly understand the company's customers and sincerely and passionately strive to meet their wants and needs?

Brand Positioning Investigation

Brand auditors should assess the strength of an organization's mission and vision and the strength of its brand's essence, promise, archetype, and personality (especially in relationship to the organization's stakeholders and their perceptions of the organization). As part of the process, the auditor should investigate how congruently each of the following groups or sources articulate or manifest these organizational and brand attributes:

- Company leaders
- Official documents
- Internal and external communications
- Marketers
- Salespeople
- Customer service employees
- Other employees
- Business partners
- Each and every point of contact the brand makes with its clients/customers

Who Performs the Audit?

BRAND AUDITOR SKILL SET

Ideally, the company performing the audit has broad and deep experience (as line managers and as consultants) in each of the following areas:

- Brand research
- Brand strategy and positioning
- Brand identity system and standards
- Brand advertising
- Organization design

SIZE OF AUDIT TEAM

Audits will vary from company to company based on the company's unique needs, organizational complexity, marketing competency, and other factors. Given the large amount of work required to complete the audit in a reasonable period of time, the audit team should consist of at least three people. The more marketing experience each team member has, the better.

A CAUTION

Weaknesses to look out for in self-proclaimed brand auditors are:

- Strength in other areas of marketing (e.g., advertising, promotion), but not in brand management

- Primary focus on brand research, strategy, and positioning, but little knowledge of how to design an organization to deliver on the brand promise

- Strong knowledge of brand management but little understanding of organization design

- Lack of brand research experience

COST AND DURATION OF A BRAND AUDIT

Audit Cost. Audit costs may vary from a low of $150,000 to more than $1 million depending on the global reach of the business, complexity of the brand and product structure, amount of proprietary research required, project's duration, number of people assigned, and the audit firm's profit margin and billing rate, among other factors. If an audit company provides an estimate much lower than that, it indicates a lack of understanding of the scope and complexity of this type of project.

Audit Duration. The project may last anywhere from a month (fast track with concentrated interviews and little to no additional research) to six months.

AREAS INVESTIGATED IN A BRAND AUDIT

A brand audit should identify strengths, weaknesses, opportunities, and threats in the following areas:

- Brand strategy and positioning

- Brand equity

- Ability to leverage the brand for business growth

- Capacity of the organization to manage and market the brand effectively

- Alignment of the organization's structure and systems to deliver the brand's promise

Bottom-Line Questions

Here are some questions that a strong brand auditor will attempt to answer:

- Does this company have a profound understanding of its consumers?

- Is the brand well positioned in its marketplace? Does it own a relevant and compelling point of difference?

- Do the leaders of this company have a vision for their brand(s)?

- Is this company's marketing staff competent?

- Is the organization mobilized to deliver on its brand's promise?

- Does the corporate culture reinforce the brand essence, promise, and personality?

- Are the brand identity system and standards simple, robust, and powerful?

- Does this organization accurately and consistently reinforce its brand's identity and positioning in internal and external communication?

- Does the brand create an emotional connection with its consumers?

www.marketingsherpa.com—MarketingSherpa is a research institute specializing in tracking what works in all aspects of marketing, offering practical case studies, research, and training for marketers.

webmarketingtoday.com—The mission of Web Marketing Today is to publish down-to-earth articles, tutorials, webinars, and podcasts to help smaller, local businesses succeed online. Its authors are Internet marketing experts.

ONLINE BRAND-RELATED PUBLICATIONS

adage.com—*AdvertisingAge*

www.adweek.com—*Adweek*

thearf.org/jar—*Journal of Advertising Research*

www.brandingmagazine.com—Independent daily brand journal

www.emeraldinsight.com (select the Journals and Books menu)—*The Journal of Product & Brand Management*

www.marketingpower.com—American Marketing Association

www.palgrave-journals.com/bm—*Journal of Brand Management*

www.salesandmarketing.com—*Sales and Marketing Management*

ONLINE ADVERTISING RESOURCES

Here is a list of online advertising resources, with brief descriptions (some taken straight from the websites themselves).

www.aaaa.org—Founded in 1917, the 4A's (American Association of Advertising Agencies) is a national trade association in the United States. Its membership produces approximately 80 percent of the total advertising volume placed by agencies nationwide. Although virtually all of the large, multinational agencies are members of the 4A's, more than 60 percent of its membership bills less than $10 million per year.

www.aaf.org—The American Advertising Federation (AAF), the nation's oldest national advertising trade association, and the only association representing all facets of the advertising industry, is headquartered in Washington, D.C., and acts as the "unifying voice for advertising." To accomplish its objectives, AAF initiatives include:

- Advertising Hall of Fame
- Advertising Hall of Achievement

APPENDIX B
Online Brand Management and Advertising Resources

ONLINE BRAND MANAGEMENT RESOURCES

www.brandingstrategyinsider.com—Branding Strategy Insider helps ma oriented leaders and professionals build strong brands. It focuses on thought-provoking expertise that promotes an elevated conversatio discipline of branding and fosters community among marketers.

www.clickz.com—Marketing news and expert advice, with a compr archive of articles on all aspects of marketing.

www.iab.net—The Interactive Advertising Bureau (IAB) is com more than 500 leading media and technology companies that are re for selling 86 percent of online advertising in the United States. The cates marketers, agencies, media companies, and the wider busines nity about the value of interactive advertising.

www.mad.co.uk—Mad.co.uk is a group subscription service rath individual news site that connects marketing, advertising, desig media industry professionals to:

- News, in-depth analysis, case studies, and best practice from ing industry websites
- Jobs through the Madjobs portal
- Exclusive discounts and benefits to conferences, training, a
- VIP networking events

marketing.about.com—About Marketing: articles, forums, cha

www.marketingprofs.com—The MarketingProfs editorial te experts and in-the-trenches marketers who know what they ar and delivers practical advice that you can actually use through conferences, seminars, podcast, articles, and webcasts.

- ADDY Awards

- American Advertising Conference

- Executive Summit

- Government Affairs Conference

- Great Brands Campaign

- Most Promising Minority Students Program

- NSAC (National Student Advertising Competition): College World Series of Advertising

- Principles and Recommended Practices for Effective Advertising in the American Multicultural Marketplace

www.adage.com—For more than sixty-five years, *Advertising Age* has been the preeminent source of marketing, advertising, and media news, information, and analysis.

www.adforum.com—With nearly half a million users monthly, AdForum.com gathers information on 20,000 agencies and 150,000 campaigns (TV, print, and interactive).

www.adslogans.co.uk—Founded in 1990 by adman and author Timothy Foster, AdSlogans has built a growing and unique database of many thousands of advertising slogans, straplines, taglines, endlines, and claims in the English language. These lines have appeared all over the world, during the last fifty years. The resource also carries many historical lines and covers all brand categories in all media.

www.ahaa.org—AHAA: The Voice of Hispanic Marketing represents the best minds and resources dedicated to Hispanic-specialized marketing. Over the last two decades, AHAA has been a long-standing champion for corporate investment in Hispanic marketing and, since its inception in 1996, has increased Hispanic budget allocations twelvefold.

www.ana.net—Founded in 1910, ANA (Association of National Advertisers) leads the marketing community by providing its members with insights, collaboration, and advocacy. ANA's membership includes more than 500 companies with 10,000 brands that collectively spend more than $250 billion in marketing and advertising. The ANA strives to communicate marketing best practices, lead industry initiatives, influence industry practices, manage industry affairs, and advance, promote, and protect all advertisers and marketers.

thearf.org—The Advertising Research Foundation (ARF) is an association for practitioners from every avenue of advertising—agency, academia, marketer, media, and research—who want to exchange ideas and research strategies. It was founded in 1936 by the ANA and the 4A's to establish an open-minded, unbiased environment, free of partisan interests. Its principal mission is to improve the practice of advertising, marketing, and media research in pursuit of smarter and more effective marketing communications for business growth.

www.clioawards.com—The CLIO is the world's most recognized international awards competition for advertising, design, interactive media, and communications. CLIO maintains its original commitment to celebrate and reward creative excellence, while continuing to evolve with the industry to acknowledge the most current breakthrough work.

www.commarts.com—Founded in 1959, Communication Arts (CA) is the premier source of inspiration for graphic designers, art directors, design firms, corporate design departments, advertising agencies, interactive designers, illustrators, and photographers—everyone involved in visual communication.

http://creativity-online.com/adcritic—AdCritic.com is a business-to-business and business-to-consumer knowledge resource for the advertising industry and related industries. Peter Beckman, founder, developed the concept of AdCritic.com to be a premiere screening service for television commercials using broadband video in 1999. Today, the site serves a need for agencies seeking creative talent, for creative talent to be found, and for consumers to give valuable feedback, survey data and rating of advertising collateral.

www.ecreativesearch.com—A comprehensive database of directors, production, and postproduction services from around the world, plus thousands of spots and credits. eCreativeSearch is a subscription-based Internet service for the commercial broadcast production industry. It provides access to a searchable and comprehensive database of talent (directors, production companies, music) and support services, as well as commercials.

www.effie.org—Effie Worldwide stands for effectiveness in marketing communications, spotlighting marketing ideas that work and encouraging thoughtful dialogue about the drivers of marketing effectiveness. The Effie network works with some of the top research and media organizations worldwide to bring its audience relevant and first-class insights into effective marketing strategy.

www.iaaglobal.org—The International Advertising Association is the world's only globally focused, integrated advertising trade association with membership representing advertisers, agencies, and the media. The IAA has corporate members, organizational members, educational affiliates, as well as fifty-six chapters with individual members and young professionals from seventy-six countries, including the top ten economies in the world.

www.oneclub.org—The One Club produces the One Show, an annual advertising competition judged by a group of the advertising industry's most reputable creative directors. Every year, a different team of top creative directors judges ads sent in from all over the world.

www.shots.net—Launched in 1990, it is the world's leading commercials title, providing ideas and inspiration for creatives internationally, as well as being the foremost source of information for the industry.

http://strategyonline.ca—This site uncovers and shares the "bold vision, brand new ideas" of Canada's national marketing community. It delivers on this tagline through the monthly *strategy* magazine, *strategy* events, as well as various initiatives with industry partners, from the CASSIES and PROMO! Awards to its presence at Cannes.

www.warc.com—The World Advertising Research Center (WARC) provides knowledge and data to the global advertising, marketing, and media industries through its websites, print publications, and conferences.

APPENDIX C

REFERENCES/FURTHER READING

Aaker, David A. *Building Strong Brands.* New York: Free Press, 1995.

————. *Managing Brand Equity.* New York: Free Press, 1991.

Aaker, David A., and Erich Joachimsthaler. *Brand Leadership.* New York: Free Press, 2000.

Aitchison, Jim. *Cutting Edge Advertising: How to Create the World's Best Print for Brands in the 21st Century.* Singapore: Prentice Hall, 1999.

Baldinger, Allan L., and Joel Rubinson. "Brand Loyalty: The Link Between Attitude and Behavior." The NPD Group, *Journal of Advertising Research,* November/December 1996, pp. 22–34.

Baltes, Michael. "Measuring Non-Financial Assets." *Wharton Alumni Magazine,* Winter 1997.

Banet-Weiser, Sarah. *Authentic™: The Politics of Ambivalence in a Brand Culture.* New York: New York University Press, 2012.

Barwise, Patrick. "Editorial: Brands in a Digital World." *The Journal of Brand Management* 4, no. 4 (Spring 1997).

Bean, Jeofrey, and Sean Van Tyne. *The Customer Experience Revolution.* St. Johnsbury, VT: Brigantine Media, 2012.

Bedbury, Scott, with Stephen Fenichell. *A New Brand World: 8 Principles for Achieving Brand Leadership in the 21st Century.* New York: Viking, 2002.

Bell, Tom. "Virtual Trade Dress: A Very Real Problem." *Maryland Law Review* 56, no. 384 (1997). http://digitalcommons.law.umaryland.edu/mlr/vol56/iss2/4.

Berger, Jonah. *Contagious: Why Things Catch On.* New York: Simon & Schuster, 2013.

Bettles, Jennie. "Branding Amid the Noise." *ClickZ Network,* http://www.clickz.com/clickz/column/1697513/branding-amid-the-noise.

Blankenship, A. B., George Breen, and Alan Dutka. *State of the Art Marketing Research*. Lincolnwood, IL: NTC Business Books, 1998.

Boyce, Rick. "Brand Building with Internet Media." AdTech Report # 8. January 26, 1998. www.o-a.com.

Brand Building and Communication Consortium Benchmarking Study. American Productivity & Quality Center and American Marketing Association, 1998.

"Brand Building on the Web." Ericsson Connexion, no. 4, December 1998.

"Brand Management: From Print to Broadcast to the Web." Seybold San Francisco/Publishing, Web Publishing Conference, September 1, 1998.

Bruzzone, Donald E., and Deborah J. Tallyn. "Linking Tracking to Pretesting with an 'Arm.'" Proceedings of the Advertising Research Foundation Advertising and Brand Tracking Workshop, November 12–13, 1996: 169–177.

"Building Your Brand Online." Advantage Internet. www.aibn.com/build-brand.html.

Cannon, Hugh M. "Addressing New Media with Conventional Media Planning." *Journal of Interactive Advertising* 1, no. 2 (Spring 2001).

Carbone, Lewis P. "Total Customer Experience Drives Value." *American Management Association International*, July/August 1998, 62–63.

Chassaing, Thierry, David C. Edelman, and Lynn Segal. "Customer Retention: Beyond Bribes and Golden Handcuffs." The Boston Consulting Group pamphlet, 1998. http://www.bcgtelaviv.com/documents/file13295.pdf.

Cialdini, Robert B., Ph.D. *Influence: The Psychology of Persuasion*. New York: Quill/William Morrow, 1993.

Clancy, Kevin J., and Peter C. Krieg. *Counter-Intuitive Marketing: Achieve Great Results Using Uncommon Sense*. New York: Free Press, 2000.

Clancy, Kevin J., and Robert S. Shulman. *Marketing Myths That Are Killing Business: The Cure for Death Wish Marketing*. New York: McGraw-Hill, 1994.

Cristol, Steven M., and Bob Johnson. "Building Brand Equity on the World Wide Web." Summary of a Presentation to the Business Week Corporate Branding Symposium, Chicago, June 17, 1997.

Czerniawski, Richard D., and Michael W. Maloney. *Creating Brand Loyalty: The Management of Power Positioning and Really Great Advertising*. New York: AMACOM, 1999.

Davis, Scott M. *Brand Asset Management: Driving Profitable Revenue Growth Through Your Brands.* San Francisco: Jossey-Bass, 2000.

Durgee, Jeffery F. "Depth Interview Techniques for Creative Advertising." *Journal of Advertising Research* 25, no. 6 (1986), 29–37.

Ehrenberg, Andrew. "Description and Prescription." *Journal of Advertising Research,* November/December 1997, 17–22.

Ehrenberg, Andrew, Neil Barnard, and John Scriven. "Differentiation or Salience." *Journal of Advertising Research,* November/December 1997, 7–14.

Eisenberg, Daniel. "It's an Ad, Ad, Ad World." *Time.com,* September 2, 2002.

Ellwood, Iain. *The Essential Brand Book: Over 100 Techniques to Increase Brand Value.* London: Kogan Page, 2000.

Erdem, Tulin. "An Empirical Analysis of Umbrella Branding." *Journal of Marketing Research* 35 (August 1998), 339–351.

Ericson, Paul, Randy Gorgman, and Mike Verma. "How to Get in the News." In the *News-Media Relations: Ad Council Academy of Rochester: Enhancing Professional Know-How,* Advertising Council of Rochester, 2001.

Farquhar, Peter H., Julia Y. Han, and Yuji Ijiri. "Brands on the Balance Sheet: Brand Values Belong in Financial Statements. Recognized Measurement Standards Are All That Business Needs." *Marketing Management,* Winter 1992, 16–22.

Finskud, Lars. "Bringing Discipline to Brand Value Management." *Financial Times Retail & Consumer Publishing,* London: Vanguard Brand Management, 1998. http://www.vanguardstrategy.com/images/pdf/discipline.pdf.

Fischler, Michael. "Round-Up at the Branding Ranch." *ClickZ Network,* http://www.clickz.com/clickz/column/1692270/round-up-at-the-branding-ranch.

Fishman, Stephen, and Rich Stim. *Nondisclosure Agreements: Protect Your Trade Secrets and More.* Berkeley, CA: Nolo, 2001.

"Five Common Myths About Trademarks: Don't Get Burned by Trademark Ignorance." *Business Wire,* February 9, 2000.

Flowers, Jim. "Ideation: It's More Than Just Brainstorming." http://jcflowers1.iweb.bsu.edu/rlo/brainstorming2.htm.

Fortini-Campbell, Lisa, Ph.D. *Hitting the Sweet Spot: How Consumer Insights Can Inspire Better Marketing and Advertising.* Chicago: The Copy Workshop, 2001.

"From Transactions to Relationships: A Relationship-Building Model of Communication." Saatchi & Saatchi Strategic Planning.

Gad, Thomas. *4-D Branding: Cracking the Corporate Code of the Network Economy.* London: Financial Times/Prentice Hall, 2001.

Gelb, Gabriel M. "The Nuts and Bolts of Business-to-Business Marketing Research." CRM University Learning Center, Chicago, Business Marketing Association, 1996,www.techmar.com/u_busmktresearchbma.asp.

Georgiou, Paul, and Stephen Miller."10 Years of Advertising Tracking in the Rent-A-Car Business." Proceedings of the Advertising Research Foundation Advertising and Brand Tracking Workshop, November 12–13, 1996: 1–12.

Gitomer, Jeffrey. *Customer Satisfaction Is Worthless, Customer Loyalty Is Priceless: How to Make Customers Love You, Keep Them Coming Back and Tell Everyone They Know.* Austin, TX: Bard Press: 1998.

Gladwell, Malcolm. *The Tipping Point: How Little Things Can Make a Big Difference.* Boston: Little, Brown, 2000.

Gobé, Marc. *Emotional Branding: The New Paradigm for Connecting Brands to People.* New York: Allworth Press, 2001.

Gosling, Sam. *Snoop: What Your Stuff Says About You.* New York: Basic Books, 2008.

Gregory, James R., with Jack G. Wiechmann. *Leveraging the Corporate Brand.* Lincolnwood, IL: NTC Business Books, 1997.

Haigh, David. "Brand Valuation or Brand Monitoring? That Is the Question." *The Journal of Brand Management* 4, no. 5 (1997), 311–319.

Hankinson, Philippa, and Graham Hankinson. "Managing Successful Brands: An Empirical Study Which Compares the Corporate Cultures of Companies Managing the World's Top 100 Brands with Those Managing Outsider Brands." *Journal of Marketing Management* 15, no. 1–3 (January–April 1999), 135–155.

Harding, Carlos, and Patrick Le Brigand. "Brand Tracking Is Good, but Is It Good Enough?" Proceedings of the Advertising Research Foundation Advertising and Brand Tracking Workshop, November 12–13, 1996: 92–104.

"Harley-Davidson Declares Victory in the Court of Public Opinion—Drops Federal Trademark Application." *Business Wire Business,* June 20, 2000.

Hebard, Amy J., and Joel Rubinson. "Value and Loyalty Measurement at AT&T." Proceedings of the Advertising Research Foundation Advertising and Brand Tracking Workshop, November 12–13, 1996: 47–71.

Hester, Edward L. *Successful Marketing Research: The Complete Guide to Getting and Using Essential Information About Your Customers and Competitors.* New York: John Wiley, 1995.

Hill, Sam, and Chris Lederer. *The Infinite Asset: Managing Brands to Build New Value.* Boston: Harvard Business School Press, 2001.

"How Distinctive Is It?…The Inherently Distinctive Test as Applied to Trademarks, Service Marks and Product Designs." Sheldon Mak & Anderson archive. http://www.usip.com/pdf/Article_Trademarks/inherent.pdf.

"How Search Engines Rank Web Pages." www.searchenginewatch.com.

Hutchinson, Alan. "Use Return on Investment for Quantifying Marketing Results," Marketing Resources Ltd., May 1998. http://www.mrlweb.com/tips/roi.html.

Ind, Nicholas. *Living the Brand: How to Transform Every Member of Your Organization into a Brand Champion.* London: Kogan Page, 2001.

Jassin, Lloyd J. "Trade Dress Protection: How to Tell a Book by Its Cover." www.CopyLaw.com.

———. "Trademark Basics." www.CopyLaw.com.

Javed, Naseem. *Naming for Power: Creating Successful Names for the Business World.* New York: Linkbridge Publishing, 1993.

Jensen, David. "Communication as Value Builder." Ketchum white paper, 2001.

Jensen, Rolf. *The Dream Society: How the Coming Shift from Information to Imagination Will Transform Your Business.* New York: McGraw-Hill, 1999.

Joachimsthaler, Erich, and David A. Aaker. "Building Brands Without Mass Media." *Harvard Business Review,* January–February 1997, 39–50.

Jobst, Joseph. "Branding on the Net." *Global Internet Marketing News.*

John, Deborah Roedder, Barbara Loken, and Christopher Joiner. "The Negative Impact of Extensions: Can Flagship Products Be Diluted?" *Journal of Marketing* 62 (January 1998), 19–32.

Kalin, Sari. "Brand New Branding: Forget What You Knew About Branding. The Web Changes Everything. Four Experts Explain How and Why." *Darwin* (July 2001), 62–68.

Kalra, Ajay, and Ronald C. Goodstein. "The Impact of Advertising Positioning Strategies on Consumer Price Sensitivity." *Journal of Marketing Research* 35 (May 1998), 210–224.

Kania, Deborah. *Branding.com*. Chicago: NTC Business Books in conjunction with the American Marketing Association, 2001.

Kapferer, Jean-Noel. *The New Strategic Brand Management*, 5th. ed. London: Kogan Page, 2012.

Keller. *Strategic Brand Management: Building, Measuring, and Managing Brand Equity*, 4th ed. Upper Saddle River, NJ: Prentice Hall, 2012.

———. "Brand Mantras: Rationale, Criteria, and Examples." *Journal of Marketing Management* 15, no.1–3 (January–April 1999), 43–51.

Keller, Kevin Lane, Susan E. Heckler, and Michael J. Houston. "The Effects of Brand Name Suggestiveness on Advertising Recall." *Journal of Marketing* 62 (January 1998), 48–57.

Kim, W. Chan, and Renée Mauborgne. *Blue Ocean Strategy: How to Create Uncontested Market Space and Make Competition Irrelevant*. Boston: Harvard Business School Publishing, 2005.

Klein, Naomi. *No Logo: Taking Aim at the Brand Bullies*. New York: Picador, 1999.

Knapp, Duane E. *The Brand Mindset: How Companies Like Starbucks, Whirlpool, and Hallmark Became Genuine Brands and Other Secrets of Branding Success*. New York: McGraw-Hill, 2000.

Lindstrom, Martin, Martha Rogers, and Don Peppers. *Clicks, Bricks & Brands: The Marriage of Online and Offline Brands*. Dover, NH: Kogan Page (U.S.), 2001.

———. "Offline Versus Online Brands—The Winners and Losers." *ClickZ Network*. http://www.clickz.com/clickz/column/1708486/offline-versus-online-brands-the-winners-losers.

Longman, Kenneth A. "If Not Effective Frequency, Then What?" *Journal of Advertising Research*, July/August 1997, 44–50.

Luntz, Frank I. *What Americans Really Want…Really: The Truth About Our Hopes, Dreams, and Fears*. New York: Hyperion, 2009.

MacRae, Chris. *The Brand Chartering Handbook: How Brand Organizations Learn "Living Scripts."* Harlow, England: Addison-Wesley, 1996.

———. "Brand Reality Editorial." *Journal of Marketing Management* 15, no. 1–3 (January–April 1999), 1–24.

Malone, Chris, and Susan Fiske. *The Human Brand: How We Relate to People, Products, and Companies*. San Francisco: Jossey-Bass, 2013.

Managing Reputation with Image and Brands. The Conference Board, 1998.

Managing the Corporate Brand. The Conference Board, 1998.

Mark, Margaret and Carol S. Pearson. *The Hero and the Outlaw: Building Extraordinary Brands Through the Power of Archetypes.* New York: McGraw-Hill, 2001.

Martin, David N. *Romancing The Brand: The Power of Advertising and How to Use It.* New York: AMACOM, 1989.

————. *Be the Brand: How to Find a Powerful Identity and Use It to Drive Sales.* Richmond, VA: New Marketplace, 2000.

McEwen, Rob. "Brand Interaction: The Oft-Neglected Element of Online Branding." *Web Commerce Today* 15 (October 15, 1998).

————. "The Little Things That Make a Difference." *ClickZ Network.* http://www.clickz.com/clickz/column/1716608/the-little-things-that-make-a-difference.

"Measuring the Future: The Value Creation Index." Cap Gemini Ernst & Young Center for Business Innovation, 2000. http://www.cbi.cgey.com/research/index.html.

Michaels, Nancy, and Debbi J. Karpowicz. *Off-the-Wall Marketing Ideas: Jumpstart Your Sales Without Busting Your Budget.* Holbrook, MA: Adams Media, 2000.

Michelli, Joseph. *The New Gold Standard: 5 Leadership Principles for Creating a Legendary Customer Experience Courtesy of Ritz-Carlton Hotel Company.* New York: McGraw-Hill, 2008.

Mikunda, Christian. *Brand Lands, Hot Spots & Cool Spaces: Welcome to the Third Place and the Total Marketing Experience.* London: Kogan Page Limited, 2004.

Mitchell, Alan. "Out of the Shadows." *Journal of Marketing Management* 15, no. 1–3 (January–April 1999), 25–42.

Montgomery, Diane, Kay Sather Bull, and Sarah Leigh Kimball. "Stimulating Creativity in Computer Mediated Learning: Individual and Collaborative Approaches." Oklahoma State University, August 4, 2001.

Morgan, Adam. *Eating the Big Fish: How Challenger Brands Can Compete Against Brand Leaders.* New York: John Wiley, 1999.

Moskin, Jonathon E. "Innovation Is Key to Fending Off Copycats." *Advertising Age*, May 26,1997, 24.

Murphy, William. "Implementing a Plan to Protect Your Company's Trade Secrets." www.alllaw.com/articles/intellectual_property/article7.asp.

Nagle, Thomas T., and Reed K. Holden. *The Strategy and Tactics of Pricing: A Guide to Profitable Decision Making.* Upper Saddle River, NJ: Prentice Hall, 1995.

"Naming Strategies: 33 Tips & Tactics for Generating Names." *The Naming Newsletter.* Rivkin & Associates. www.namingnewsletter.com.

Ogilvy, David. *Ogilvy On Advertising.* New York: Vintage Books, 1985.

Osborne, Dawn. "Trademarks on the Internet—Not Just a Matter of Domain Names and Meta Tags." INT Media Group. http://www.icbtollfree.com/article.cfm?articleId=4485.

"Patents, Trademarks, Copyrights, and Trade Secrets: A Primer for Business Executives, Entrepreneurs, and Research Administrators." Olive & Olive, P.A. www.oliveandolive.com.

Peters, Tom. *The Circle of Innovation.* New York: Alfred A. Knopf, 1997.

Pine, B. Joseph II, and James H. Gilmore. "Welcome to the Experience Economy." *Harvard Business Review,* July–August 1998.

Plsek, Paul. "The Eight Basic Heuristics of Directed Creativity." www.directedcreativity.com/pages/Heuristics.html.

Poffenberger, Albert T., Ph.D. *Psychology in Advertising.* Chicago: A. W. Shaw Company, 1925.

Pratkanis, Anthony, and Elliot Aronson. *Age of Propaganda: The Everyday Use and Abuse of Persuasion.* New York: W. H. Freeman, 2000.

Quek, Patrick. "Return on Marketing Dollars." http://www.hotel-online.com/Neo/Trends/PKF/Special/MarketingDollars_Nov99.html.

Rabuck, Michael J., and Karl E. Rosenberg. "Some Observations on Advertising for Large Brands." *Journal of Advertising Research,* May/June 1997, 17–25.

Rapaille, Clotaire. *The Culture Code: An Ingenious Way to Understand Why People Around the World Live and Buy as They Do.* New York: Broadway Books, 2006.

Ries, Al, and Laura Ries. *The 22 Immutable Laws of Branding: How to Build a Product or Service into a World-Class Brand.* New York: HarperCollins, 1998.

———. *The 11 Immutable Laws of Internet Branding.* New York: HarperCollins, 2000.

Ries, Al, and Jack Trout. *The 22 Immutable Laws of Marketing: Violate Them at Your Own Risk!* New York: HarperCollins, 1993.

Rosen, Emanuel. *The Anatomy of Buzz: How to Create Word of Mouth Marketing.* New York: Doubleday, 2000.

Sachs, Jonah. *Winning the Story Wars: Why Those Who Tell—and Live—the Best Stories Will Rule the Future.* Boston: Harvard Business Review Press, 2012.

Sapherstein, Michael B. "The Trademark Registrability of the Harley-Davidson Roar: A Multimedia Analysis." October 11, 1998. http://www.bc.edu/bc_org/avp/law/st_org/iptf/articles/content/1998101101.html.

Schmitt, Bernd, and Alex Simonson. *Marketing Aesthetics.* New York: Free Press, 1997.

Schultz, Don, and Anders Gronstedt. "Making Marcom an Investment: Market-Driven Accounting System Splits Spending into Business-Building and Brand-Building Activities." *Marketing Management,* Fall 1997, 41–49.

Schultz, Don E., and Scott Bailey. "Customer/Brand Loyalty in an Interactive Marketplace." *Journal of Advertising Research,* May–June 2000, 41–52.

Schultz, Don E., Stanley I. Tannenbaum, and Robert F. Lauterborn. *Integrated Marketing Communications.* Lincolnwood, IL: NTC Business Books, 1995.

Schultz, Don E., and Jeffrey S. Walters. *Measuring Brand Communication ROI.* New York: Association of National Advertisers, 1997.

Settle, Robert B., and Pamela L. Alreck. *Why They Buy: American Consumers Inside and Out.* New York: John Wiley, 1986.

Silverstein, Michael. "Creating a Flawless Brand Experience." The Boston Consulting Group pamphlet.

Simon, Carol J., and Mary W. Sullivan. "The Measurement and Determinants of Brand Equity: A Financial Approach." *Marketing Science* 12, no. 1 (Winter 1993), 28–52.

Spoelstra, Jon. *Marketing Outrageously: How to Increase Your Revenues by Staggering Amounts!* Austin, TX: Bard Press, 2001.

Stengel, Jim. *Grow: How Ideals Power Growth and Profit at the World's Greatest Companies.* New York: Crown Business, 2011.

Stalk, George, Jr., David K. Pecaut, and Benjamin Burnett. "Breaking Compromises, Breakaway Growth." *Harvard Business Review,* September–October 1996, 131–139.

Steidl, Peter. *Neurobranding.* CreateSpace, 2012.

Stolzenberg, Martin, and Peggy Lebenson. "Tracking the Obvious: New Ways of Looking at Old Problems." Proceedings of the Advertising Research

Foundation Advertising and Brand Tracking Workshop, November 12–13, 1996: 148–168.

Sulham, Priscilla L. "Trademark Infringement: Take Steps to Protect Company Brand Online." *Puget Sound Business Journal,* July 16, 1999. http://www.bizjournals.com/seattle/stories/1999/07/19/focus12.html.

Sullivan, Luke. *Hey Whipple, Squeeze This: A Guide to Great Ads.* New York: John Wiley, 1998.

Sutherland, Max, and Stephen Holden. "Slipstream Marketing." *The Journal of Brand Management* 4, no. 6 (1997), 401–406.

Sutherland, Max, and Alice K. Sylvester. *Advertising and the Mind of the Consumer: What Works, What Doesn't and Why.* St. Leonards, NSW, Australia: Allen & Unwin, 2009

Tchong, Michael. "Branding on the Web." *ICONOCLAST: Business 2.0's Newsletter for Internet Marketing Executives,* August 12, 1998.

Temporal, Paul. *Branding in Asia: The Creation, Development and Management of Asian Brands for the Global Market.* Singapore: John Wiley (Asia) Pte Ltd, 2001.

Thomas L. Harris/Impulse PR Client Survey 1999.

Tilley, Catherine. "Built-in Branding: How to Engineer a Leadership Brand." *Journal of Marketing* Management 15, no. 1–3 (January–April 1999), 181–191.

"Tips & Tactics: 10 Do's and Don'ts For Smart Naming." *The Naming Newsletter.* Rivkin & Associates. www.namingnewsletter.com.

Travis, Daryl. *Emotional Branding: How Successful Brands Gain the Irrational Edge.* Roseville, CA: Prima Venture, 2000.

Trout, Jack. *Big Brands Big Trouble: Lessons Learned the Hard Way.* New York: John Wiley, 2001.

———. *Differentiate or Die: Survival in Our Era of Killer Competition.* Hoboken, NJ: John Wiley, 2000, 2008.

———. *In Search of the Obvious: The Antidote for Today's Marketing Mess.* Hoboken, NJ: John Wiley, 2008.

Trout, Jack, with Steve Rivkin. *The New Positioning: The Latest on the World's #1 Business Strategy.* New York: McGraw-Hill, 1997.

Tvede, Lars, and Peter Ohnemus. *Marketing Strategies for the New Economy.* Chichester, West Sussex, England: John Wiley, 2001.

Upshaw, Lynn B. Building *Brand Identity: A Strategy for Success in a Hostile Marketplace.* New York: John Wiley, 1995.

Van Praet, Douglas. *Unconscious Branding: How Neuroscience Can Empower (and Inspire) Marketing.* New York: Palgrave Macmillan, 2012.

Verbeke, Willem, Paul Ferris, and Roy Thurik. "The Acid Test of Brand Loyalty: Consumer Response to Out-of-Stocks for Their Favourite Brands." *The Journal of Brand Management* 5, no. 1 (1997), 43–52.

Wansink, Brian. "Making Old Brands New." *American Demographics,* December 1997, 53–58.

Weilbacher, William M. *Brand Marketing.* Lincolnwood, IL: NTC Business Books, 1995.

Wells, Melanie. "Cult Brands." Forbes.com, April 16, 2001. http://www.forbes.com/forbes/2001/0416/198.html.

Williams, Roy H. *Secret Formulas of the Wizard of Ads.* Austin, TX: Bard Press, 1999.

Wong, Thomas. *101 Ways to Boost Your Web Traffic: Internet Promotion Made Easier.* Union City, CA: Intesync, 2000.

NOTES

CHAPTER 2: Understanding the Language of Branding

1. American Marketing Association Dictionary, https://www.ama.org/resources/Pages/Dictionary.aspx?dLetter=B.

2. Kevin Lane Keller, *Strategic Brand Management: Building, Measuring, and Managing Brand Equity,* 4th ed. (Upper Saddle River, NJ: Prentice Hall, August 2012).

3. Kristin Zhivago, "Marketing Technology," (newsletter), July/August 1994.

4. This definition of brand identity is courtesy of Lister Butler Consulting, New York.

5. Courtesy of Lister Butler Consulting.

6. Maureen Azzato, "Store Brands Drive Differentiation and Profit," *Store Brands Decisions,* June 13, 2009, http://www.storebrandsdecisions.com/news/2009/06/13/store-brands-drive-differentiation-and-profit.

7. Urban Wallace Associates, "Key Issues to Covered in a Marketing Plan," 2005, http://www.uwa.com/compadv_c_001.pdf.

CHAPTER 3: Brand Management Process: An Overview

1. Michael Porter, *Competitive Advantage: Creating and Sustaining Superior Performance* (New York: Free Press, 1998).

CHAPTER 4: Understanding the Consumer

1. Robert Arp, ed., *1001 Ideas That Changed the Way We Think* (New York: ATRIA Books, 2013), 747.

CHAPTER 6: Brand Design

1. David Reyes-Guerra, manager of corporate identity and product naming for Xerox, at IQPC's Maximizing Brand Value Through Internal Communication conference, Chicago, May 24–25, 1999.

2. Richard D. Czerniawski and Michael W. Maloney, *Creating Brand Loyalty: The Management of Power Positioning and Really Great Advertising* (New York: AMACOM, 1999), 161.

3. Adam Morgan, *Eating the Big Fish: How Challenger Brands Can Compete Against Brand Leaders* (New York: John Wiley, 1999), 31.

4. Jonah Sachs, *Winning the Story Wars: Why Those Who Tell—and Live—the Best Stories Will Rule the Future* (Boston: Harvard Business Review Press, 2012), 174.

5. Morgan, *Eating the Big Fish,* 74.

CHAPTER 7: Brand Identity System and Standards

1. Steve Rivkin, "33 Tips & Tactics for Generating Names," *Branding Strategy Insider,* June 11, 2009, http://www.brandingstrategyinsider.com/2009/06/33-tips-tactics-for-generating-names.html#.UzrfINxT5Fw.

2. The primary source for this discussion is Kendra Cherry, "Color Psychology: How Colors Impact Moods, Feelings, and Behaviors," About.com, 2014, http://psychology.about.com/od/sensationandperception/a/colorpsych.htm.

3. Joe Hallock, "Color Assignment," November 11, 2013, http://www.joehallock.com/edu/COM498/associations.html.

4. Hallock, "Color Assignment," is also the primary source for the findings on favorite colors of men and women and the other qualities associated with colors.

CHAPTER 8: Driving the Consumer from Brand Awareness to Brand Insistence

1. Much of this section (especially the list of factors that decrease and increase price sensitivity) is informed by Thomas T. Nagle, John Hogan, and Joseph Zale's book, *The Strategy and Tactics of Pricing: A Guide to Profitable Decision Making* (Upper Saddle River, NJ: Prentice Hall, 2010). It also largely draws on my experience crafting pricing strategy for Hallmark.

2. Jonah Berger, *Contagious: Why Things Catch On* (New York: Simon & Schuster, 2013), 170–171.

3. Nagle, Holden, and Zale, *Strategy and Tactics of Pricing.*

4. Rolf Jensen, *The Dream Society: How the Coming Shift from Information to Imagination Will Transform Your Business* (New York: McGraw-Hill, 1999).

CHAPTER 9: Brand Advertising

1. "Advertising Agency Search Tips," AgencyFinder.com, April 6, 2014, http://www.agencyfinder.com/advertisers/advertising-agency-search-tips/.

2. Richard D. Czerniawski and Michael W. Maloney, *Creating Brand Loyalty: The Management of Power Positioning and Really Great Advertising* (New York: AMACOM, 1999), 194–215. Also, David Olgilvy, *Ogilvy on Advertising* (New York: Vintage Books, 1985), 103–113.

3. Chris McLeod and James Neil, "Comparative Advertising: Tips and Traps," *Clayton Utz Insights,* August 30, 2012, http://www.claytonutz.com/publications/edition/30_august_2012/20120830/comparative_advertising_tips_and_traps.page.

4. Mark Lightowler, "Storytelling Maps- Storytelling Creating Tools," May 17, 2012, newbrandstories.com/2012/05/17/storytelling-pharma.

5. Chris Vogler, *The Writers Journey: Mythic Structure for Writers,* adapted this now commonly used storytelling structure from Joseph Campbell's 1949 book, *The Hero with the Thousand Faces.*

6. Oliver Rimoldi, "The impact of 'likeability' on advertising effectiveness: To what extent does liking an advert have a persuasive influence on consumer behavior?" (degree thesis, University of Nottingham, UK, 2008), http://www.psychology.nottingham.ac.uk/staff/ddc/c8cxpa/further/dissertation_examples/rimoldi_08.pdf.

7. Paul A. Scipione, "Too Much or Too Little? Public Perceptions of Advertising

Expenditures," *Journal of Advertising Research* 24, no. 6 (December 1984/January 1985), 23–26.

8. William M. Luther, *The Marketing Plan: How to Prepare and Implement It,* 4th ed. (New York: AMACOM, 2011), 103–108.

9. Christian Harper, managing director of BSMG Worldwide, commenting on the PR budget.

10. Hugh M. Cannon, "Addressing New Media with Conventional Media Planning," *Journal of Interactive Advertising* 1, no. 2 (Spring 2001), 3deec518bef64ee980.pdf.

11. Virginia Nussey, "The Six-Step Emotional Appeal," Raven (blog), March 16, 2011, http://blog.raventools.com/the-6-step-emotional-appeal/.

12. Max Sutherland and Alice K. Sylvester, *Advertising and the Mind of the Consumer: What Works, What Doesn't and Why,* 3rd ed. (St. Leonards, NSW: Allen & Unwin, 2009), 63–64.

13. Sterling Anthony, CPP, "Bettering the Packaging-Advertising Connection," Packaging World, January 11, 2013, http://www.packworld.com/package-design/graphic/bettering-packaging-advertising-connection.

14. David W. Stewart and David H. Furse, "Analysis of the Impact of Executional Factors in Advertising Performance," *Journal of Advertising Research* 27, no. 6 (December 1987/January 1988), 45–50.

15. David W. Stewart and David H. Furse, "Analysis of the Impact of Executional Factors in Advertising Performance," *Journal of Advertising Research* 40, no. 6 (November/December 2000), 85–88.

16. Millward Brown, "Do TV Ads 'Wear Out'?" WPP plc, 2012, www.wpp.com/wpp/marketing/advertising/do-tv-ads-wear-out/.

17. Paul Georgiou and Stephen Miller, "Ten Years of Advertising Tracking in the Rent-A-Car Business," transcript of proceedings, *Advertising Research Foundation Advertising and Brand Tracking Workshop,* November 12–13, 1996, 3.

18. Sutherland and Sylvester, *Advertising and the Mind of the Consumer,* 54.

19. Ibid. 14.

20. Georgiou and Miller, "Ten Years for Advertising Tracking in the Rent-A-Car Business," 7.

21. Kevin J. Clancy and Robert S. Shulman, *Marketing Myths That Are Killing Business: The Cure for Death Wish Marketing* (New York: McGraw-Hill, 1995), 151–153.

22. YuMe, Inc., "Ads Need to Work Harder to Break Through to Millennials, Says New Study from IPG Media Lab and YuMe," news release, April 6, 2014, www.yume.com/news/press-releases/ads-need-work-harder-break-through-millennials-says-new-study-ipg-media-lab-and-.

23. Douglas Van Praet, "The Distraction of Data: How Brand Research Misses the Real Reasons Why People Buy," Fast Company, April 6, 2014, http://www.fastcocreate.com/1683398/the-distraction-of-data-how-brand-research-misses-the-real-reasons-why-people-buy.

24. Georgiou and Miller, "Ten Years for Advertising Tracking in the Rent-A-Car Business," 10–11.

25. Ibid. 10.

26. Ibid. 10.

27. Sutherland and Sylvester, *Advertising and the Mind of the Consumer,* 9.

28. Ibid. 7, 200.

29. Ibid. 12.

30. Cannon, "Addressing New Media with Conventional Media Planning."

CHAPTER 10: Nontraditional Marketing Approaches That Work

1. "Designer Stores, in Extra Large," *Wall Street Journal,* June 6, 2001, B1, B12.

2. David Olgilvy, *Ogilvy on Advertising* (New York: Vintage Books, 1985), 90.

3. Adam Morgan, *Eating the Big Fish: How Challenger Brands Compete Against Brand Leaders* (New York: John Wiley, 1999), 168–169.

4. Emanuel Rosen, *The Anatomy of Buzz: How to Create Word of Mouth Marketing* (New York: Doubleday, 2000), 119.

5. Ibid. 182–183.

6. Morgan, *Eating the Big Fish,* 117–118.

7. Spike Jones, "Report: 93% of Word of Mouth Happens Offline," Ask Spike (blog), November 11, 2013, http://askspike.com/2010/09/28/report-93-of-word-of-mouth-happens-offline/.

8. Rosen, *Anatomy of Buzz,* 177.

9. Daniel Eisenberg, "It's an Ad, Ad, Ad World," *TIME.com,* September 2, 2002.

10. Sarah Brookhart, "Persuasion and the 'Poison Parasite,'" *Observer* 14, no. 8, October 2001, http://www.psychologicalscience.org/observer/1001/cialdini.html.

11. Eisenberg, "It's an Ad, Ad, Ad World."

12. Jonah Berger, *Contagious: Why Things Catch On* (New York: Simon & Schuster, 2013), 33, 64, 169

13. Ray Jutkins, "13 Platinum Advantages Direct Response Marketing Offers the 21st Century Marketer," November 17, 2001, http://www.rayjutkins.com/baker/baker24.html.

14. Diane Montgomery, Kay Sather Bull, and Sarah Leigh Kimball, "Stimulating Creativity in Computer Mediated Learning: Individual and Collaborative Approaches," Oklahoma State University, August 4, 2001.

CHAPTER 11: Online Brand Building

1. The Footprint Chronicles, Patagonia.com, April 9, 2014, http://www.patagonia.com/us/footprint?assetid=23429&ln=451.

2. Our Ambassadors, Patagonia. com, April 9, 2014, http://www.patagonia.com/us/ambassadors.

3. Lorrie Thomas, *The McGraw-Hill 36-Hour Course: Online Marketing* (New York: McGraw-Hill, 2011), 137.

4. Millward Brown: Knowledge Point, How Should Your Brand Capitalize on Social Media? August 2011, http://www.millwardbrown.com/Libraries/MB_Knowledge_Points_Downloads/MillwardBrown_KnowledgePoint_SocialMedia.sflb.ashx.

5. Jason Weaver, *Manager's Guide to Online Marketing* (New York: McGraw-Hill, 2013), 188, citing Juniper Research.

6. "The Incredible Growth of the Internet Since 2000," Royal Pingdom (blog), October 22, 2010, http://royal.pingdom.com/2010/10/22/incredible-growth-of-the-internet-since-2000/.

7. Wikipedia, "Global Internet Usage," http://en.wikipedia.org/wiki/Global_Internet_usage.

CHAPTER 12: Developing a Brand Building Organization

1. "Southwest Airlines Careers" and "Purpose" video, http://www.southwest.com/html/about-southwest/careers/.

2. Michael Porter, *The Competitive Advantage: Creating and Sustaining Superior Performance* (New York: Free Press, 1998).

CHAPTER 14: Creating the Total Brand Experience

1. Starbucks Corporation, Green Apron Book, http://starbucksmarkdavid.wordpress.com/2011/02/02/green-apron-book/.

2. Jeffrey Gitomer, "Why Starbucks Works," *Business Record,* July 11, 2009, http://www.businessrecord.com/Content/Default/Archives/Article/Why-Starbucks-works/-3/988/38454.

3. John Quelch, "How Starbucks Growth Destroyed Brand Value," *Harvard Business Review,* July 2, 2008, http://blogs.hbr.org/2008/07/how-starbucks-growth-destroyed/.

4. Marc Gobé, *Emotional Branding: The New Paradigm for Connectiong Brands to People* (New York: Allworth Press, 2001; new edition 2010).

5. David Hanna, "How GM Destroyed Its Saturn Success," *Forbes,* March 8, 2010, http://www.forbes.com/2010/03/08/saturn-gm-innovation-leadership-managing-failure.html.

6. Robert Reiss, "How Ritz-Carlton Stays at the Top," *Forbes,* October 30, 2009, http://www.forbes.com/2009/10/30/simon-cooper-ritz-leadership-ceonetwork-hotels.html.

7. Ibid.

8. Greg Palast, "BP Covered Up Blow-Out Two Years Prior to Deadly Deepwater Horizon Oil Spill," EcoWatch, April 19, 2012, http://ecowatch.com/2012/04/19/bpcoverup/.

CHAPTER 17: Brand Research

1. This section is largely based on the work of Dan Vandenberg, president of Consumer Vision, Inc. "Naming Method" and "Latency Method" are terms first used by Peter Farquhar.

2. Dan Vandenberg, referencing Peter Farquhar's characterization of brand extension.

3. Olson Zaltman Associates, "The Olson Zaltman Difference," http://www.olsonzaltman.com/oza-difference.htm.

4. The source is my experience in conducting hundreds of focus groups and other qualitative research.

5. Carmen Nobel, "Neuromarketing: Tapping into the 'Pleasure Center' of Consumers," *Forbes,* February 1, 2013, http://www.forbes.com/sites/hbsworkingknowledge/2013/02/01/neuromarketing-tapping-into-the-pleasure-center-of-consumers/.

6. Steria/Business Intelligence Maturity Audit (biMA), 2013 survey, as reported in Charles McLellan, "Big Data: An Overview," ZDNet.com, October 1, 2013, http://www.zdnet.com/big-data-an-overview-7000020785.

7. Jonathan Shaw, "Why 'Big Data' Is a Big Deal," *Harvard Magazine,* March–April 2014, 30, 34.

8. Jason Frand, "Data Mining: What Is Data Mining?" Anderson Graduate School of Management at UCLA, Spring 1996, http://www.anderson.ucla.edu/faculty/jason.frand/teacher/technologies/palace/datamining.htm.

CHAPTER 18: Brand Equity Measurement

1. "Measuring the Future: The Value Creation Index," Cap Gemini Ernst & Young, Center for Business Innovation, 2000.

2. Michael Baltes, "Measuring Non-Financial Assets," *Wharton Alumni Magazine,* Winter 1997, http://whartonmagazine.com/issues/winter-1997/measuring-non-financial-assets/.

3. Ibid.

4. Don E. Schultz, Ph.D., "Managing and Measuring Brand Value," white paper.

CHAPTER 19: How Organization Age and Size Affect Brand Management Issues

1. Bhimrao M. Ghodeswar, "Building Brand Identity in Competitive Markets: A Conceptual Model," *Journal of Product & Brand Management* 17, no. 1 (2008), 4–12, http://www.iei.liu.se/fek/svp/mafo/artikelarkiv/1.310120/Building_brand.pdf; and my personal experience in working at both Hallmark and Element K.

CHAPTER 20: Legal Issues in Brand Management

1. "False Advertising: Lanham Act—Section 43(a): Full Text," Advertising Compliance Service, http://lawpublish.com/false-advertising-lanham-act.html.

2. "Truth in Advertising," Federal Trade Commission, http://www.ftc.gov/news-events/media-resources/truth-advertising.

3. "False Advertising: Lanham Act."

CHAPTER 21: Common Brand Problems

1. David N. Martin, *Be the Brand* (Richmond, VA: New Marketplace, 2000), 44.

INDEX